ROCKVILLE PUBLIC LIBRARY
3 4035 14544 0737
W9-DFS-263
DISCARDED

how i discovered poetry

marilyn nelson

illustrations by Hadley Hooper

speak

SPEAK
An imprint of Penguin Random House LLC
375 Hudson Street
New York, New York 10014

First published in the United States of America by Dial Books,
an imprint of Penguin Group (USA) LLC, 2014
Published by Speak, an imprint of Penguin Random House LLC, 2016

Text copyright © 2014 by Marilyn Nelson
Illustrations copyright © 2014 by Hadley Hooper

Penguin supports copyright. Copyright fuels creativity, encourages diverse voices, promotes free speech, and creates a vibrant culture. Thank you for buying an authorized edition of this book and for complying with copyright laws by not reproducing, scanning, or distributing any part of it in any form without permission. You are supporting writers and allowing Penguin to continue to publish books for every reader.

THE LIBRARY OF CONGRESS HAS CATALOGED THE DIAL BOOKS EDITION AS FOLLOWS:
Nelson, Marilyn, date, author.
[Poems, Selections]
How I discovered poetry/Marilyn Nelson ; illustrations by Hadley Hooper.
pages cm
ISBN 978-0-8037-3304-6 (hc)
1. Nelson, Marilyn, date—Poetry. 2. Authorship—Poetry.
3. Poetry—Authorship. I. Hooper, Hadley, illustrator. II. Title.
PS35 2013005289

Speak ISBN 978-0-14-751005-1

Printed in the United States of America

3 5 7 9 10 8 6 4 2

To my corporeal and soul siblings, Jennifer and Mel,

and to my other sisters and brothers

—M.N.

Rockville Public Library
52 Union Street
Vernon, CT 06066

how i discovered poetry

Blue Footsies

(Cleveland, Ohio, 1950)

Once upon a time. Upon a time?
Something got on a time? What is a time?
When it got on a time, could it get off?
Could it get on a time two times? Three times?
Three times upon a time . . . Times on a time . . .
Three times on time . . . Or three times on three times . . .
I hear Jennifer's breath. Our room is dark.
Mama's voice questions and Daddy's answers,
a sound seesaw through the wall between us.
If there was, once upon a time, a fire,
and I could only rescue one of them,
would I save him, or her? Or Jennifer?
Four-year-old saves three people from hot flames!
God bless Mama, Daddy, and Jennifer . . .

Church

(Cleveland, Ohio, 1950)

Why did Lot have to take his wife and flea
from the bad city, like that angel said?
Poor Lot: imagine having a pet flea.
I'd keep mine on a dog. But maybe fleas
were bigger in the olden Bible days.
Maybe a flea was bigger than a dog,
more like a sheep or a goat. Maybe they had
flea farms back then, with herds of giant fleas.
Jennifer squirms beside me on the pew,
sucking her thumb, nestled against Mama.
Maybe Lot and his wife rode saddled fleas!
Or drove a coach pulled by a team of fleas!
I giggle soundlessly, but Mama swats
my leg, holding a finger to her lips.

Called Up

(Cleveland, Ohio, 1951)

Folding the letter and laying it down,
Daddy says, "Well, Baby, I've been called back up."
Mama pauses, then puts my bowl of beans
in front of me. Jennifer eats and hums
across from me on two telephone books.
Mama says, "Pray God you won't see combat."
Jennifer, stop singing at the table,
I hiss. Her humming's driving me crazy.
She looks up from her bowl with dreaming eyes:
Huh? Mama says, "My darling, we're going, too."
Stop singing! "I'll take a leave from law school,"
he says, "and you'll take a leave from your job."
We've been called up. Our leaves become feathers.
With wings we wave good-bye to our cousins.

Texas Protection

(James Connally AFB, Texas, 1951)

America goes on and on and on and on,
and on the land are cities, towns, and roads
that stream under your wheels like stripy snakes
and end up in Texas, with new people.
Our dog, Pudgy, found a new family.
Mayflower School feels like something I dreamed
before I woke up wanting cowboy boots
and craving the cap pistol's puff of smoke.
Mama says, "We're walking on eggshells here."
Daddy returns the faceless men's salutes.
But I would tiptoe in my cowboy boots,
I promise, without breaking any eggs!
And if I had a gun and a holster
I could protect us from the Communists!

Telling Time

(James Connally AFB, Texas, 1951)

Mama reminds me I'm a big girl now:
I'm five years old. I can watch Jennifer
for five minutes; they'll just be down the street.
They tuck us in. I hear the door lock click.
Five minutes. "Just five minutes," Daddy said.
My first-grade class is learning to read clocks,
so I know minutes are the little lines
between numbers. Clocks are how you tell time.
Past is before now; future is after.
Now is a five-minute eternity,
Jennifer and I howling in pajamas
in the front yard of the housing unit,
surrounded by concerned faceless strangers
who back away, now our parents are here.

Bomb Drill

(Lackland AFB, Texas, 1952)

Nothing belongs to us in our new house
except Mama's piano and our clothes.
I'm the new girl in *Dick and Jane* country,
the other children faceless as grown-ups.
I read through recess and take some books home.
I read to Jennifer while Mama plays.
I read while the television talker
talks about *career* and the *hide drajen bomb*.
Mama says she's going to vote for Ike.
Daddy says, *"Woman, you just think he's cute!"*
We ducked and covered underneath our desks,
hiding from drajen bombs in school today.
Maybe drajens would turn into butter
if they ran really fast around a tree.

Pink Menace

(Lackland AFB, Texas, 1952)

The Bomb Drill bell is not the Fire Drill bell
or the Tornado bell or the Recess
bell or the bell that says Time to Go Home.
Everybody's motto is Be Prepared,
so we practice Tragic Catastrophes,
hoping they won't come. (*Keep your fingers crossed.*)
My many secret good-luck rituals
seem to be working okay. (*Knock on wood.*)
I never step on cracks in the sidewalk:
America's safe from The Red Menace.
I touch a finger to the car window
whenever we drive over railroad tracks:
the Menace turns pink and fuzzy. At night,
I'm asleep before the end of my blessing list.

A Snake

(Lowry AFB, Colorado, 1953)

As soon as we got here, we turned around
and drove back through the no-guardrail mountains,
connecting the dots of farm mailboxes
to towns and faceless people who don't count.
Mama hugged Aunt Carma and Uncle George.
Daddy wiped his tears with his handkerchief.
Oneida wasn't in her pink bedroom.
She wasn't in the hospital, either.
They said she was in that box. She was dead.
We drove back through the frightening mountains.
Jennifer and I chanted *There's a snake!*
to keep ourselves from looking at the huge
and scaredy-fying emptiness.
When you die, you go to a different school.

Your Own

(Smoky Hill AFB, Kansas, 1953)

Our new house, Officers' Quarters 42,
connects to other quarters and mowed yards
connecting to wheat fields and wilderness
waiting to be explored by kids and dogs.
Sometimes we don't come in until we're called
by someone's mom. They say *Mom,* not *Mama*.
Hazel, Charlotte, Jeannie, Tommy, and Charles:
as soon as we hear the School's Over bell
we flock together like migrating birds,
catching grasshoppers, gathering bouquets,
or just plain running into breathlessness.
I don't know why Mama looked sad tonight
while I was washing up, or why she said,
"Be careful: Don't like them more than your own."

Bad Name

(Smoky Hill AFB, Kansas, 1954)

The dishes washed and dried, my homework done,
and *Amos 'n' Andy* still an hour away,
I kneel with crayons at the coffee table,
drawing and coloring. Round head, round eyes,
half-circle eyebrows, and half-circle mouths.
Segregation means people are kept apart
and *integration* means they're together.
TV is black-and-white, but people aren't.
There's a bad name mean people might call you,
but words aren't sticks and stones. At school today,
James told Mrs. Liebel he didn't say
that name at me. He said he said, "Don't be
a *noogie-hitter*." That's when you just poke
the tetherball instead of punching it.

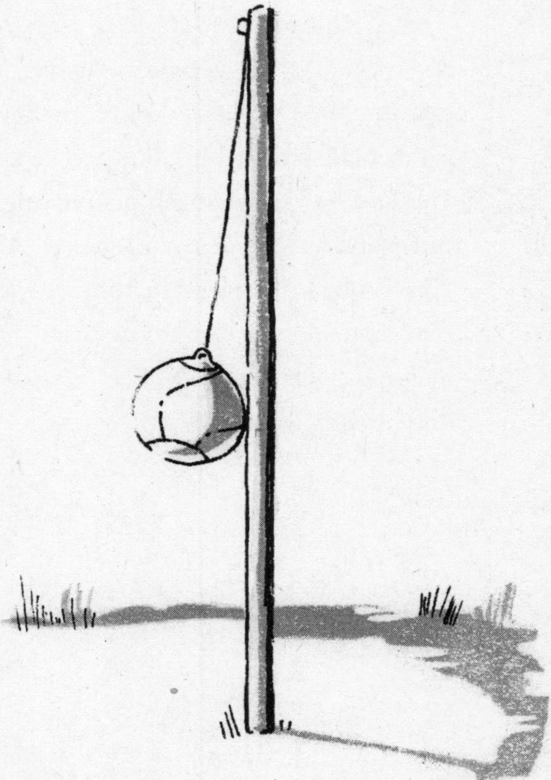

Sonic Boom

(Smoky Hill AFB, Kansas, 1954)

My best friend's name is Tommy Avery.
His mom talks funny because she's English.
They have a little toy Winston Churchill
that puffs real smoke when she lights its cigar.
She made Tommy's fancy birthday dinner
from a recipe in a magazine:
Fiesta Peach Spam Loaf with canned string beans.
Eight candles on his chocolate birthday cake.
Lieutenant Avery was in uniform
and Tommy was wearing his Cub Scout neckerchief.
His mom said, "We can all sleep well at night,
safeguarded by such good-looking soldiers."
While we were singing, a jet made a sonic boom,
like a hammer on an iron curtain.

Career Girl

(Smoky Hill AFB, Kansas, 1954)

Mama's what people call a "career girl."
That's a mother that doesn't stay at home.
She teaches second grade in the base school.
Her all-white class may be a Negro First.
School days start when she zips on her girdle
and calls, "Good morning, chickadees, rise and shine!"
We race to get dressed. Mama braids our hair
as we spoon our cornflakes. The other moms
cook scrambled eggs, pack their kids' lunch boxes
with crustless sandwiches and homemade treats.
They don't shoo their kids out of the kitchen.
They don't frown over red-penciled papers.
They don't say they're too busy for checkers.
They don't care about Making History.

Making History

(Smoky Hill AFB, Kansas, 1955)

Somebody took a picture of a class
standing in line to get polio shots
and published it in the *Weekly Reader*.
We stood like that today. And it did hurt.
Mrs. Liebel said we were Making History,
but all I did was sqwunch up my eyes and wince.
Making History takes more than standing in line
believing little white lies about pain.
Mama says First Negroes are History:
First Negro Telephone Operator,
First Negro Opera Singer at the Met,
First Negro Pilots, First Supreme Court Judge.
That lady in Montgomery just became a First
by sqwunching up her eyes and sitting there.

Fruit
Cake

Gold Box

(Smoky Hill AFB, Kansas, 1955)

I list things I'd take to a bomb shelter
if we had a bomb shelter, which we don't,
so why would I keep working on my list
except because it holds the things I love
so tightly in my mind, they can't fall out?
I keep the list in my gold fruitcake tin.
Jennifer has one for her treasures, too.
I'd take my gold box to a bomb shelter,
but we don't have one. Nobody we know
has a bomb shelter. But they still make bombs.
There's TV talk about them every night
before the good shows come on, and I laugh
at *I Love Lucy* and *Sergeant Bilko*
or lose myself in *The Ed Sullivan Shew*.

Kemo Sabe

(Smoky Hill AFB, Kansas, 1955)

We're watching *The Lone Ranger* on TV.
I'd like to marry Tonto when I grow up:
He's so handsome. I love how he says *how*.

Mama grew up in Indian Country.
"Your grandmother taught in a Creek-Seminole school,"
she says. *Blah, blah . . .* "As a matter of fact,
for a while in high school, a Creek boy was sweet on me."

Daddy says, "Lucky you got out of there
and met me! Marilyn, you could have been
named Pocahontas!"
The room disappears.
A me with another name? An Indian me?
Could I be someone else, but think my thoughts?
How different could I be, and still be me?
The music throbs. They ride toward the sunset.

Mississippi

(Smoky Hill AFB, Kansas, 1955)

Over the river and through the woods, for miles
of four-lane highways, slowed by blowing snow,
through towns named for long-vanquished Indians,
to Aunt Charlie's house in Omaha we go.
Hypnotized by the rhythm of tire chains,
I eat a sandwich passed from the front seat,
where Mama and Daddy are talking about a boy
named Emmett. Jennifer, whispering to her doll,
crosses the line between her side and mine,
and when I poke her just a little bit,
she howls as if it hurts, out of sheer spite.
"BEHAVE!"
Lost again in the inwardness of thought
and my five senses, I add to my list:
Thank you for not stationing us in Mississippi.

Glow-in-the-Dark

(Smoky Hill AFB, Kansas, 1956)

Some TV Negroes have shine-in-the-dark
white eyes and teeth and are afraid of ghosts.
I slip out of my twin bed, tiptoe to
our dresser mirror, and grin in the dark.
To my relief, my teeth and eyes don't shine.
In the no-lights-on-at-midnight mirror,
I'm a darker outline against darkness.
Behind my silhouette, my Sunday School
Attendance Award cross is still glowing
in the shadowed cubicle of my headboard,
between my gold plastic music box clock
and my gold fruitcake tin full of treasures.
Guided by its dying phosphorescence,
I slide back into my warm blanket nest.

Traveling Light

(Smoky Hill AFB, Kansas, 1956)

In memory, Pudgy is just a tail
brushing my thighs as we surveyed the shelves
in the icebox. "Pudgy," Daddy explained,
"went to live with a different family;
she's fed and happy." Lady welcomed us
to one Officers Housing, where she lived
under our unit. She was a good dog.
She seemed almost sad when we drove away
behind the moving van. And General
did have a knack for causing us trouble:
He dug up gardens, dragged whole clotheslines home.
"He'll be happier with his new family,"
Daddy explains. We've been transferred again.
We stand numb as he gives away our toys.

Just Pick a Name

(On the Road, 1956)

The miles enter my eyes and disappear
like cigarette smoke from the car window.
The sky seems to be bigger in the West.
I'm growing bigger inside to take it in.
The landscape feeds my hungry eyes a feast
beyond imagining. Who lived before
in places streaming past like scenery?
What if I left a note in a mailbox
out in the boonies, far from any town,
that said, *I know it's hard. You're doing fine.*
I wonder: Would that make things different?
You could just pick a name from the phone book
of any of these bypassed Podunk towns
and send a postcard signed, *Be happy. God.*

Say It

(Mather AFB, California, 1956)

Base Housing is a little ranch house town
with smooth sidewalks perfect for roller skates.
I'm the best reader in Mrs. Krull's class.
Helene's parents are Mama and Daddy's friends
from way back when both men were cadets;
now they're the only Negro officers
on base. But there are two here, not just one.
Helene's a year ahead of me in school.
She's going to be a nurse when she grows up.
We were strolling in the NCO neighborhood
today, when a blond girl jeered from her yard
that she could say a word that would make us mad.
Helene said, "Say it." And when the girl did,
Helene thumped a lump on her forehead before she was done.

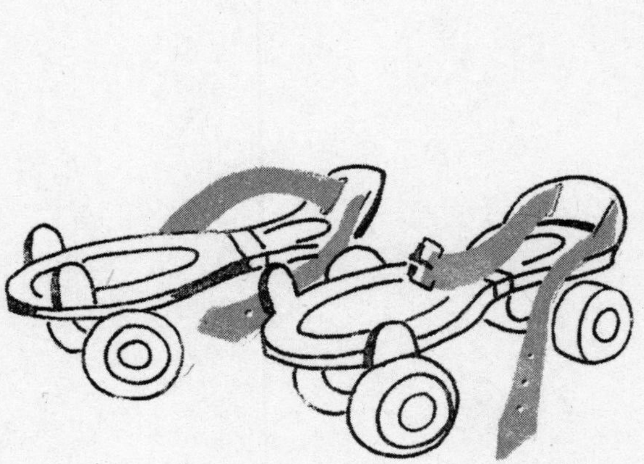

Moonlily

(Mather AFB, California, 1956)

When we play horses at recess, my name
is Moonlily and I'm a yearling mare.
We gallop circles around the playground,
whinnying, neighing, and shaking our manes.
We scrape the ground with scuffed saddle oxfords,
thunder around the little kids on swings
and seesaws, and around the boys' ball games.
We're sorrel, chestnut, buckskin, pinto, gray,
a herd in pastel dresses and white socks.
We're self-named, untamed, untouched, unridden.
Our plains know no fences. We can smell spring.
The bell produces metamorphosis.
Still hot and flushed, we file back to our desks,
one bay in a room of palominos.

Cloud-Gathering

(Mather AFB, California, 1956)

Mama makes me close the book and go play.
Sometimes I join a pack of officers' kids
roaming the dry fields around Base Housing
and making traps for blue-bellied lizards.
Sometimes I lie among the cornflowers
and wild poppies, dreaming as clouds unfold:
Our baby has *the Mongolian spot* . . .
I'm glad they don't make me change his diapers . . .
White people down South want segregation . . .

They think brown is a contagious disease . . .
A mob attacked a girl for going to school . . .
I'd give anything to have a pony!
I'd call him Prince and feed him sugar cubes
and brush his mane and tail and ride bareback!

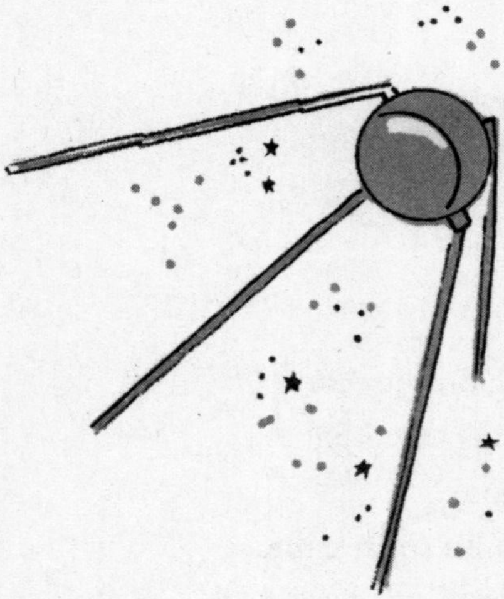

Sputnik

(Mather AFB, California 1957)

My Base School classmates play musical chairs:
sudden absences when dads get transferred,
friends who'll meet from now on only by chance.
Tonight might be the last slumber party
I'll giggle through with my best friend, Helene.
Tomorrow I'll feel lonely as *Sputnik*.
This girl in my class, Joanne, is pretty nice.
She invited me over after school.
But as soon as we got in her room, she closed the door,
opened the window, lit a cigarette,
and passed it to me. What's the point of that?
The grown-ups smoke: So what? I'd rather talk.
Helene talks about the kids in Little Rock:
how brave they are, how lonely they must feel.

Darkroom

(Mather AFB, California, 1957)

Tonight with Daddy in the dark bathroom,
I held my breath, watching science magic.
From white paper bathed in developer,
Jennifer and I on the piano bench
in a cloud of crisp, frothy crinolines
and other Easter finery emerged:
our hands in white gloves folded in our laps,
our patent Mary Janes and crossed anklets,
our temporary curling-iron curls.

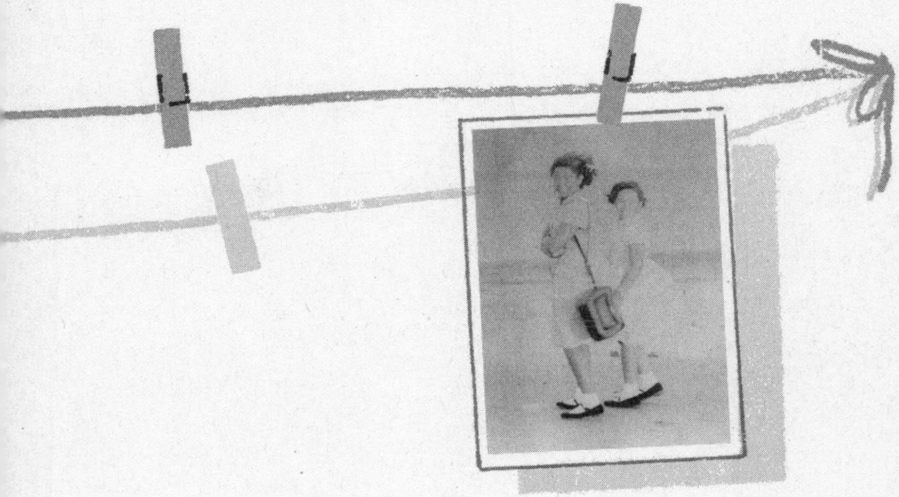

After the stop bath and fixer, we hang
with clothespins on a line over the tub,
living colors reduced to black-and-white,
a lived moment captured in memory
Mama will put in the photo album.

Nelsons

(On the Road, 1957)

Daddy's handsome: uniform, new haircut.
But the travel baby bed in our seat
crowds me and Jennifer. We kept asking,
"Are we there yet?" every few endless miles,
until Daddy shouted, "HEY!" and braked. We braced
ourselves. We skidded, turned, and spit gravel
up a long driveway ending at a barn.
Barking dogs. Mama whispered Daddy's name.
A light-haired man came out. He calmed the dogs,
and looked at Daddy with inquiring eyes.
Daddy called, "Hello! We saw your mailbox!
We're Nelsons, too! I fly B-52s!
Would you mind letting my girls see your farm?"
That's why I'm here petting this stupid cow.

Fieldwork

(Portsmouth, New Hampshire, 1957)

Before he was sent to England for training,
Daddy said, "Let's pretend we're researching
an unknown civilian Caucasian tribe."
We live in a town apartment building
with shouting children clattering on the stairs.
For school lunch, they bring baked-bean sandwiches.
Some families eat for dinner only pie.
The sixth-grade boy next door is named Carrol;
his favorite lunch is onion on rye bread.
They say *tonic* for pop and *pock* for park.
They say our baby's *cunning*, meaning cute.
They say I look like Althea Gibson,
the First Negro to win the Wimbledon,
so I should start taking tennis lessons.

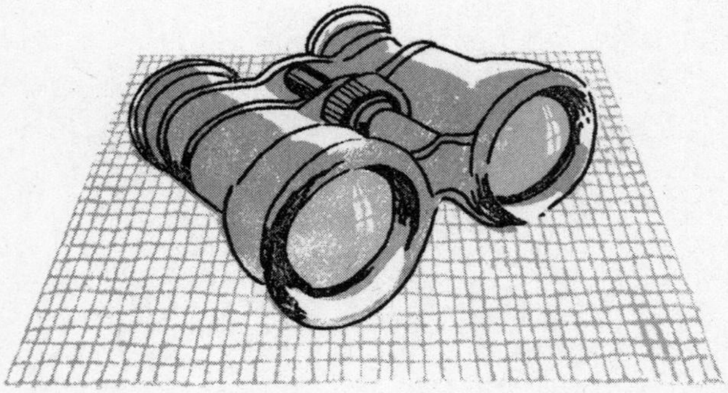

Caucasian Dinner

(Kittery Point, Maine, 1958)

Mama's rented a colonial house
a block from the ocean, in a village
where we're the First Negroes of everything.
We're the First Negro Family in Town,
the First Negro Children in the Town's School.
The Baylisses live in the house next door;
their mantel has photos of dead people
in their coffins. Uncle Ed sits all day
in their bay window with binoculars,
then comments on what we had for dinner.
Aunt Flossie asks us over for cookies.
Sometimes Mama lets me and Jennifer cook.
Tonight we made a Caucasian dinner:
cauliflower, broiled cod, mashed potatoes.

Ghost

(Kittery Point, Maine 1958)

This house in Kittery Point has felt like home
since the first night I slept in my own room,
furnished with bed, dresser, a vanity,
and framed art museum reproductions
of Renaissance paintings. It feels like home:
the first time I've felt like this in my life.
The deep front lawn perfect for badminton,
the wallpaper's somber floral designs,
the town library just across the street,
the Atlantic close enough to walk to:
It really feels like home. My one complaint
is that, on full-moon nights, a ghost appears.
She's hovering right now, near my closet,
daring me to call Jennifer again.

Attic Window

(Kittery Point, Maine, 1958)

Sweet Land of Liberty. Home of the Free.
The Melting Pot. The American Dream.
The Tooth Fairy. Adam and Eve. The Virgin Birth.
The more time I spend in the library,
the less sure I am about everything.
Did the Indians invite the Pilgrims
to their Thanksgiving feast? If so, I bet
the Pilgrims went home with the leftovers.
I read by the window in the attic,
and things people believe in are unmasked
like movie stars whose real names are revealed
in their obituaries. Jennifer
is such a baby, with her stuffed tiger
and that letter she's writing to Santa.

Paper Dolls

(Kittery Point, Maine, 1958)

I keep my area neatly policed
and always pass Saturday inspections.
You can't see the floor of Jennifer's room,
for all her clutter and her paper dolls.
I've heard her whispering voices for them,
tabbing on their cut-out paper outfits
and turning them into a puppet play.
She's too old to still be playing with dolls.
Besides, her mess drifts across the border
into my room, and she won't pick it up.
Today I took her stupid paper dolls
out to the burn-barrel in the backyard.
Daddy was burning documents and trash.
The flames rose in me as the dolls caught fire.

Queen of the Sixth Grade

(Kittery Point, Maine, 1958)

There was an accident in school today.
I shudder when I remember the crunch
of tibia and fibula and wood
as Jamie tried to get off the seesaw
and got her forearm accidentally
caught under her own weight and the up-kick
on the other end, increased by the force
Ellie and I used pushing her end down
so her seesaw seat slammed the blacktop hard
two or three times before she realized
what a mistake it was to say that name
she learned in some civilian school down South
before they got transferred and she came here
to this school, where I'm Queen of the Sixth Grade.

Aooga

(Kittery Point, Maine, 1958)

Visiting, Daddy found a Model T
buried under old furniture and junk
in Uncle Ed and Aunt Flossie's red barn,
in the meadow between their house and ours.
Uncle Ed said, "That cah's been dead for yee-ahs."
Daddy thought they might bring it back to life.
After several weekends of tinkering,
its sputter sparked into a miracle.
Now we chug off, Daddy behind the wheel,
on Sunday afternoon drives on back roads.
Uncle Ed and Aunt Flossie smile and wave
to neighbors generations intertwined.
Aunt Flossie wipes tears with her handkerchief.
Her veiny cheeks flush pink. Her white hair flows.

Beautiful Hair

(Kittery Point, Maine, 1958)

Second week of two at a summer camp
in the Maine woods somewhere, where there's a lake,
a lodge, sleeping cabins, and outhouses.
(The less you eat and drink, the less you go.)
I haven't seen Jennifer very much:
Our cabins are in different divisions.
I brought books, but there isn't time to read
because we're all so busy having fun.
My cabin-mates say they wish they were tan
like me. They say, "Your hair is beautiful;
can I touch it?" None of us understand
why integrating schools is a big deal.
When Mama and Daddy came on Parents' Day,
Mama screamed quietly, "My God! Your hair!"

Critic

(Kittery Point, Maine, 1959)

Daddy pulled a puppy from the pocket
of his flight jacket, and we imprinted
like a gosling to a goose. Speida's my dog,
though he's impartially affectionate.
Either he likes poems, or he likes my voice:
I read aloud from the anthology
I found with Daddy's other college books
and he sits, cocks his head, and wags his tail.
My teacher, Mrs. Gray, told me about
the famous poetess who lived near here.
She says I'll be a famous poet, too.
Today I read Speida one of my poems.
His face got a look of so much disgust
I laughed and forgot we're being transferred.

Parking Lot Dawn

(On the Road, 1959)

After the cousins came the long drive west.
Car games, sing-alongs, and conversation,
alternating drivers, meals in the car.
Gas station restrooms, or behind a tree.
Daddy corrects white men who call him boy.
Even when they're in police uniforms.
Even though the radio updates news
of sit-ins and white citizens' councils.

I ride behind his beautiful close-cropped head,
my window slightly cracked for Speida's nose.
Last night, awake alone, he parked the car
in the Grand Canyon visitors' parking lot.
And this morning, he woke us up to dawn.
There's more beauty on Earth than I can bear.

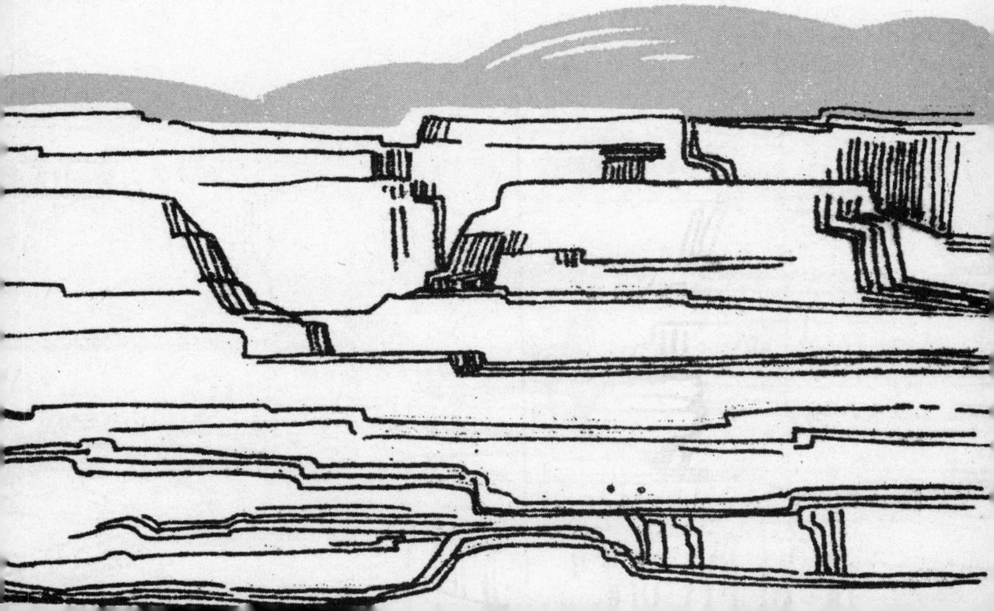

A Drift of Girlfriends

(Sacramento, California, 1959)

We've moved to a neighborhood of new homes
being built to be sold to Negro families.
Mama said she's proud we're landowners now,
like her papa was in Oklahoma,
his red dirt farm stretching fertile acres.
Daddy plowed our bare yard in the Lincoln,
breaking up the clods with its white-walled tires.
I walk to and from school, books to my chest,
with a drift of girlfriends, none of them mine.
I'm learning that Negro is a language
I don't speak. And I don't know how to dance.
At home, we listen to Miles and Coltrane,
Tchaikovsky and Chopin. I get good grades
because I'm curious and I like to read,
and NOT because I'm "trying to be white."

Africans

(Sacramento, California, 1959)

Mama brings Africans home from grad school,
like a kid who keeps finding lost puppies.
She's so proud of their new independence.
She brings home smooth-faced mahogany men,
dressed in suits like beautiful pajamas,
so Jennifer and I can shake their hands.
Nodding polite answers to her questions,
they go to town on her catfish and grits.
Later, while Daddy drives them to their dorms,
she washes and Jennifer and I dry.
"Some of the greatest wrongs of history
are being righted now," she says. "These are
our people." As I put a plate away,
I ask myself who is not my people.

Bitter Apple

(Sacramento, California, 1959)

Who should be transferred here but Helene's dad!
Miracle of miracles! Thank you, God!
Last night, the first of what we vow will be
many sleepovers, she explained to me
in whispers that excluded Jennifer
something she's learned since our last heart-to-heart
when we were stationed here two years ago:
how to get a boy's love, and how to kiss.
I don't know what she said: It's hard to hear
when someone's words are breath tickling your ear.
But what I understood has made me taste
the bitter apple of disappointment.
To think souls touching is so trivial
you can practice it with a Coke bottle.

The History of Tribal Suppression

(On the Road, 1959)

We drive through Indian territory,
every vista inhabited by ghosts
almost visible on the horizon.
Daddy says he has some Indian blood;
something he thinks his mother told him once.
Mama, as co-pilot, reads from the map
the history of tribal suppression.
Plump, brown-faced weavers sit along the road.
At last, Daddy pulls over. TRADING POST.
I choose a turquoise and silver bracelet;
Jennifer picks an authentic tom-tom.
Too many miles later to turn around,
she sees the tom-tom says "Made in Japan."
And my wrist is beginning to turn green.

Sinfonia Concertante

(Fort Worth, Texas, 1959)

Daddy's here on temporary duty,
so Mama's piano is in storage.
Home is a four-room third-floor apartment
in a Negro quarter of the city.
My all-black classmates act like I'm from Mars.
Are you the girl from California?
Talk for us. And these boys act like I'm cute!
Miss Jackson saw me pretend piano
and had me put into a music class.
String quartet: two violins, cello,
and on viola, me, sawing away.
Daddy says my squawks set his teeth on edge,
so I practice out on the balcony,
genius on view all up and down the block.

Mischievious

(Fort Worth, Texas, 1959)

Between classes, teachers patrol the halls,
slapping their palms with short, thick leather straps.
Some tell kids to "assume the position,"
then whack them with perforated paddles.
My English teacher uses a ruler
to smack the palms of kids who mispronounce.
His bugbear's *mischievous,* which every kid
who reads it pronounces *mischievious.*
That added syllable drives the man mad.
He blew his stack when I corrected him:
"They're *eu-cal-YP-tus*, not *eu-CAL-yp-tus*, trees."
(I guess I was being *mischievious.*)
He said, "Stand up and hold out your right hand."
I'm in the office now. Mama's coming.

To Miss Jackson

(Fort Worth, Texas, 1959)

Miss Jackson loans me her own poetry books:
More Hughes, Cullen, Johnson. Gwendolyn Brooks,
First Negro Poet to Win the Pulitzer Prize.
(Maybe she's trying to tell me something.)
Isolated by temporariness
and unable to wholly comprehend
the things boys say to me under their breath
when we pass by each other in the hall
so close that we can sense each other's heat,
I flee into the arms of poetry.
I take my books to bed. I read so late
Daddy shouts, "Lights OUT!" Then Mama urges,
"Get the Man's hand out of your dad's pocket!"
I lie in the dark. My head whirls with words.

Let Me Count the Ways

(On the Road, 1959)

A sleeping princess startled from a dream
of tall, dark, handsome fifteen-year-old boys
surrounding me, like Gidget on the beach,
with warm eyes and begging-to-be-kissed lips,
cute, eager, willing . . . I'm back in my place
in the backseat, my face a fist because
I've been robbed of such tantalizing fruit.
Odessa's brother told her he likes me.
Now I won't find out if he's my true love.
I'm so bummed out. Life is passing me by.
Texas is becoming Oklahoma.
What if Odessa's brother was my prince?
How might I have loved him, given the chance?
I count the ways as miles and time streak past.

A Quartet of Geeks

(Clinton-Sherman AFB, Oklahoma, 1959)

All Hell seems to be breaking out down South!
My days start with radio news; they end
blessing the students integrating schools
and giving thanks for the National Guard.
Here, in God-Forsaken, Oklahoma,
we live on-base in the good neighborhood.
Majors and Colonels get bigger homes,
NCOs have an apartment complex.
We're assigned three bedrooms, two baths, garage.
There's no school on the base. We have to go
to schools in town: our teachers' First Negroes
(though I doubt they pronounce the word that way),
and the First Negroes of most of the kids.
But I've found a place in the seventh-grade cliques
with three best friends: We're a quartet of geeks.

Dances With Doorknobs

(Clinton-Sherman AFB, Oklahoma, 1959)

When Daddy's in control of the high-fi,
we listen to his favorite jazz albums.
Sometimes Mama talks about way back when
the greats were just young musicians on tour,
unwelcome in hotels. How this one stayed
with them once or twice, before I was born;
how that one loved her chicken and dumplings.
Sunday afternoons, Mama's in control
of which LP will release its music:
Marian Anderson, Mahler, Heifetz.
But I have a transistor radio,
the latest thing. One hand on the doorknob,
I jitterbug alone in our bedroom
when Jennifer's not here. Not often enough.

5 6 7 8 10 14 16

My Friends

(Clinton-Sherman AFB, Oklahoma, 1959)

My friends all live in the same neighborhood
because our dads are officers. We're stars
in all classes except gym, and, outside
of school, part of each other's families.
Cheryl dropped by last Saturday afternoon,
as Mama finished straightening our hair,
and said she smelled hair burning. Jennifer said,
"We put our heads in the oven once a week."
The other day at lunch, John blurted out,
"Your eyes aren't black, they're brown!" He'd just noticed
that he hadn't really been seeing me.
His mom talks to me as if we're equals.
Last night Kim, Cheryl, and I slept outside
in Kim's yard, giggling under the stars.

The Baby Picture Guessing Game

(Clinton-Sherman AFB, Oklahoma, 1959)

The Home Ec Baby Picture Guessing Game
ended soon for me: Everyone could see
which baby I was. They all looked alike.
When all the babies were identified,
they gave the Cutest Baby prize to me
and we ate the cupcakes we'd baked and iced.
My classmates voted down a class party
at the Elk City Theatre because
Negroes have to sit in the balcony.
Oh, it's not a bed of thornless roses:
Some of the farm boys punch each other's arms
and make kissy sounds when they walk past me.
But Mama and Daddy tell me every day
that I'm a cygnet in a flock of ducks.
And anyway, it isn't Little Rock.

Safe Path Through Quicksand

(Clinton-Sherman AFB, Oklahoma, 1959)

I belong to the Protestant Youth Group
and go to chapel on Sunday mornings.
Do I believe? Well, let's just say I hope.
I think Jesus is an elder brother
whose footsteps mark a safe path through quicksand.
Maybe we're already in "Heaven" now:
Every place I've been holds its own beauty.
But I do hope to God there is a hell
waiting for some people. For racist cops.
For grandmothers who spit hate at children.
A hell for mean, sneering, slicked-back-hair guys
like Rick Havard and Donald Goeringer.
A hell for Mr. and Mrs. Purdy,
who smile at me in class, and do evil.

How I Discovered Poetry

(Clinton-Sherman AFB, Oklahoma, 1959)

It was like soul-kissing, the way the words
filled my mouth as Mrs. Purdy read from her desk.
All the other kids zoned an hour ahead to 3:15,
but Mrs. Purdy and I wandered lonely as clouds borne
by a breeze off Mount Parnassus. She must have seen
the darkest eyes in the room brim: The next day
she gave me a poem she'd chosen especially for me
to read to the all-except-for-me white class.
She smiled when she told me to read it, smiled harder,
said oh yes I could. She smiled harder and harder
until I stood and opened my mouth to banjo-playing
darkies, pickaninnies, disses and dats. When I finished,
my classmates stared at the floor. We walked silent
to the buses, awed by the power of words.

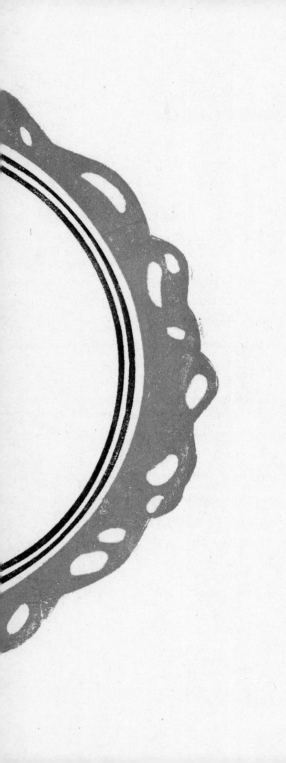

Thirteen-Year-Old American Negro Girl

(Clinton-Sherman AFB, Oklahoma, 1959)

My face, as foreign to me as a mask,
allows people to believe they know me.
Thirteen-Year-Old American Negro Girl,
headlines would read if I was newsworthy.
But that's just the top-of-the-iceberg me.
I could spend hours searching the mirror
for clues to my truer identity,
if someone didn't pound the bathroom door.
You can't see what the mirror doesn't show:
for instance, that after I close my book
and turn off my lamp, I say to the dark:
Give me a message I can give the world.
Afraid there's a poet behind my face,
I beg until I've cried myself to sleep.

Author's Note

This book is a late-career retrospective, a personal memoir, a "portrait of the artist as a young American Negro Girl." The poems cover the decade of the fifties, from 1950, when I was four years old, to 1960, when I was fourteen.

I prefer to call the girl in the poems "the Speaker," not "me." Although the poems describe a girl whose life is very much like mine, the incidents the poems describe are not entirely or exactly "memories." They are sometimes much enhanced by research and imagination.

The Speaker's growing awareness of personal and racial identity are set against the tensions America experienced during the fifties. Some of the poems that seem to be "about me" are as much about the "Red Scare," the shadow of the atom bomb, racism, the rise of the Civil Rights Movement, or the first stirrings of women's empowerment.

Each of the poems is built around a "hole" or "gap" in the Speaker's understanding. As she grows older, the holes are less obviously evident, but they are always there. Her maturing voice, growing self-awareness, and broadening interests are a major theme of the book.

This is also the story of military family life. Though this is the specific story of the wife and children of one of the first African American career officers in the Air Force, most military families share some of the experiences described here. Their frequent transfers cause a sense of rootlessness, as the extended family and friends are more and more often seen waving good-bye as the family drives away. For most military children, home is something more longed for than known.

Another theme of the book is the Speaker's increasing fascination with language. In the last poem, at approximately the age of Confirmation or Bat Mitzvah, she realizes, with a feeling of awe and responsibility, that she may grow up to be a poet. As that poet, I have written this book as a sequence of fifty unrhymed sonnets. Like other sonnets, these have fourteen lines, and are roughly iambic pentameter (ten syllables per line), but they don't rhyme, and they don't always have the traditional volta, or "turn" from one thought to another thought, in the middle.

I'd like to thank my sister, Jennifer Nelson, for helping me remember things; and to thank my friends Inge Pedersen and Stephen Roxburg for giving me good advice; and to thank my editor, Lauri Hornik, for pushing me to develop my original idea; and to thank my agent, Regina

Brooks of Serendipity Literary Agency, for cheering me on; and to thank my friend Pamela Espeland for thinking through things with me and making me laugh as I worked on the poems.

Who's Who in the family photos:

page 46, left: Marilyn's mama and daddy, Johnnie and Melvin Nelson, Melvin's aunts Edith and Effie, Marilyn, and younger sister Jennifer; right: Marilyn, Mama, and Jennifer in the Painted Desert

page 47: Marilyn and Jennifer on the Pacific coast

back cover: Marilyn's parents, Lt. Melvin Nelson and Johnnie Mitchell Nelson, newlyweds

The author gratefully acknowledges the editors of the following publications, in which some of these poems first appeared:

Fields of Praise: New and Selected Poems by Marilyn Nelson, copyright 1994, 1995, 1996, 1997, Louisiana State University Press: "How I Discovered Poetry"

Beloit Poetry Journal (Vol. 62, No. 3, Spring 2012) *Split This Rock Chapbook 2012:* "Called Up," "Your Own," "Making History"

"30 Poets/30 Days: April 2012," GottaBook blog (gottabook.blogspot.com): "Telling Time"

Tygerburning Literary Journal (No. 2, Summer 2013): "Pink Menace," "Mississippi"

Saranac Review (No. 8, 2013–2014): "Career Girl"

Cimarron Review (No. 180, Summer 2012): "Nelsons," "Parking Lot Dawn," "Thirteen-Year-Old American Negro Girl"

Complicated Kris Northern

"This image illustrates some of the best qualities of fractals—infinity, reiteration, and self similarity."– **Kris Northern**

GRADE 2

Differentiation and Intervention Guide

Investigations

IN NUMBER, DATA, AND SPACE®

This work is protected by United States copyright laws and is provided solely for the use of teachers and administrators in teaching courses and assessing student learning in their classes and schools. Dissemination or sale of any part of this work (including the World Wide Web) will destroy the integrity of the work and is not permitted.

PEARSON

Glenview, Illinois • Boston, Massachusetts
Chandler, Arizona • Upper Saddle River, New Jersey

TERC

The Investigations curriculum was developed by TERC, Cambridge, MA.

NSF

This material is based on work supported by the National Science Foundation ("NSF") under Grant No.ESI-0095450. Any opinions, findings, and conclusions or recommendations expressed in this material are those of the author(s) and do not necessarily reflect the views of the National Science Foundation.

ISBN-13: 978-0-328-62339-6

ISBN-10: 0-328-62339-3

Copyright © 2011 Pearson Education, Inc., or its affiliates. All Rights Reserved. Printed in the United States of America. This publication is protected by copyright, and permission should be obtained from the publisher prior to any prohibited reproduction, storage in a retrieval system, or transmission in any form or by any means, electronic, mechanical, photocopying, recording, or likewise. The publisher hereby grants permission to reproduce pages R1–R89, in part or in whole, for classroom use only, the number not to exceed the number of students in each class. Notice of copyright must appear on all copies. For information regarding permissions, write to Pearson Curriculum Group Rights & Permissions, One Lake Street, Upper Saddle River, New Jersey 07458.

Pearson, Scott Foresman, and Pearson Scott Foresman are trademarks in the U.S. and/or other countries, of Pearson Education, Inc., or its affiliates.

4 5 6 7 8 9 10 V042 14 13 12 11

Contents

Overview

The *Differentiation and Intervention Guide* is a flexible and versatile component that supplements the *Investigations* curriculum units. An Intervention, Practice, and Extension activity is provided for every Investigation. The differentiation activities presented in this guide can be used anytime after the session referenced, such as during Math Workshops, or outside of math time. In addition, a Quiz is available to use as a formative assessment after an Investigation is completed.

Teachers may also assign multiple activities for an Investigation to a single student. For example, after a student completes the Practice activity, it may be appropriate for that student to work on the Extension activity. Similarly, Practice and Extension activities can also be used to reinforce and extend Intervention suggestions, either during the Investigation or later in the unit.

Within each curriculum unit, a feature titled "Differentiation: Supporting the Range of Learners" appears regularly. This feature offers ideas for Intervention, Extension, and ELL related to the content of that session. The *Differentiation and Intervention Guide* expands many of these existing Intervention and Extension suggestions by providing teaching suggestions and/or student masters. The *Differentiation and Intervention Guide* also provides additional Practice activities for all students.

Curriculum Unit 1, p. 22

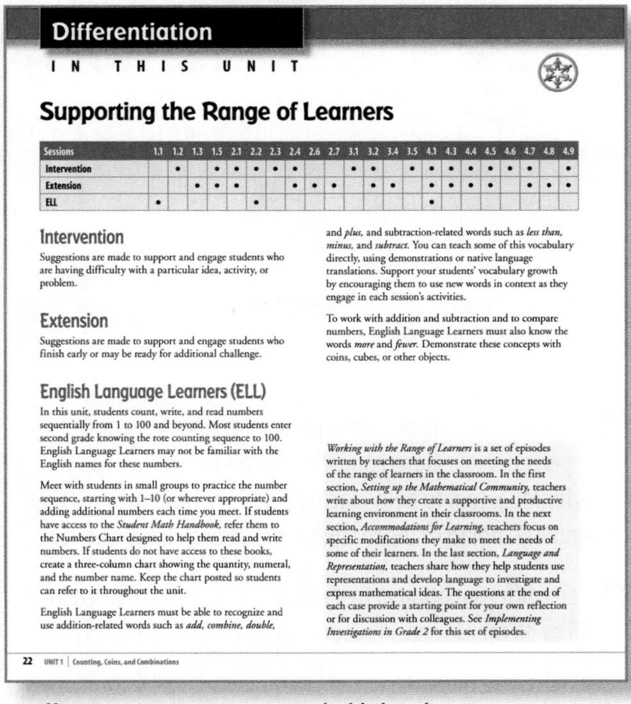

Differentiation

IN THIS UNIT

Supporting the Range of Learners

Sessions	1.1	1.2	1.3	1.5	2.1	2.2	2.3	2.4	2.6	2.7	3.1	3.2	3.4	3.5	4.1	4.3	4.4	4.5	4.6	4.7	4.8	4.9
Intervention		•		•	•	•	•	•			•	•		•	•	•	•	•	•	•		•
Extension			•	•	•			•	•	•		•	•		•	•	•	•		•	•	•
ELL	•					•									•							

Intervention

Suggestions are made to support and engage students who are having difficulty with a particular idea, activity, or problem.

Extension

Suggestions are made to support and engage students who finish early or may be ready for additional challenge.

English Language Learners (ELL)

In this unit, students count, write, and read numbers sequentially from 1 to 100 and beyond. Most students enter second grade knowing the rote counting sequence to 100. English Language Learners may not be familiar with the English names for these numbers.

Meet with students in small groups to practice the number sequence, starting with 1–10 (or wherever appropriate) and adding additional numbers each time you meet. If students have access to the *Student Math Handbook,* refer them to the Numbers Chart designed to help them read and write numbers. If students do not have access to these books, create a three-column chart showing the quantity, numeral, and the number name. Keep the chart posted so students can refer to it throughout the unit.

English Language Learners must be able to recognize and use addition-related words such as *add, combine, double,* and *plus,* and subtraction-related words such as *less than, minus,* and *subtract.* You can teach some of this vocabulary directly, using demonstrations or native language translations. Support your students' vocabulary growth by encouraging them to use new words in context as they engage in each session's activities.

To work with addition and subtraction and to compare numbers, English Language Learners must also know the words *more* and *fewer.* Demonstrate these concepts with coins, cubes, or other objects.

Working with the Range of Learners is a set of episodes written by teachers that focuses on meeting the needs of the range of learners in the classroom. In the first section, *Setting up the Mathematical Community,* teachers write about how they create a supportive and productive learning environment in their classrooms. In the next section, *Accommodations for Learning,* teachers focus on specific modifications they make to meet the needs of some of their learners. In the last section, *Language and Representation,* teachers share how they help students use representations and develop language to investigate and express mathematical ideas. The questions at the end of each case provide a starting point for your own reflection or for discussion with colleagues. See *Implementing Investigations in Grade 2* for this set of episodes.

22 UNIT 1 | Counting, Coins, and Combinations

Differentiation suggestions are embedded in the curriculum units.

Curriculum Unit 1, p. 118

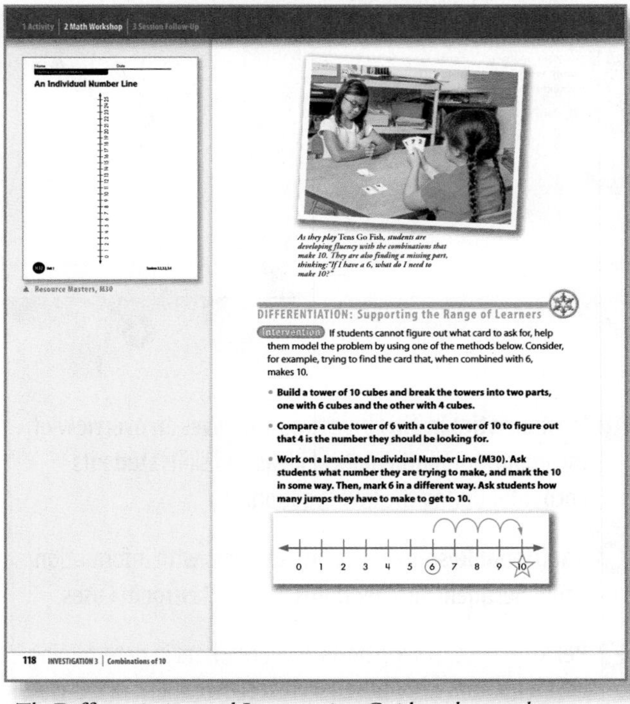

1 Activity | 2 Math Workshop | 3 Session Follow-Up

An Individual Number Line

▲ Resource Masters, M30

As they play Tens Go Fish, *students are developing fluency with the combinations that make 10. They are also finding a missing part, thinking: "If I have a 6, what do I need to make 10?"*

DIFFERENTIATION: Supporting the Range of Learners

Intervention If students cannot figure out what card to ask for, help them model the problem by using one of the methods below. Consider, for example, trying to find the card that, when combined with 6, makes 10.

- **Build a tower of 10 cubes and break the towers into two parts, one with 6 cubes and the other with 4 cubes.**
- **Compare a cube tower of 6 with a cube tower of 10 to figure out that 4 is the number they should be looking for.**
- **Work on a laminated Individual Number Line (M30). Ask students what number they are trying to make, and mark the 10 in some way. Then, mark 6 in a different way. Ask students how many jumps they have to make to get to 10.**

0 1 2 3 4 5 6 7 8 9 10

118 INVESTIGATION 3 | Combinations of 10

The Differentiation and Intervention Guide *enhances the existing differentiation suggestions in the curriculum units.*

Understanding This Guide

The *Differentiation and Intervention Guide* contains support pages for every Investigation in the curriculum units. The first page provides teachers with an overview of the key mathematics in the Investigation and descriptions of student performance. The remaining three pages provide easy-to-use activities based on the Math Focus Points in the Investigation. Each activity features built-in ELL support and resource masters for students.

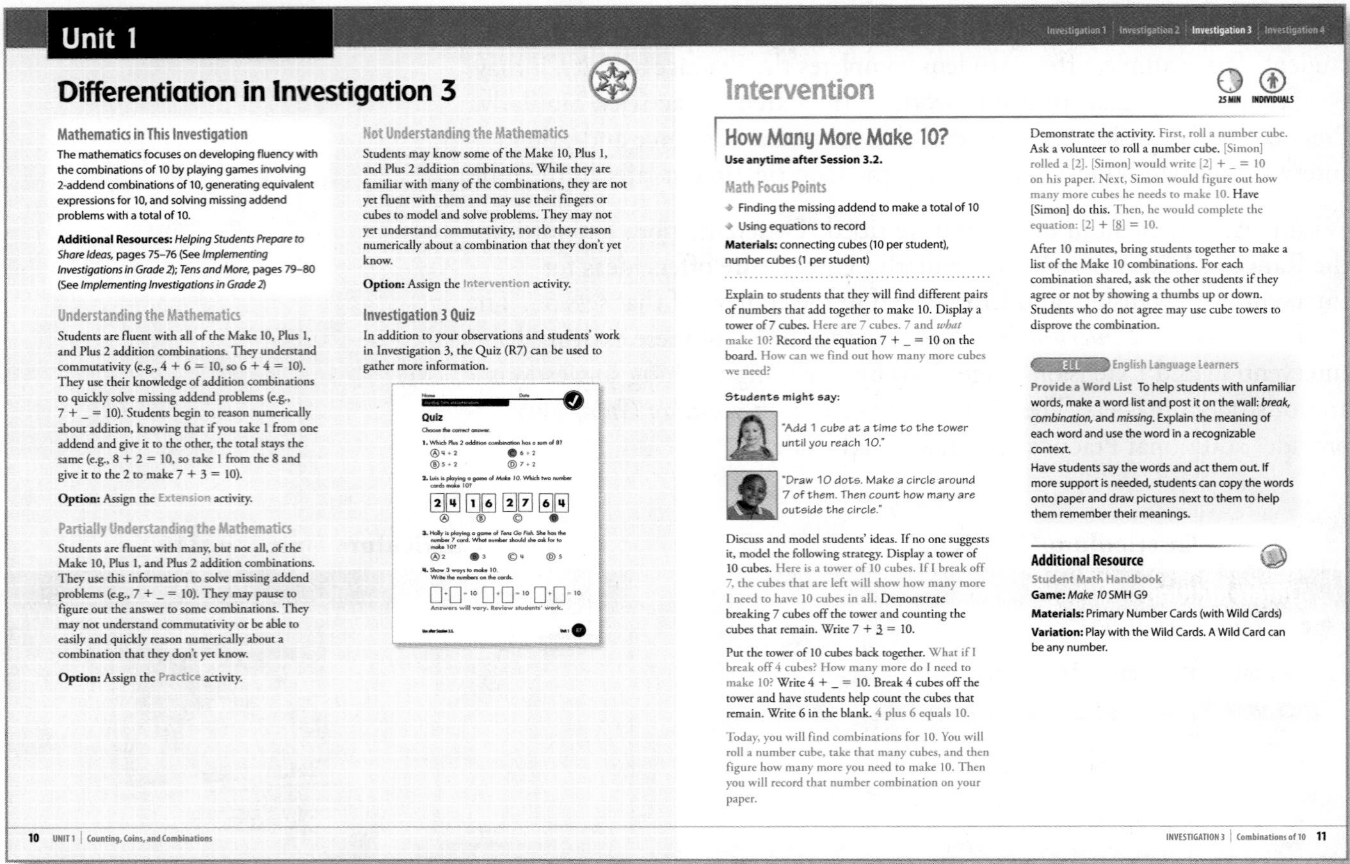

Unit 1

Investigation 1 | Investigation 2 | Investigation 3 | Investigation 4

Differentiation in Investigation 3

Mathematics in This Investigation

The mathematics focuses on developing fluency with the combinations of 10 by playing games involving 2-addend combinations of 10, generating equivalent expressions for 10, and solving missing addend problems with a total of 10.

Additional Resources: *Helping Students Prepare to Share Ideas*, pages 75–76 (See *Implementing Investigations in Grade 2*); *Tens and More*, pages 79–80 (See *Implementing Investigations in Grade 2*)

Understanding the Mathematics

Students are fluent with all of the Make 10, Plus 1, and Plus 2 addition combinations. They understand commutativity (e.g., 4 + 6 = 10, so 6 + 4 = 10). They use their knowledge of addition combinations to quickly solve missing addend problems (e.g., 7 + _ = 10). Students begin to reason numerically about addition, knowing that if you take 1 from one addend and give it to the other, the total stays the same (e.g., 8 + 2 = 10, so take 1 from the 8 and give it to the 2 to make 7 + 3 = 10).

Option: Assign the Extension activity.

Partially Understanding the Mathematics

Students are fluent with many, but not all, of the Make 10, Plus 1, and Plus 2 addition combinations. They use this information to solve missing addend problems (e.g., 7 + _ = 10). They may pause to figure out the answer to some combinations. They may not understand commutativity or be able to easily and quickly reason numerically about a combination that they don't yet know.

Option: Assign the Practice activity.

Not Understanding the Mathematics

Students may know some of the Make 10, Plus 1, and Plus 2 addition combinations. While they are familiar with many of the combinations, they are not yet fluent with them and may use their fingers or cubes to model and solve problems. They may not yet understand commutativity, nor do they reason numerically about a combination that they don't yet know.

Option: Assign the Intervention activity.

Investigation 3 Quiz

In addition to your observations and students' work in Investigation 3, the Quiz (R7) can be used to gather more information.

Quiz

Choose the correct answer.

1. Which Plus 2 addition combination has a sum of 8?
   (A) 4 + 2 (B) 6 + 2 (C) 5 + 2 (D) 7 + 2
2. Lois is playing a game of *Make 10*. Which two number cards make 10?
   (A) 2 4 (B) 1 6 (C) 2 7 (D) 6 4
3. Holly is playing a game of *Tens Go Fish*. She has the number 7 card. What number should she ask for to make 10?
   (A) 2 (B) 3 (C) 4 (D) 5
4. Show 3 ways to make 10. Write the numbers on the cards.
   □ + □ = 10 □ + □ = 10 □ + □ = 10
   Answers will vary. Review students' work.

10 UNIT 1 | Counting, Coins, and Combinations

Intervention

25 MIN INDIVIDUALS

How Many More Make 10?

Use anytime after Session 3.2.

Math Focus Points

- Finding the missing addend to make a total of 10
- Using equations to record

Materials: connecting cubes (10 per student), number cubes (1 per student)

Explain to students that they will find different pairs of numbers that add together to make 10. Display a tower of 7 cubes. Here are 7 cubes. 7 and *what* make 10? Record the equation 7 + _ = 10 on the board. How can we find out how many more cubes we need?

Students might say:

"Add 1 cube at a time to the tower until you reach 10."

"Draw 10 dots. Make a circle around 7 of them. Then count how many are outside the circle."

Discuss and model students' ideas. If no one suggests it, model the following strategy. Display a tower of 10 cubes. Here is a tower of 10 cubes. If I break off 7, the cubes that are left will show how many more I need to have 10 cubes in all. Demonstrate breaking 7 cubes off the tower and counting the cubes that remain. Write 7 + 3 = 10.

Put the tower of 10 cubes back together. What if I break off 4 cubes? How many more do I need to make 10? Write 4 + _ = 10. Break 4 cubes off the tower and have students help count the cubes that remain. Write 6 in the blank. 4 plus 6 equals 10.

Today, you will find combinations for 10. You will roll a number cube, take that many cubes, and then figure how many more you need to make 10. Then you will record that number combination on your paper.

Demonstrate the activity. First, roll a number cube. Ask a volunteer to roll a number cube. [Simon] rolled a [2]. [Simon] would write [2] + _ = 10 on his paper. Next, Simon would figure out how many more cubes he needs to make 10. Have [Simon] do this. Then, he would complete the equation: [2] + [8] = 10.

After 10 minutes, bring students together to make a list of the Make 10 combinations. For each combination shared, ask the other students if they agree or not by showing a thumbs up or down. Students who do not agree may use cube towers to disprove the combination.

ELL English Language Learners

Provide a Word List To help students with unfamiliar words, make a word list and post it on the wall: *break*, *combination*, and *missing*. Explain the meaning of each word and use the word in a recognizable context.

Have students say the words and act them out. If more support is needed, students can copy the words onto paper and draw pictures next to them to help them remember their meanings.

Additional Resource

Student Math Handbook

Game: *Make 10* SMH G9

Materials: Primary Number Cards (with Wild Cards)

Variation: Play with the Wild Cards. A Wild Card can be any number.

INVESTIGATION 3 | Combinations of 10 11

1. **Mathematics in This Investigation** gives an overview of the important mathematical ideas and skills students encounter during the Investigation.
2. **Additional Resources** provide teachers with information about pertinent Teacher Notes and/or Classroom Cases.
3. **Performance descriptions** assist teachers in determining differentiation activities based on observations of students throughout the Investigation and analyzing students' work.
4. The **Quiz** consists of 3 multiple-choice questions and 1 performance-based question. It can be used as an additional tool to help teachers identify students' levels of understanding of the mathematics in each Investigation.
5. Each differentiation activity is designed to be covered in 15 to 30 minutes in small groups, pairs, or as individuals.

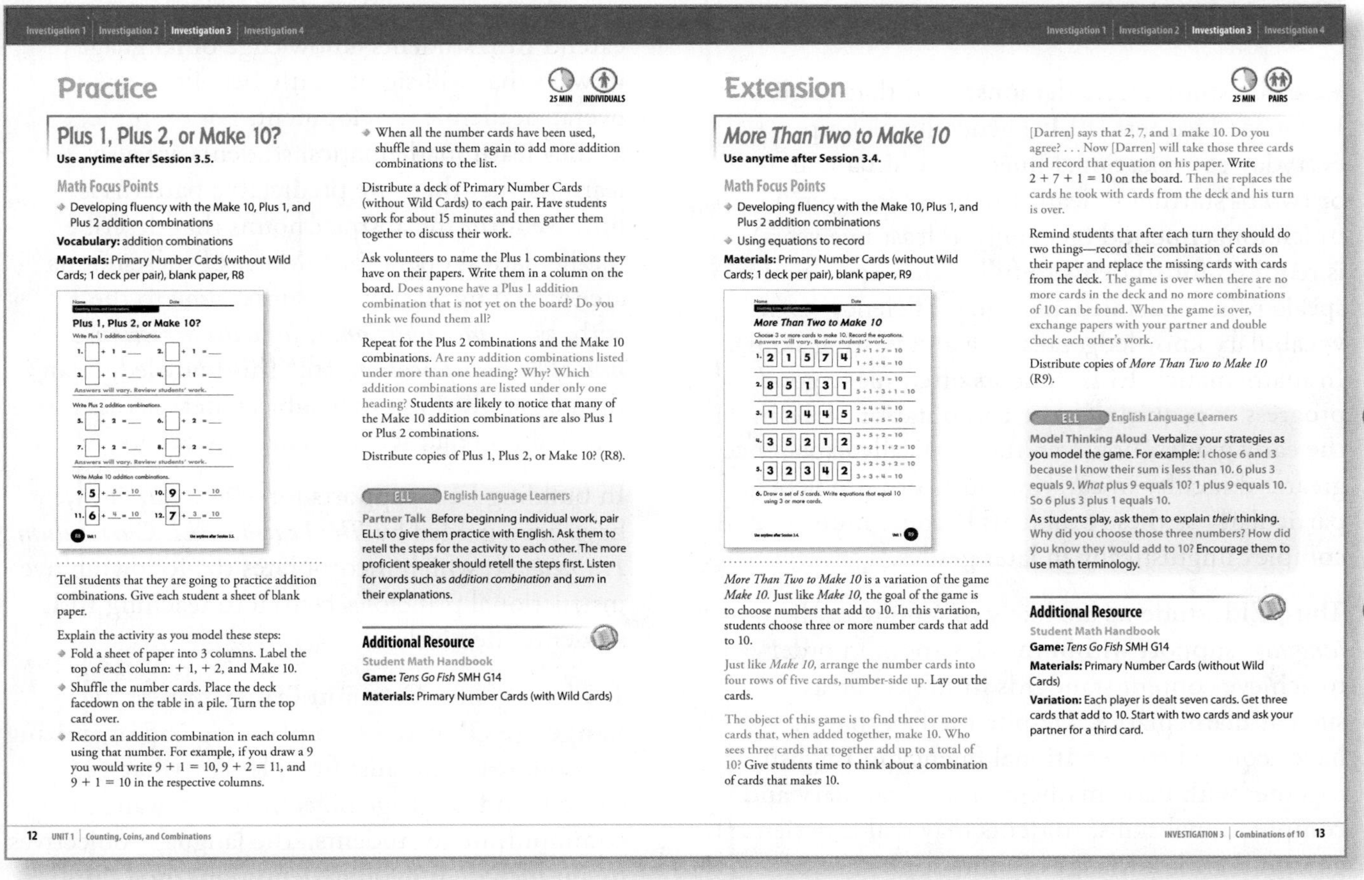

Investigation 1 | Investigation 2 | Investigation 3 | Investigation 4

Practice

25 MIN INDIVIDUALS

Plus 1, Plus 2, or Make 10?

Use anytime after Session 3.5.

Math Focus Points

- Developing fluency with the Make 10, Plus 1, and Plus 2 addition combinations

Vocabulary: addition combinations

Materials: Primary Number Cards (without Wild Cards; 1 deck per pair), blank paper, R8

Plus 1, Plus 2, or Make 10?

Write Plus 1 addition combinations.

Answers will vary. Review students' work.

Write Plus 2 addition combinations.

Answers will vary. Review students' work.

Write Make 10 addition combinations.

9. 5 + 5 = 10 10. 9 + 1 = 10

11. 6 + 4 = 10 12. 7 + 3 = 10

Tell students that they are going to practice addition combinations. Give each student a sheet of blank paper.

Explain the activity as you model these steps:

- Fold a sheet of paper into 3 columns. Label the top of each column: + 1, + 2, and Make 10.
- Shuffle the number cards. Place the deck facedown on the table in a pile. Turn the top card over.
- Record an addition combination in each column using that number. For example, if you draw a 9 you would write $9 + 1 = 10$, $9 + 2 = 11$, and $9 + 1 = 10$ in the respective columns.
- When all the number cards have been used, shuffle and use them again to add more addition combinations to the list.

Distribute a deck of Primary Number Cards (without Wild Cards) to each pair. Have students work for about 15 minutes and then gather them together to discuss their work.

Ask volunteers to name the Plus 1 combinations they have on their papers. Write them in a column on the board. Does anyone have a Plus 1 addition combination that is not yet on the board? Do you think we found them all?

Repeat for the Plus 2 combinations and the Make 10 combinations. Are any addition combinations listed under more than one heading? Why? Which addition combinations are listed under only one heading? Students are likely to notice that many of the Make 10 addition combinations are also Plus 1 or Plus 2 combinations.

Distribute copies of Plus 1, Plus 2, or Make 10? (R8).

ELL English Language Learners

Partner Talk Before beginning individual work, pair ELLs to give them practice with English. Ask them to retell the steps for the activity to each other. The more proficient speaker should retell the steps first. Listen for words such as *addition combination* and *sum* in their explanations.

Additional Resource

Student Math Handbook

Game: *Tens Go Fish* SMH G14

Materials: Primary Number Cards (with Wild Cards)

12 UNIT 1 | Counting, Coins, and Combinations

Investigation 1 | Investigation 2 | Investigation 3 | Investigation 4

Extension

25 MIN PAIRS

More Than Two to Make 10

Use anytime after Session 3.4.

Math Focus Points

- Developing fluency with the Make 10, Plus 1, and Plus 2 addition combinations
- Using equations to record

Materials: Primary Number Cards (without Wild Cards; 1 deck per pair), blank paper, R9

More Than Two to Make 10

Choose 3 or more cards to make 10. Record the equations.

Answers will vary. Review students' work.

1. 2 1 5 7 4 — $2 + 1 + 7 = 10$; $1 + 5 + 4 = 10$
2. 8 5 1 3 1 — $8 + 1 + 1 = 10$; $5 + 1 + 3 + 1 = 10$
3. 1 2 4 4 5 — $2 + 4 + 4 = 10$; $1 + 4 + 5 = 10$
4. 3 5 2 1 2 — $3 + 5 + 2 = 10$; $5 + 2 + 1 + 2 = 10$
5. 3 2 3 4 2 — $3 + 2 + 3 + 2 = 10$; $3 + 3 + 4 = 10$
6. Draw a set of 5 cards. Write equations that equal 10 using 3 or more cards.

More Than Two to Make 10 is a variation of the game *Make 10.* Just like *Make 10,* the goal of the game is to choose numbers that add to 10. In this variation, students choose three or more number cards that add to 10.

Just like *Make 10,* arrange the number cards into four rows of five cards, number-side up. Lay out the cards.

The object of this game is to find three or more cards that, when added together, make 10. Who sees three cards that together add up to a total of 10? Give students time to think about a combination of cards that makes 10.

[Darren] says that 2, 7, and 1 make 10. Do you agree? . . . Now [Darren] will take those three cards and record that equation on his paper. Write $2 + 7 + 1 = 10$ on the board. Then he replaces the cards he took with cards from the deck and his turn is over.

Remind students that after each turn they should do two things—record their combination of cards on their paper and replace the missing cards with cards from the deck. The game is over when there are no more cards in the deck and no more combinations of 10 can be found. When the game is over, exchange papers with your partner and double check each other's work.

Distribute copies of *More Than Two to Make 10* (R9).

ELL English Language Learners

Model Thinking Aloud Verbalize your strategies as you model the game. For example: I chose 6 and 3 because I know their sum is less than 10. 6 plus 3 equals 9. *What* plus 9 equals 10? 1 plus 9 equals 10. So 6 plus 3 plus 1 equals 10.

As students play, ask them to explain *their* thinking. Why did you choose those three numbers? How did you know they would add to 10? Encourage them to use math terminology.

Additional Resource

Student Math Handbook

Game: *Tens Go Fish* SMH G14

Materials: Primary Number Cards (without Wild Cards)

Variation: Each player is dealt seven cards. Get three cards that add to 10. Start with two cards and ask your partner for a third card.

INVESTIGATION 3 | Combinations of 10 13

6 Activities can be used anytime after the session content is covered giving increased flexibility to teachers.

7 **Resource Masters** provide additional practice or are used as a recording sheet.

8 **ELL notes** provide teachers with suggestions to support students with language and vocabulary.

9 **Additional Resources** for students provide useful Student Math Handbook references or games to play for extra practice.

Supporting ELL Students

English Language Learners in the Math Classroom

Dr. Jim Cummins
University of Toronto

Research studies have demonstrated that English Language Learners (ELLs) generally pick up everyday conversational fluency within a year or two of starting to learn English. However, a much longer period (generally at least five years) is required for students to fully catch up to native speakers in academic language proficiency (e.g., vocabulary knowledge, reading and writing skills). In mathematics, ELL students often make good progress in acquiring basic computation skills in the early grades; however, they typically experience greater difficulty in carrying out word problems particularly as these problems become more complex linguistically in later grades.

Thus, ELL students are likely to require explicit *language* support within the classroom in order to achieve content standards in subject areas such as mathematics. Despite the fact that they have acquired conversational fluency in English together with basic mathematical vocabulary and computational skills, students may still experience gaps in their knowledge of more sophisticated vocabulary, syntax, and discourse features of mathematical language.

The linguistic challenges faced by ELL students in learning math reflect the fact that language is central to the teaching of virtually every school subject. The concepts embedded in the curriculum are inseparable from the language we use to teach these concepts to our students. For example, most mathematical problems require students to understand prepositions and logical relations that are expressed through language.

This fusion of language and content across the curriculum presents both challenges and opportunities in teaching ELL students. The challenges are to provide the instructional supports to enable ELL students to understand math content and carry out math tasks and operations. However, math instruction also provides teachers with the opportunity to extend ELL students' knowledge of language in ways that will significantly benefit their overall academic development. For example, as they learn mathematics, students are also learning that there are predictable patterns in how we form the abstract nouns that describe mathematical operations. Many of these nouns are formed by adding the suffix *–tion* to the verb, as in *add/addition, subtract/subtraction, multiply/multiplication,* etc. This knowledge can then be applied in other subject areas across the curriculum (e.g., science, language arts).

In building ELL supports for *Investigations*, we have been guided by *The Pearson ELL Curriculum Framework*, which incorporates the following five instructional principles central to teaching ELL students effectively.

1. Identify and Communicate Content and Language Objectives In planning and organizing a lesson, teachers must first identify what content and language objectives they want to communicate to students. The language objectives might include providing definitions, descriptions, examples, and visual supports for explaining vocabulary.

2. Frontload the Lesson Frontloading refers to the use of prereading or preinstructional strategies that prepare ELL students to understand new academic content. Frontloading strategies include activating prior knowledge, building background, previewing text, preteaching vocabulary, and making connections.

3. Provide Comprehensible Input Language and content that students can understand is referred to as comprehensible input. Teachers make use of nonlinguistic supports to enable students to understand language and content that would otherwise have been beyond their comprehension. Typical supports include visuals, models, and manipulatives.

4. Enable Language Production Language production complements comprehensible input and is an essential element in developing expertise in academic language. Use of both oral and written language enables students to solve problems, generate insights, express their ideas, and obtain feedback from teachers and peers.

5. Assess for Content and Language Understanding Finally, the instructional cycle flows into assessing what students have learned and then spirals upward into further development of students' content knowledge and language expertise.

These principles come to life in the *Differentiation and Intervention Guide* in the form of seven specific instructional strategies.

- ***Model Thinking Aloud*** When ELL students articulate their thinking processes through language, they are enabled to complete activities, identify gaps in their knowledge, and receive feedback from teachers. Teachers, however, must model this process in order for students to learn how to use it effectively. When modeling thinking aloud, it is important for teachers to use visuals and gestures.
- ***Partner Talk*** When it comes to working on a math activity of any kind, two heads are often better than one. Partner talk provides an audience for students' thinking aloud and an opportunity for the teacher to direct students to listen for particular vocabulary and linguistic structures as they engage in a task with their partner.
- ***Provide a Word List*** When students make a list of relevant vocabulary in a lesson with examples of how these words are used, it reinforces their knowledge of this vocabulary and provides an opportunity for teachers to monitor their understanding and provide additional explanation as needed. Paying special attention to homophones, such as *sum* and *some*, is particularly helpful for ELL students.
- ***Provide Sentence Stems*** Sentence stems provide support for ELL students to gain access to the sequence of steps in an activity, and they expand students' knowledge of how to communicate their thinking processes to the teacher and their peers.
- ***Rephrase*** Students struggling with vocabulary and language acquisition are often confused by extra details in word problems or overly wordy statements. Rephrasing statements in a different way that utilizes simpler language, shorter sentences, and eliminates unnecessary information helps students focus on and understand the important information needed to work through an activity.
- ***Suggest a Sequence*** Sequencing of steps is crucial to solving many math problems, and ELL students may need additional help in this process. Providing struggling ELL students with a sequence of steps to follow provides them with a guide for how to complete an activity or report their findings. When suggesting a sequence, be sure to use concise language.
- ***Use Repetition*** Repetition of instructions or explanations may also be required to enable ELL students to fully understand instruction. Because students are still in the process of learning English, they may need repetition, paraphrasing, or elaboration to understand teacher talk containing new vocabulary or structures.

Differentiation in Investigation 1

Mathematics in This Investigation

The mathematics focuses on developing number sense through counting and comparing quantities. It is assumed that students entering Grade 2 can identify, read, write, and sequence numbers to 100, count a set of 40–50 objects by ones, compose and decompose numbers to 15, and solve simple addition and subtraction story problems.

Additional Resource: *Seizing the Moment,* pages 76–77 (See *Implementing Investigations in Grade 2*)

Understanding the Mathematics

Students organize and count a set of 50–60 objects. They have strategies for organizing and keeping track of the count, and they know the counting sequence. They use numbers to record how many, and identify numbers on the 100 chart and number line.

Option: Assign the **Extension** activity.

Partially Understanding the Mathematics

These students may vary in their counting skills. For example, some students may have solid counting strategies up to a certain amount but may need support and practice with counting larger sets (e.g., greater than 40 objects). Other students may be inconsistent in how they organize and keep track of what has or has not been counted.

Option: Assign the **Practice** activity.

Not Understanding the Mathematics

Students who do not have accurate counting strategies are likely to be very inconsistent in utilizing strategies for counting and keeping track of a larger set of objects. They are likely to vary in more than one of the following skills: organize and keep track of what has or has not been counted, know the counting sequence up to at least 50, and/or know that the last number they say represents the total number of objects in the set.

Option: Assign the **Intervention** activity.

Investigation 1 Quiz

In addition to your observations and students' work in Investigation 1, the Quiz (R1) can be used to gather more information.

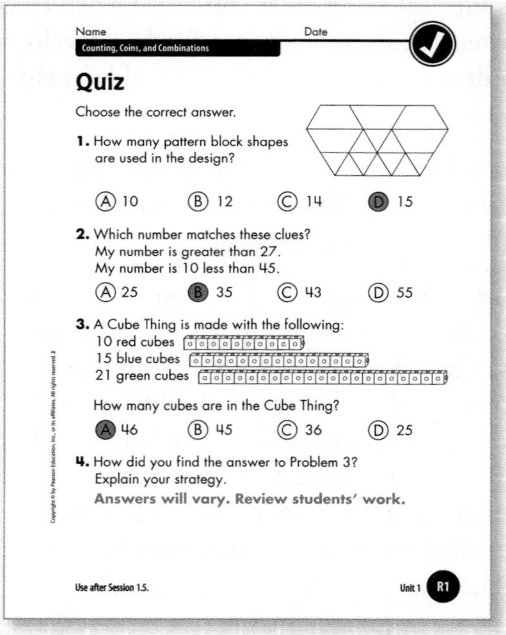
Name Date
Counting, Coins, and Combinations

Quiz

Choose the correct answer.

1. How many pattern block shapes are used in the design?

(A) 10 (B) 12 (C) 14 (D) 15

2. Which number matches these clues?
My number is greater than 27.
My number is 10 less than 45.

(A) 25 (B) 35 (C) 43 (D) 55

3. A Cube Thing is made with the following:
10 red cubes
15 blue cubes
21 green cubes

How many cubes are in the Cube Thing?

(A) 46 (B) 45 (C) 36 (D) 25

4. How did you find the answer to Problem 3? Explain your strategy.
Answers will vary. Review students' work.

Use after Session 1.5. Unit 1 R1

Intervention

20 MIN PAIRS

Strategies for Counting

Use anytime after Session 1.2.

Math Focus Points

- Counting sets of up to 60 objects

Materials: connecting cubes (60 per student); 5 index cards labeled with the numbers 25, 32, 40, 51, 60 (1 set per pair); class number line; R88

Extend the Building Cube Things activity (page 36) by having students use Blank Ten-Frames (R88) to organize and then count several sets of cubes. It is important to identify the baseline amount that students can count accurately and build from there.

Distribute a copy of R88 and at least 60 cubes to each student and a set of numbered index cards to each pair of students.

Ask students to find the card with the number 25. Let's find 25 on our class number line. Ask a volunteer to mark 25 on the class number line. If students have difficulty, have them begin at 1 and count up to 25.

Today you and a partner are going to count out several sets of cubes. You will organize your cubes on these ten-frames. Place one cube in each square of a ten-frame and count out 25 cubes for your partner. When you think you have 25, your partner will double-check your work.

Once students have finished assembling their set of 25 cubes and double-checking their partner's set, ask them to share strategies for counting 25 cubes.

Students might say:

"I counted every cube."

"I could see that there are 10 cubes in every full ten-frame so I counted 10, 20. Then I counted the other extra cubes—21, 22, 23, 24, 25."

Discuss how the ten-frame is a helpful tool for organizing and keeping track while counting a set of objects. A ten-frame organizes cubes into groups of 5 and 10. It may help students to see these subsets and use them to count.

Repeat with a new number card, adjusting the amount for each student depending on their accuracy. Remind students that for each new number they first locate the number on their number line, count out a set of cubes using the ten-frames, and then switch sets with their partner.

After pairs have counted at least three sets, they can choose one set to build a Cube Thing.

ELL English Language Learners

Model Thinking Aloud If students have difficulty counting the appropriate number of cubes, model your actions as you share your thought processes aloud. I put a cube in each square of my ten-frame. Each ten-frame holds 10 cubes, so I have 10. I can fill another ten-frame to get 20. Another full ten-frame would be too much, so I add one cube at a time until I have 25 in all.

Additional Resource

Student Math Handbook pages 33–34

Practice

25 MIN INDIVIDUALS

Cube Buildings

Use anytime after Session 1.3.

Math Focus Points

- Counting sets of up to 60 objects

Materials: connecting cubes, R2

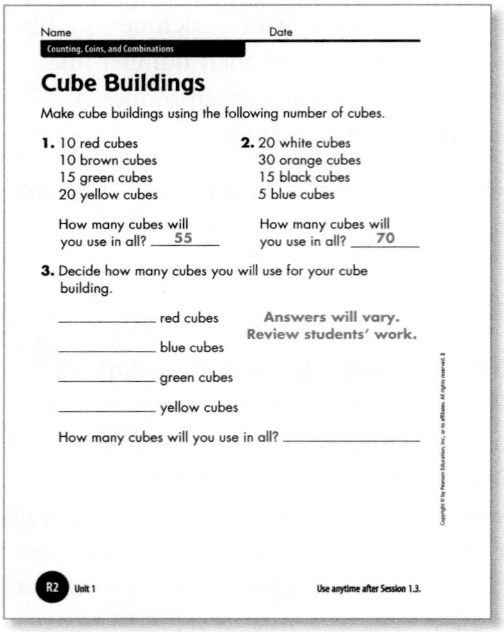

Name Date

Counting, Coins, and Combinations

Cube Buildings

Make cube buildings using the following number of cubes.

1. 10 red cubes
   10 brown cubes
   15 green cubes
   20 yellow cubes

   How many cubes will you use in all? 55

2. 20 white cubes
   30 orange cubes
   15 black cubes
   5 blue cubes

   How many cubes will you use in all? 70

3. Decide how many cubes you will use for your cube building.

   ______ red cubes
   ______ blue cubes
   ______ green cubes
   ______ yellow cubes

   Answers will vary. Review students' work.

   How many cubes will you use in all? ______

R2 Unit 1 Use anytime after Session 1.3.

This activity gives students additional practice counting larger sets of objects using a specified number of objects.

Today you will build a cube building using a list that tells how many of each color cube to use.

Distribute a copy of Cube Buildings (R2) to each student. Write the list for the first cube building on the board.

First you should count out the number of cubes for each color, then you should determine how many cubes you will use in all. How many cubes will you use in all for the first cube building? Have students share strategies for counting the total number of cubes.

Students might say:

"I know that 10 and 10 is 20 so there are 20 reds and browns. Then I would count 21, 22, 23, 24, ... until all of the cubes were counted."

"I would start with the 20 yellows and then count the reds and then the browns. When I count I would keep them in their color piles and move each pile after I counted it."

Each student should count out the specified number of cubes and determine the total number of cubes. Then have them make a cube building.

After students have created their cube buildings, have them find a partner and discuss the following questions. How are your cube buildings the same? How are they different? Students should realize that both cube buildings have the same number of cubes even if their designs are different.

Then have partners take turns explaining how they know their cube buildings have the correct number of cubes.

ELL English Language Learners

Model Thinking Aloud Some English Language Learners may have difficulty describing similarities and differences between cube buildings. Beginner ELLs may only be able to say phrases like "same number" or "different shape." Model responses to each question. Keith and I used the same number of cubes. The shapes are different. My building is a large cube but Keith's is long and skinny.

Additional Resource

Student Math Handbook pages 33–34

Extension

25 MIN INDIVIDUALS

Cube Building Riddles

Use anytime after Session 1.3.

Math Focus Points

- Counting sets of up to 60 objects

Materials: connecting cubes, R3

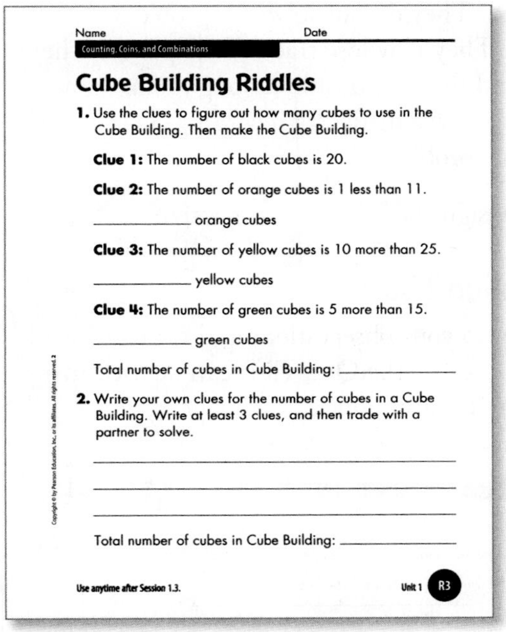
Name Date

Counting, Coins, and Combinations

Cube Building Riddles

1. Use the clues to figure out how many cubes to use in the Cube Building. Then make the Cube Building.

Clue 1: The number of black cubes is 20.

Clue 2: The number of orange cubes is 1 less than 11.

________ orange cubes

Clue 3: The number of yellow cubes is 10 more than 25.

________ yellow cubes

Clue 4: The number of green cubes is 5 more than 15.

________ green cubes

Total number of cubes in Cube Building: ________

2. Write your own clues for the number of cubes in a Cube Building. Write at least 3 clues, and then trade with a partner to solve.

____

____

____

Total number of cubes in Cube Building: ________

Use anytime after Session 1.3. Unit 1 R3

Write the following clues on the board.

Clues

1. The number of red cubes is 10.
2. The number of green cubes is 5 more than the number of red cubes.
3. The number of brown cubes is 1 more than 14.
4. The number of white cubes is 10 more than the red cubes plus green cubes.

Just as we used number clues to play *Guess My Number*, we can also use number clues to determine the number of cubes you will need to make a cube building.

Present each of the following clues and discuss strategies for finding the correct number of cubes for each color. Clue 1 tells us that there are 10 red cubes. Clue 2 says, "The number of green cubes is 5 more than the number of red cubes." How many green cubes will there be? How do you know?

Students might say:

"I know that 10 plus 5 is 15."

"I counted 10, 11, 12, 13, 14, 15 and I used my fingers to keep track of the 5."

Clue 3 tells us that the number of brown cubes is 1 more than 14. How many brown cubes will there be? How do you know? Clue 4 says, "The number of white cubes is 10 more than the number of red cubes plus green cubes." How many white cubes will there be? How do you know?

After each clue has been discussed, record the number of each color cube on the board.

After you figure out each clue, take that number of cubes and figure out the total number of cubes in your building. Discuss strategies for determining the total number of cubes.

Distribute copies of Cube Building Riddles (R3).

ELL English Language Learners

Rephrase If students have difficulty finding the correct number of cubes based on the clues, it may help to shorten or rephrase the clues. For example: There are 5 more green cubes than red cubes.

Additional Resource

Student Math Handbook pages 33–34

Differentiation in Investigation 2

Mathematics in This Investigation

The mathematics focuses on counting a set of up to 60 objects by 1s and by groups. It also focuses on developing an understanding of addition and subtraction by interpreting and solving story problems with totals up to 45.

Understanding the Mathematics

Students count a set of 60 or more objects in at least one way with strategies for organizing and keeping track of the count. They are able to interpret a story problem and solve it accurately. Students may model the problem with cubes or circles and count all. Some students may be able to solve the problem by counting on (or back) or reason about the quantities based on what they already know.

Option: Assign the **Extension** activity.

Partially Understanding the Mathematics

Students may vary in their counting skills and may need practice with organizing and counting larger sets. They may be able to interpret a story problem, but they make mistakes as they count or combine the numbers. These students may be able to find and correct errors on their own. Some students may understand what the problem is asking, but they struggle with where to start and stop when counting on or back. These students may be losing the connection between the numbers and the situation.

Option: Assign the **Practice** activity.

Not Understanding the Mathematics

Students may not be able to accurately count a large set of objects. They may lose track of their count, not know the number sequence to 60, or not know that the last number they say represents the total in the set. Students may have difficulty interpreting a story problem and need support to make sense of what is being asked. They do not solve the problem accurately. They may lose track of the parts of the problem and the relationship among them. Some students may have difficulty recording their strategy for solving a problem.

Option: Assign the **Intervention** activity.

Investigation 2 Quiz

In addition to your observations and students' work in Investigation 2, the Quiz (R4) can be used to gather more information.

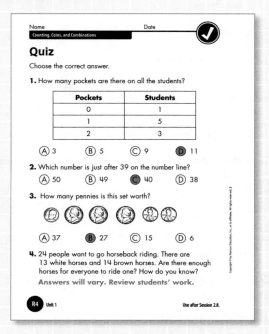

Name Date

Counting, Coins, and Combinations

Quiz

Choose the correct answer.

1. How many pockets are there on all the students?

Pockets	Students
0	1
1	5
2	3

Ⓐ 3 Ⓑ 5 Ⓒ 9 Ⓓ 11

2. Which number is just after 39 on the number line?

Ⓐ 50 Ⓑ 49 Ⓒ 40 Ⓓ 38

3. How many pennies is this set worth?

Ⓐ 37 Ⓑ 27 Ⓒ 15 Ⓓ 6

4. 24 people want to go horseback riding. There are 13 white horses and 14 brown horses. Are there enough horses for everyone to ride one? How do you know?

Answers will vary. Review students' work.

Copyright © by Pearson Education, Inc., or its affiliates. All rights reserved. 2

R4 Unit 1 Use after Session 2.8.

Intervention

20 MIN PAIRS

Will Each Person Get One?

Use anytime after Session 2.1.

Math Focus Points

- Comparing two amounts under 45 to find the difference

Materials: connecting cubes (15 per pair plus 20 extra), bags (1 per pair plus 1 extra), R88

Materials to Prepare: Fill a bag with 8–15 cubes for each pair, putting a different number in each bag. Prepare one extra bag containing 7 cubes for demonstration purposes.

Simplify the situation in Enough for the Class? (page 65) as follows. There are 10 people sitting at a table. Show students Blank Ten-Frames (R88). I'm going to draw a face for each person. How many faces should I draw? Explain that the faces represent the people at the table. Count to verify that there are exactly 10 faces. Hold up the bag of 7 cubes. Let's find out if there are enough cubes in this bag for each person at the table to get one.

Pour the cubes from the bag and have students count to verify the total. Then, starting at the top left, place one cube on each face as everyone counts: 1, 2, 3, . . . 7.

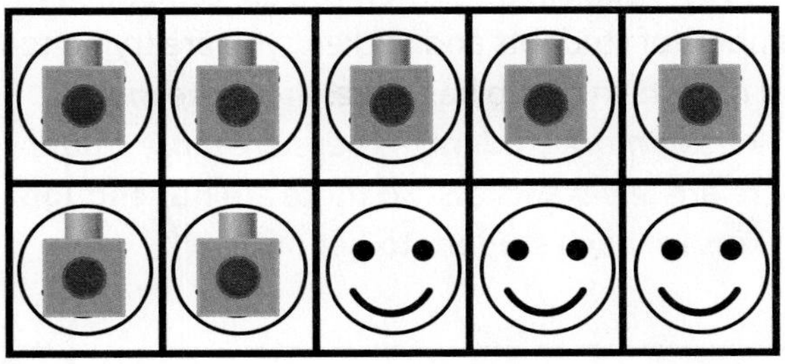

Are there enough cubes for each person at the table to get one? How many more do we need? How can we find out?

Students might say:

"Count how many faces don't have cubes."

"I can see that 3 faces don't have a cube."

So, if we have 10 people and 7 cubes, there are not enough cubes in the bag for each person to get one.

Repeat the problem using the bag of 16 cubes. Remind students that there are still 10 people at the table. After determining the number of cubes in the bag and if there are enough cubes for the people at the table, discuss how many extra cubes there are.

Distribute a bag of cubes and a copy of R88 to each pair of students. Have them work together to draw 10 faces on one blank ten-frame. They count the number of cubes in their bag and determine if there are enough cubes for the 10 people to each get one. Then have the pairs find out how many more they need or how many extras there are.

ELL English Language Learners

Model Thinking Aloud As you demonstrate the problem with 7 cubes, model your thinking aloud. First, I put one cube on top of each face. I used all of the cubes in the bag but there are still some faces without cubes. There are not enough cubes for every person to get one. Next, I count the faces that don't have a cube: 1, 2, 3. I need 3 more cubes for every person to get one.

As pairs solve other problems, ask probing questions to help them explain their thinking. For example: [Anita and Chen], I see that you put one cube on top of each face. Why did you do that?

Additional Resource

Student Math Handbook pages 33–34

Practice

25 MIN INDIVIDUALS

Enough or Not Enough?

Use anytime after Session 2.2.

Math Focus Points

- Comparing two amounts under 45 to find the difference

Materials: connecting cubes (as needed), R5

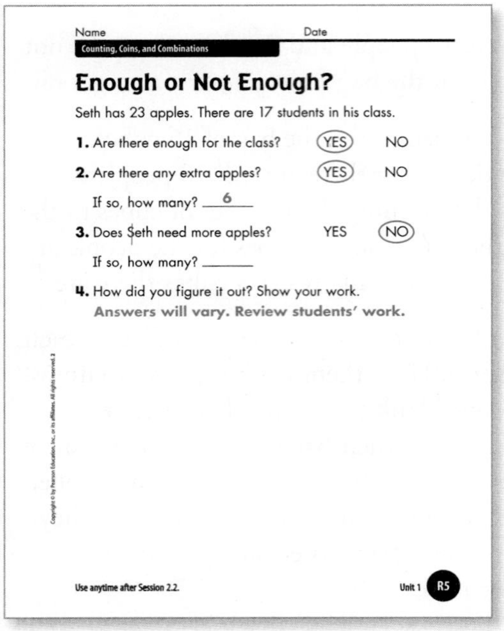

Name Date

Counting, Coins, and Combinations

Enough or Not Enough?

Seth has 23 apples. There are 17 students in his class.

1. Are there enough for the class? (YES) NO

2. Are there any extra apples? (YES) NO

If so, how many? 6

3. Does Seth need more apples? YES (NO)

If so, how many? ______

4. How did you figure it out? Show your work.

Answers will vary. Review students' work.

Use anytime after Session 2.2. Unit 1 R5

Read the following problem aloud. Mrs. Reed has 23 stickers. There are 13 boys and 14 girls in her class. Are there enough stickers for each student in her class to get one?

Review the information in the problem. Write it on the board. What does the problem tell us? What do we know? What do we need to find out?

Discuss the steps for solving the problem. First, we need to find out how many students are in Mrs. Reed's class. How could we do that? Next, we need to compare the number of students with the number of stickers. How could we do that?

Students might say:

"Make a cube tower for the stickers and a cube tower for the students. It shows there are more students."

"Show the students and the stickers on a number line. Since 23 is less than 27, there are not enough stickers."

How many more stickers does Mrs. Reed need? How did you find out? Ask students to explain their strategies. Record them on the board.

Present a second problem for students to solve on their own. There are 32 basketballs. There are 15 boys and 12 girls in gym class. Are there enough basketballs for each student to get one?

After students have solved the problem, bring them together to discuss their solutions. Are there enough basketballs for each student to get one? How many extras are there? How did you find out? If any new strategies are mentioned, add them to the list on the board.

Distribute copies of Enough or Not Enough? (R5).

ELL English Language Learners

Rephrase Explain that when you are *comparing* the numbers of students and stickers, you are trying to find out which group has *more*. Are there *more* stickers or *more* students? There are *more* students. There are *fewer* stickers. So there are not enough stickers for each student to get one.

Additional Resource

Student Math Handbook pages 23–24

Extension

20 MIN INDIVIDUALS

Two or More Bones

Use anytime after Session 2.1.

Math Focus Points

- Comparing two amounts under 45 to find the difference

Materials: connecting cubes (30–55 per student), R6 (2 per student)

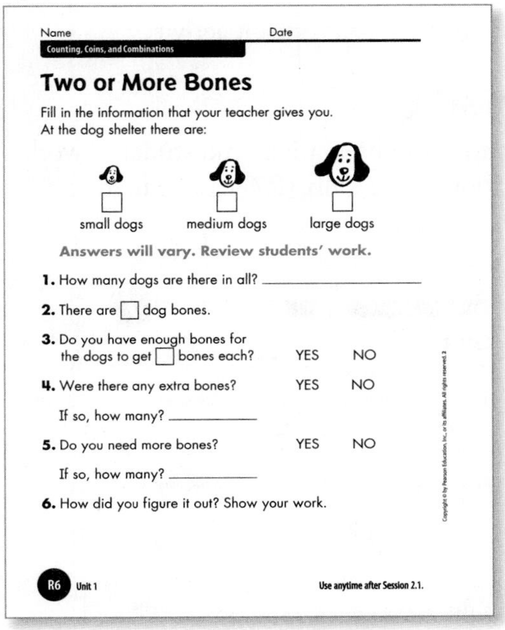

Name Date

Counting, Coins, and Combinations

Two or More Bones

Fill in the information that your teacher gives you.
At the dog shelter there are:

☐ small dogs ☐ medium dogs ☐ large dogs

Answers will vary. Review students' work.

1. How many dogs are there in all? ________

2. There are ☐ dog bones.

3. Do you have enough bones for the dogs to get ☐ bones each? YES NO

4. Were there any extra bones? YES NO

If so, how many? ________

5. Do you need more bones? YES NO

If so, how many? ________

6. How did you figure it out? Show your work.

R6 Unit 1 Use anytime after Session 2.1.

Materials to Prepare: On the board, draw 3 simple, different-sized dogs. Label as shown below.

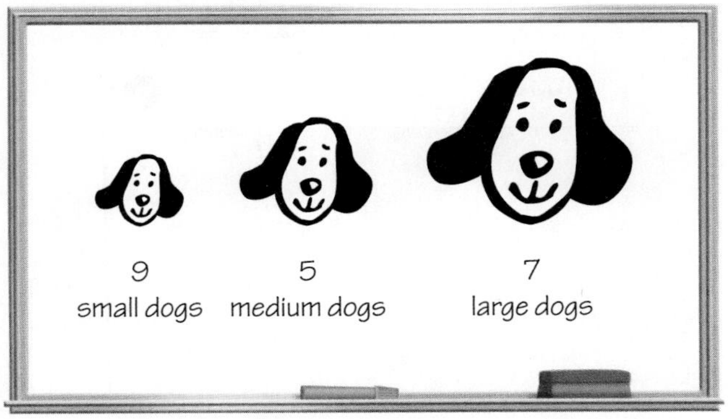

Distribute a copy of Two or More Bones (R6) to each student. Read the following problem aloud. A pet store has dogs for sale. This picture shows how many small, medium, and large dogs there are. You have 44 dog bones. Do you have enough for each dog at the pet store to get 2 bones each? Direct students to fill in the information about this problem on R6. Students should fill in the number of each type of dog, the total number of bones *(44),* and number of bones each dog gets *(2).*

Students work individually to solve the problem. After students solve the problem, discuss multiple ways of solving the problem. Is there another way to solve the problem? Who did it a different way?

Distribute another copy of R6 to each student. Use the same story above but tell students that this time each dog gets 3 bones. This resource can be used repeatedly by changing one or more of the variables in the problem.

ELL English Language Learners

Suggest a Sequence Support English Language Learners in explaining their strategies by helping them sequence their steps. What did you do *first*? What did you do *next*? What did you do *after* that? Record students' answers to help them understand their own thinking processes.

Additional Resource

Student Math Handbook

Game: *Guess My Number on the 100 Chart* SMH G8

Materials: 100 chart

Variation: After guessing each number, have students show the number in 3 different ways.

Differentiation in Investigation 3

Mathematics in This Investigation

The mathematics focuses on developing fluency with the combinations of 10 by playing games involving 2-addend combinations of 10, generating equivalent expressions for 10, and solving missing addend problems with a total of 10.

Additional Resources: *Helping Students Prepare to Share Ideas,* pages 75–76 (See *Implementing Investigations in Grade 2*); *Tens and More,* pages 79–80 (See *Implementing Investigations in Grade 2*)

Understanding the Mathematics

Students are fluent with all of the Make 10, Plus 1, and Plus 2 addition combinations. They understand commutativity (e.g., $4 + 6 = 10$, so $6 + 4 = 10$). They use their knowledge of addition combinations to quickly solve missing addend problems (e.g., $7 + \_ = 10$). Students begin to reason numerically about addition, knowing that if you take 1 from one addend and give it to the other, the total stays the same (e.g., $8 + 2 = 10$, so take 1 from the 8 and give it to the 2 to make $7 + 3 = 10$).

Option: Assign the **Extension** activity.

Partially Understanding the Mathematics

Students are fluent with many, but not all, of the Make 10, Plus 1, and Plus 2 addition combinations. They use this information to solve missing addend problems (e.g., $7 + \_ = 10$). They may pause to figure out the answer to some combinations. They may not understand commutativity or be able to easily and quickly reason numerically about a combination that they don't yet know.

Option: Assign the **Practice** activity.

Not Understanding the Mathematics

Students may know some of the Make 10, Plus 1, and Plus 2 addition combinations. While they are familiar with many of the combinations, they are not yet fluent with them and may use their fingers or cubes to model and solve problems. They may not yet understand commutativity, nor do they reason numerically about a combination that they don't yet know.

Option: Assign the **Intervention** activity.

Investigation 3 Quiz

In addition to your observations and students' work in Investigation 3, the Quiz (R7) can be used to gather more information.

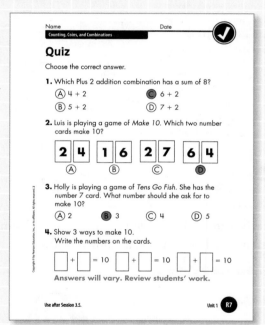

Name Date

Counting, Coins, and Combinations

Quiz

Choose the correct answer.

1. Which Plus 2 addition combination has a sum of 8?
   - Ⓐ 4 + 2
   - Ⓑ 5 + 2
   - Ⓒ 6 + 2
   - Ⓓ 7 + 2
2. Luis is playing a game of *Make 10.* Which two number cards make 10?
   - Ⓐ 2 4
   - Ⓑ 1 6
   - Ⓒ 2 7
   - Ⓓ 6 4
3. Holly is playing a game of *Tens Go Fish.* She has the number 7 card. What number should she ask for to make 10?
   - Ⓐ 2
   - Ⓑ 3
   - Ⓒ 4
   - Ⓓ 5
4. Show 3 ways to make 10. Write the numbers on the cards.

   ☐ + ☐ = 10 ☐ + ☐ = 10 ☐ + ☐ = 10

   Answers will vary. Review students' work.

Use after Session 3.5. Unit 1 R7

Intervention

25 MIN INDIVIDUALS

How Many More Make 10?

Use anytime after Session 3.2.

Math Focus Points

- Finding the missing addend to make a total of 10
- Using equations to record

Materials: connecting cubes (10 per student), number cubes (1 per student)

Explain to students that they will find different pairs of numbers that add together to make 10. Display a tower of 7 cubes. Here are 7 cubes. 7 and *what* make 10? Record the equation 7 + _ = 10 on the board. How can we find out how many more cubes we need?

Students might say:

"Add 1 cube at a time to the tower until you reach 10."

"Draw 10 dots. Make a circle around 7 of them. Then count how many are outside the circle."

Discuss and model students' ideas. If no one suggests it, model the following strategy. Display a tower of 10 cubes. Here is a tower of 10 cubes. If I break off 7, the cubes that are left will show how many more I need to have 10 cubes in all. Demonstrate breaking 7 cubes off the tower and counting the cubes that remain. Write 7 + 3 = 10.

Put the tower of 10 cubes back together. What if I break off 4 cubes? How many more do I need to make 10? Write 4 + _ = 10. Break 4 cubes off the tower and have students help count the cubes that remain. Write 6 in the blank. 4 plus 6 equals 10.

Today, you will find combinations for 10. You will roll a number cube, take that many cubes, and then figure how many more you need to make 10. Then you will record that number combination on your paper.

Demonstrate the activity. First, roll a number cube. Ask a volunteer to roll a number cube. [Simon] rolled a [2]. [Simon] would write [2] + _ = 10 on his paper. Next, Simon would figure out how many more cubes he needs to make 10. Have [Simon] do this. Then, he would complete the equation: [2] + [8] = 10.

After 10 minutes, bring students together to make a list of the Make 10 combinations. For each combination shared, ask the other students if they agree or not by showing a thumbs up or down. Students who do not agree may use cube towers to disprove the combination.

ELL English Language Learners

Provide a Word List To help students with unfamiliar words, make a word list and post it on the wall: *break, combination,* and *missing*. Explain the meaning of each word and use the word in a recognizable context.

Have students say the words and act them out. If more support is needed, students can copy the words onto paper and draw pictures next to them to help them remember their meanings.

Additional Resource

Student Math Handbook

Game: *Make 10* SMH G9

Materials: Primary Number Cards (with Wild Cards)

Variation: Play with the Wild Cards. A Wild Card can be any number.

Practice

25 MIN INDIVIDUALS

Plus 1, Plus 2, or Make 10?

Use anytime after Session 3.5.

Math Focus Points

- Developing fluency with the Make 10, Plus 1, and Plus 2 addition combinations

Vocabulary: addition combinations

Materials: Primary Number Cards (without Wild Cards; 1 deck per pair), blank paper, R8

Name Date

Counting, Coins, and Combinations

Plus 1, Plus 2, or Make 10?

Write Plus 1 addition combinations.

1. ☐ + 1 = ___ 2. ☐ + 1 = ___

3. ☐ + 1 = ___ 4. ☐ + 1 = ___

Answers will vary. Review students' work.

Write Plus 2 addition combinations.

5. ☐ + 2 = ___ 6. ☐ + 2 = ___

7. ☐ + 2 = ___ 8. ☐ + 2 = ___

Answers will vary. Review students' work.

Write Make 10 addition combinations.

9. 5 + 5 = 10 10. 9 + 1 = 10

11. 6 + 4 = 10 12. 7 + 3 = 10

R8 Unit 1 Use anytime after Session 3.5.

Tell students that they are going to practice addition combinations. Give each student a sheet of blank paper.

Explain the activity as you model these steps:

- Fold a sheet of paper into 3 columns. Label the top of each column: + 1, + 2, and Make 10.
- Shuffle the number cards. Place the deck facedown on the table in a pile. Turn the top card over.
- Record an addition combination in each column using that number. For example, if you draw a 9 you would write $9 + 1 = 10$, $9 + 2 = 11$, and $9 + 1 = 10$ in the respective columns.
- When all the number cards have been used, shuffle and use them again to add more addition combinations to the list.

Distribute a deck of Primary Number Cards (without Wild Cards) to each pair. Have students work for about 15 minutes and then gather them together to discuss their work.

Ask volunteers to name the Plus 1 combinations they have on their papers. Write them in a column on the board. Does anyone have a Plus 1 addition combination that is not yet on the board? Do you think we found them all?

Repeat for the Plus 2 combinations and the Make 10 combinations. Are any addition combinations listed under more than one heading? Why? Which addition combinations are listed under only one heading? Students are likely to notice that many of the Make 10 addition combinations are also Plus 1 or Plus 2 combinations.

Distribute copies of Plus 1, Plus 2, or Make 10? (R8).

ELL English Language Learners

Partner Talk Before beginning individual work, pair ELLs to give them practice with English. Ask them to retell the steps for the activity to each other. The more proficient speaker should retell the steps first. Listen for words such as *addition combination* and *sum* in their explanations.

Additional Resource

Student Math Handbook

Game: *Tens Go Fish* SMH G14

Materials: Primary Number Cards (with Wild Cards)

Extension

25 MIN PAIRS

More Than Two to Make 10

Use anytime after Session 3.4.

Math Focus Points

- Developing fluency with the Make 10, Plus 1, and Plus 2 addition combinations
- Using equations to record

Materials: Primary Number Cards (without Wild Cards; 1 deck per pair), blank paper, R9

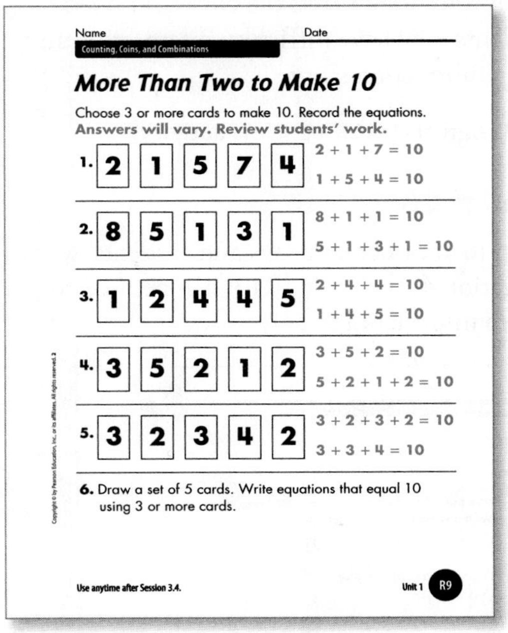

Name Date

Counting, Coins, and Combinations

More Than Two to Make 10

Choose 3 or more cards to make 10. Record the equations.
Answers will vary. Review students' work.

1. 2 1 5 7 4 — $2 + 1 + 7 = 10$; $1 + 5 + 4 = 10$
2. 8 5 1 3 1 — $8 + 1 + 1 = 10$; $5 + 1 + 3 + 1 = 10$
3. 1 2 4 4 5 — $2 + 4 + 4 = 10$; $1 + 4 + 5 = 10$
4. 3 5 2 1 2 — $3 + 5 + 2 = 10$; $5 + 2 + 1 + 2 = 10$
5. 3 2 3 4 2 — $3 + 2 + 3 + 2 = 10$; $3 + 3 + 4 = 10$
6. Draw a set of 5 cards. Write equations that equal 10 using 3 or more cards.

Copyright © by Pearson Education, Inc., or its affiliates. All rights reserved. 2

Use anytime after Session 3.4. Unit 1 R9

More Than Two to Make 10 is a variation of the game *Make 10.* Just like *Make 10,* the goal of the game is to choose numbers that add to 10. In this variation, students choose three or more number cards that add to 10.

Just like *Make 10,* arrange the number cards into four rows of five cards, number-side up. Lay out the cards.

The object of this game is to find three or more cards that, when added together, make 10. Who sees three cards that together add up to a total of 10? Give students time to think about a combination of cards that makes 10.

[Darren] says that 2, 7, and 1 make 10. Do you agree? . . . Now [Darren] will take those three cards and record that equation on his paper. Write $2 + 7 + 1 = 10$ on the board. Then he replaces the cards he took with cards from the deck and his turn is over.

Remind students that after each turn they should do two things—record their combination of cards on their paper and replace the missing cards with cards from the deck. The game is over when there are no more cards in the deck and no more combinations of 10 can be found. When the game is over, exchange papers with your partner and double check each other's work.

Distribute copies of *More Than Two to Make 10* (R9).

ELL English Language Learners

Model Thinking Aloud Verbalize your strategies as you model the game. For example: I chose 6 and 3 because I know their sum is less than 10. 6 plus 3 equals 9. *What* plus 9 equals 10? 1 plus 9 equals 10. So 6 plus 3 plus 1 equals 10.

As students play, ask them to explain *their* thinking. Why did you choose those three numbers? How did you know they would add to 10? Encourage them to use math terminology.

Additional Resource

Student Math Handbook

Game: *Tens Go Fish* SMH G14

Materials: Primary Number Cards (without Wild Cards)

Variation: Each player is dealt seven cards. Get three cards that add to 10. Start with two cards and ask your partner for a third card.

Differentiation in Investigation 4

Mathematics in This Investigation

The mathematics focuses on making sense of addition and subtraction (as removal) problems with totals up to 45. Strategies are developed for solving these problems and recording solutions.

Understanding the Mathematics

Students interpret, model, and accurately solve addition and subtraction story problems. They understand the structure of a problem, can form a mental image or build a model that represents the problem, and solve the problem. Students who count on or add by place are demonstrating a deeper understanding of the operation of addition and of the quantities in the problem than those who are counting all. Students may solve a subtraction problem by counting all, counting back, or subtracting a number in parts. Students record strategies that show clearly how they solved the problem.

Option: Assign the **Extension** activity.

Partially Understanding the Mathematics

Students may understand that the structure of an addition problem is about combining two groups and finding the total, but they make errors in their computation. Some students may struggle with knowing where to start and stop when counting on. Students may record a different strategy than the one they actually used to solve the problem but that is easier to represent (e.g., counting all). Students may understand that the structure of a subtraction problem is about removing one quantity from another and finding how many are left, but they make computational errors or have difficulty keeping track of what they need to do. Some students may not know where to start or stop when counting back or may be unsure of the counting back sequence.

Option: Assign the **Practice** activity.

Not Understanding the Mathematics

Some students may still be working on understanding the structure of a problem. They are unsure of what the problem is asking or what steps they need to take to solve it. The may know that in an addition problem the total should be more than either addend, or that in a subtraction problem the result is less than the total number they started with. They may be able to represent the quantities in a problem by drawing all the objects, but they count inaccurately and do not find the correct answer. Some students may have difficulty interpreting and modeling a subtraction story.

Option: Assign the **Intervention** activity.

Investigation 4 Quiz

In addition to your observations and students' work in Investigation 4, the Quiz (R10) can be used to gather more information.

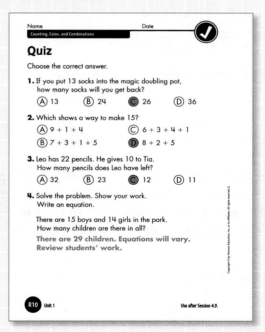

Name Date

Counting, Coins, and Combinations

Quiz

Choose the correct answer.

1. If you put 13 socks into the magic doubling pot, how many socks will you get back?

(A) 13 (B) 24 (C) 26 (D) 36

2. Which shows a way to make 15?

(A) 9 + 1 + 4 (C) 6 + 3 + 4 + 1

(B) 7 + 3 + 1 + 5 (D) 8 + 2 + 5

3. Leo has 22 pencils. He gives 10 to Tia. How many pencils does Leo have left?

(A) 32 (B) 23 (C) 12 (D) 11

4. Solve the problem. Show your work. Write an equation.

There are 15 boys and 14 girls in the park. How many children are there in all?

There are 29 children. Equations will vary. Review students' work.

Copyright © by Pearson Education, Inc., or its affiliates. All rights reserved. 2

R10 Unit 1 Use after Session 4.9.

Intervention

25 MIN INDIVIDUALS

Visualizing Story Problems

Use anytime after Session 4.4.

Math Focus Points

- Visualizing, retelling, and modeling the action of addition and subtraction (as removal) situations
- Using standard notation (+, −, =) to represent addition and subtraction situations

Vocabulary: plus sign, equal sign, minus sign

Materials: connecting cubes (as needed), pocket 100 chart, class number line, blank paper, crayons, "Story Problem Steps" chart (from Session 4.4, p. 156), "Strategies for Problem #1" chart (optional; from Session 4.1, p. 141)

Display the "Story Problem Steps" chart (page 156). Direct attention to the first step: "Read the problem. Imagine the story in your head." I'm going to read a story problem. Listen carefully. Close your eyes and try to picture what is happening. Think about the information given in the story.

Travis brought 14 juice boxes to class. Nadia brought 13 juice boxes. How many juice boxes do they have in all? After reading the problem twice, have students open their eyes.

Discuss the action in the problem. How does the story begin? What happens in the story? What is the problem asking you to find? Will there be more or fewer juice boxes in the end? Why?

How many juice boxes does Travis have? On the board, record Travis, 14 juice boxes. How many juice boxes does Nadia have? On the board, record Nadia, 13 juice boxes.

Provide students with a sheet of blank paper (folded in half) and crayons. Direct them to use the left half of their papers to record this information.

Ask students how they would solve the problem and then give them a few minutes to solve the problem. Provide cubes, as needed. Ask them to record their solutions on the right half of their papers.

Students share their solution strategies. Model how to record each strategy. [Leo] drew each juice box and then counted them all, and [Anita] showed the two groups of juice boxes using a set of 14 cubes and a group of 13 cubes.

You may want to compare today's strategies to the "Strategies for Problem #1" chart (page 141). Are any of the strategies the same? Are there any on the chart that we didn't use today?

Ask students to help you write an equation for the problem. Connect the symbols (+ and =) to the action in the story. Point to each addend in the equation. The plus sign means that the two groups of juice boxes are being put together. Point to the numbers on either side of the equal sign. The equal sign shows that two things are the same or equal.

Repeat the process using a subtraction (removal) problem. There are 28 apples on the table. Students eat 6 of them. How many apples are left? When writing the equation for the subtraction problem, explain that the minus sign in this problem means to separate some of the apples from the original amount.

ELL English Language Learners

Suggest a Sequence Some students might need help explaining their strategies. Ask questions that will help them sequence the steps they used to solve the problem. What did you do *first*? What did you do *next*? What did you do *after* that? Record students' answers to help them understand their own thinking processes.

Additional Resource

Student Math Handbook pages 59–60, 67

Practice

20 MIN INDIVIDUALS

Modeling Story Problems

Use anytime after Session 4.5.

Math Focus Points

- Solving addition and subtraction (as removal) story problems
- Using standard notation (+, −, =) to represent addition and subtraction situations

Materials: "Story Problem Steps" chart (from Session 4.4, p. 156), connecting cubes (as needed), pocket 100 chart, class number line, R11

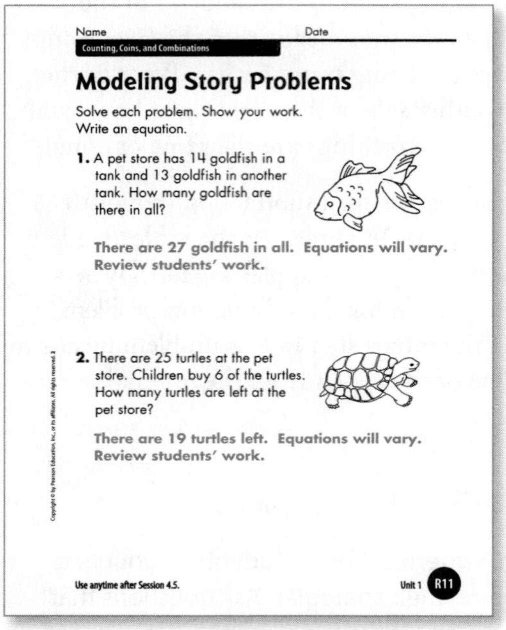

Name Date

Counting, Coins, and Combinations

Modeling Story Problems

Solve each problem. Show your work.
Write an equation.

1. A pet store has 14 goldfish in a tank and 13 goldfish in another tank. How many goldfish are there in all?

There are 27 goldfish in all. Equations will vary. Review students' work.

2. There are 25 turtles at the pet store. Children buy 6 of the turtles. How many turtles are left at the pet store?

There are 19 turtles left. Equations will vary. Review students' work.

Use anytime after Session 4.5. Unit 1 R11

Review the "Story Problem Steps" chart (page 156). Read the following problem aloud. Jeffrey had 28 seashells. He gave 13 of them to Leigh. How many seashells did Jeffrey have left?

Discuss the information given in the problem. At the beginning, how many seashells does Jeffrey have? Does Jeffrey get more seashells or are some taken away? Will Jeffrey have more than or less than 28 seashells? How do you know?

Talk about strategies for solving the problem. How would you solve the problem? What tools would you use to model the problem? Does anyone have a different way?

Students might say:

"Show 28 cubes. Take away 13 of them. Count how many are left."

"Show 28 minus 13 on a number line."

Have students share their ways of recording their strategies. [Luis] made dots to stand for the seashells. [Carla] only put the important numbers in the problem on the number line. She didn't have to write them all.

Write an equation together. What number is first? How do you know? What symbol is next? Where does the equal sign go?

Read the following addition problem aloud. Melissa had 17 seashells. Henry gave her 15 more. How many seashells did Melissa have then? Have students solve the problem, record their strategies, and write an equation. Then discuss their solutions and strategies as a group.

Distribute copies of Modeling Story Problems (R11).

ELL English Language Learners

Use Repetition Read each problem several times with students. Focus on any words with which students may be unfamiliar. Then have students retell the problem in their own words. Prompt them with supporting questions, as necessary.

Additional Resource

Student Math Handbook pages 67–68

Extension

25 MIN INDIVIDUALS

Story Problems with Multiple Parts

Use anytime after Session 4.4.

Math Focus Points

- Solving addition and subtraction (as removal) story problems
- Using standard notation (+, −, =) to represent addition and subtraction situations

Materials: connecting cubes (as needed), pocket 100 chart, class number line, R12

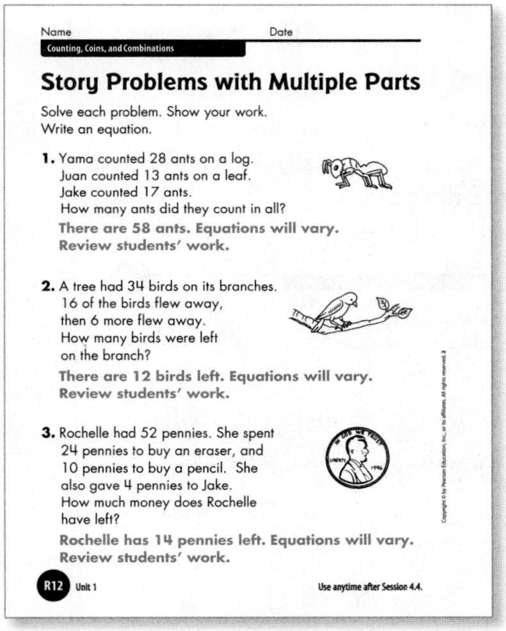

Name Date

Counting, Coins, and Combinations

Story Problems with Multiple Parts

Solve each problem. Show your work.
Write an equation.

1. Yama counted 28 ants on a log.
Juan counted 13 ants on a leaf.
Jake counted 17 ants.
How many ants did they count in all?
There are 58 ants. Equations will vary. Review students' work.

2. A tree had 34 birds on its branches.
16 of the birds flew away,
then 6 more flew away.
How many birds were left on the branch?
There are 12 birds left. Equations will vary. Review students' work.

3. Rochelle had 52 pennies. She spent 24 pennies to buy an eraser, and 10 pennies to buy a pencil. She also gave 4 pennies to Jake.
How much money does Rochelle have left?
Rochelle has 14 pennies left. Equations will vary. Review students' work.

R12 Unit 1 Use anytime after Session 4.4.

Explain to students that you will read a story problem to them and they are to take notes, writing down all the important information that they hear in the problem. Esteban has 26 marbles. Katrina has 18 marbles. Kira has 7 marbles. How many marbles do Esteban, Katrina, and Kira have in all?

Discuss the notes students wrote. What important information did you write down? What is the whole and what are the parts? What are we asked to find out? Is this an addition problem or a subtraction problem?

Students solve the problem individually, record their strategies, and write an equation. Remind them to use the problem-solving tools available to help them.

When students have finished, bring the group back together to discuss their strategies. What equation did you write? How did you solve the problem?

Students might say:

"I added 10 and 20 together for 30. I put the 8 and 6 together. That's 30 plus 14, or 44 in all. Then I added on the 7 and got 51."

"I added 18 and 7 and got 25. Then I added 26 on the 100 chart. I started at 25 and went 35, 45, 50, 51."

List students' strategies on the board. Did anyone solve the problem in a different way? Did anyone get a different answer? Guide students who got incorrect answers in retracing their steps and finding their mistakes.

Distribute copies of Story Problems with Multiple Parts (R12).

ELL English Language Learners

Partner Talk Support students in explaining their strategies by modeling steps in a clear sequence. Have students practice by explaining their strategy to a partner and acting out each step.

Additional Resource

Student Math Handbook pages 63–64

Differentiation in Investigation 1

Mathematics in This Investigation

The mathematics focuses on describing and identifying attributes of 3-D shapes. This information is used to match a 3-D shape to a 2-D image as well as to sort shapes into groups.

Understanding the Mathematics

Students correctly identify and describe the important mathematical features (e.g., number and shape of faces) of 3-D shapes and use these attributes to sort shapes into groups. They recognize the relationships within the set of Geoblocks and use this knowledge to compose or decompose the blocks into new shapes. They can easily match a single Geoblock to its 2-D image.

Option: Assign the **Extension** activity.

Partially Understanding the Mathematics

Students can describe and identify many features of 3-D shapes. While they recognize the important attributes of shapes, they may not use geometric terms to describe these attributes or use them to sort the shapes into exclusive groups. They recognize relationships within the set of Geoblocks and can use this knowledge to compose or decompose some of the blocks into new shapes. Students may not readily see and match a 3-D block to its 2-D image.

Option: Assign the **Practice** activity.

Not Understanding the Mathematics

Students are not able to accurately identify or describe the attributes of 3-D shapes. When describing a shape, they may focus on non-geometric attributes (e.g., color). They may have difficulty counting the number of faces and seeing that similar shapes have similar attributes. They may not understand that shapes can be combined or decomposed to make other shapes or recognize the relationships within the set of Geoblocks. Students are likely to be challenged by matching a single Geoblock to a 2-D image of the block.

Option: Assign the **Intervention** activity.

Investigation 1 Quiz

In addition to your observations and students' work in Investigation 1, the Quiz (R13) can be used to gather more information.

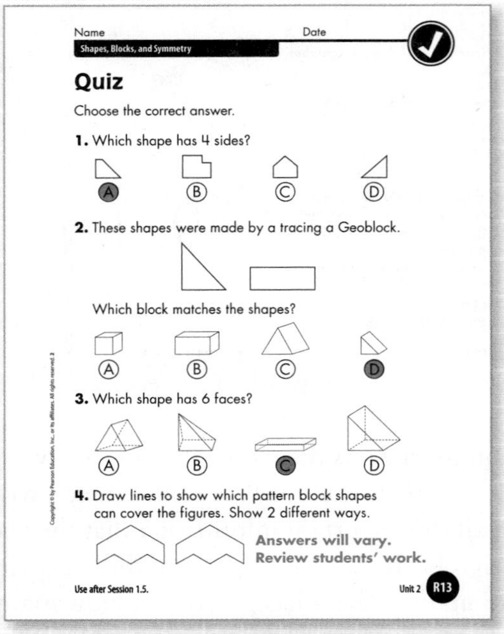
Name Date
Shapes, Blocks, and Symmetry

Quiz

Choose the correct answer.

1. Which shape has 4 sides?
(A) (B) (C) (D)

2. These shapes were made by a tracing a Geoblock.

Which block matches the shapes?
(A) (B) (C) (D)

3. Which shape has 6 faces?
(A) (B) (C) (D)

4. Draw lines to show which pattern block shapes can cover the figures. Show 2 different ways.

Answers will vary. Review students' work.

Copyright © by Pearson Education, Inc., or its affiliates. All rights reserved. 2

Use after Session 1.5. Unit 2 R13

Intervention

20 MIN PAIRS

Block Matching

Use anytime after Session 1.2.

Math Focus Points

- Attending to features of 3-D shapes, particularly the number and shape of faces

Vocabulary: face

Materials: Find the Block Task Cards 7–12 (M10–M12; 1 set per pair), Geoblocks (I, J, M, O, P, X; 1 set per pair)

Adapt the situation in Introducing Find the Block (page 32) as follows. Hold up Task Card 7 from the Find the Block Task Cards (M10–M12). Take a look at this card. It shows all the faces, or sides, of one of these Geoblocks, and was made by tracing around each face. Can you figure out by looking at this card how many faces the Geoblock has? What shapes are the faces of the Geoblock?

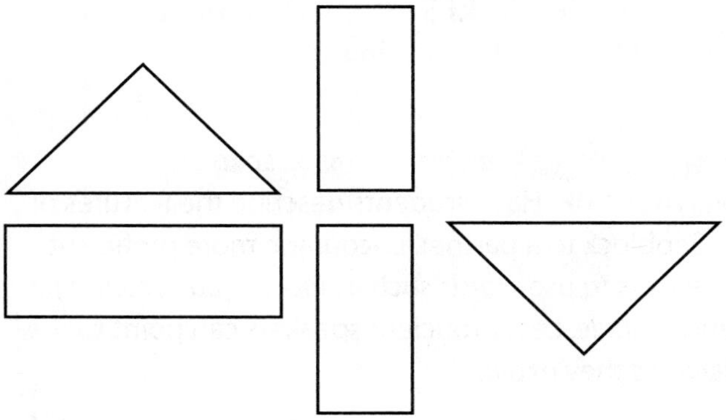

Students might say:

"The card shows 2 triangles. I need to find a Geoblock with 2 triangle faces."

"The card shows 3 rectangles. I need to find a Geoblock with 3 rectangle faces."

Show Geoblocks I, J, M, O, P, and X. Ask students to select the one that matches Task Card 7. Explain that there may be more than one block with the same shape faces, but both the shapes and sizes of the faces must match the card exactly. Show students how to check to make sure each face of a block matches one shape on Task Card 7.

This activity is called Block Matching. You will be using Task Cards 7–12. Each Task Card matches only one Geoblock. You will work with a partner to match each Geoblock with a Task Card that shows all of that block's faces.

First, you and your partner should each choose a Task Card and look for the matching block. Once you have each found a block, check each other's work. Then lay each block on top of its card and choose two new cards. Continue until each of your six Geoblocks has been matched to a card.

When students are finished, discuss Task Cards 9 and 10. How are these two Geoblocks the same? How are they different? Repeat with Task Cards 11 and 12. Emphasize that each have the same number of faces and the same shape faces but the sizes of the faces are different.

ELL English Language Learners

Use Repetition Students struggling with the English language may have difficulty understanding that the words *face* and *side* are interchangeable. Give each student a rectangular prism Geoblock. How many *faces* does this Geoblock have? How many *sides* does this Geoblock have? Emphasize that faces are sides and that the number of each is the same. Repeat with other Geoblocks.

Additional Resource

Student Math Handbook pages 124–125

Practice

20 MIN PAIRS

Describing Faces

Use anytime after Session 1.3.

Math Focus Points

- Attending to features of 3-D shapes, particularly the number and shape of faces

Vocabulary: face, square, rectangle

Materials: Geoblocks, R14

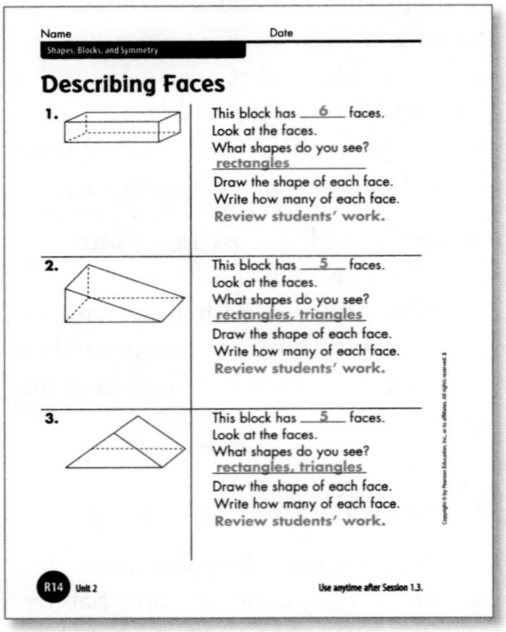

Name Date

Shapes, Blocks, and Symmetry

Describing Faces

1. This block has 6 faces.
Look at the faces.
What shapes do you see?
rectangles
Draw the shape of each face.
Write how many of each face.
Review students' work.

2. This block has 5 faces.
Look at the faces.
What shapes do you see?
rectangles, triangles
Draw the shape of each face.
Write how many of each face.
Review students' work.

3. This block has 5 faces.
Look at the faces.
What shapes do you see?
rectangles, triangles
Draw the shape of each face.
Write how many of each face.
Review students' work.

Copyright © by Pearson Education, Inc., or its affiliates. All rights reserved. 2

R14 Unit 2 Use anytime after Session 1.3.

Materials to Prepare: From the Geoblock sets, find a cube for each pair (Geoblock B, C, or D). Each pair will also need Geoblocks I, S, and X.

Distribute a cube to each pair. Does anyone know the name of this block? That's right, it's a cube. Describe it to your partner.

Record students' descriptions on the board. One of the important things to notice about 3-D shapes is the sides or faces and the number of them. How many faces does a cube have?

Agree that there are 6, then ask students to describe the shape of those faces. All the faces are square. A cube has 6 square faces.

Record the following information on the board.

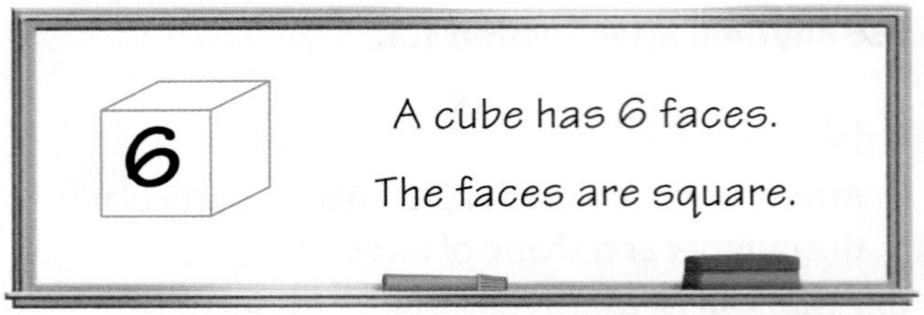
6
A cube has 6 faces.
The faces are square.

Explain that students will be recording similar information about other Geoblocks. Distribute a set of the three other Geoblocks to each pair. Students can work with a partner but each should record on his or her own copy of Describing Faces (R14).

Bring the group together to discuss the number and shapes of the faces on each block.

Hold up Geoblock S. This block has five faces. Two are triangles and three are rectangles. What do you notice about the rectangular faces?

Compare Geoblocks S and X. How are they the same? How are they different?

ELL English Language Learners

Partner Talk Have students describe the features of a Geoblock to a partner. Encourage more proficient speakers to use words such as *faces, square, rectangle,* and *triangle.* Less proficient speakers can point to the faces as they explain.

Additional Resource

Student Math Handbook pages 124–125

Extension

20 MIN GROUPS

Faces, Vertices, and Edges

Use anytime after Session 1.2.

Math Focus Points

- Attending to features of 3-D shapes, particularly the number and shape of faces

Vocabulary: faces, vertices, edges

Materials: Geoblocks (at least 10 unique blocks including 2 cubes, 4 rectangular prisms, and 4 triangular prisms), *Student Math Handbook* p. 125, R15

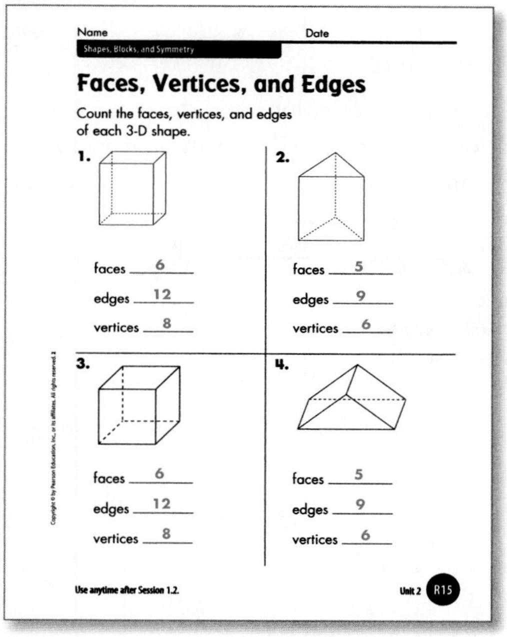
Name Date

Shapes, Blocks, and Symmetry

Faces, Vertices, and Edges

Count the faces, vertices, and edges of each 3-D shape.

1. faces 6, edges 12, vertices 8

2. faces 5, edges 9, vertices 6

3. faces 6, edges 12, vertices 8

4. faces 5, edges 9, vertices 6

Use anytime after Session 1.2. Unit 2 R15

Have students turn to page 125 of the *Student Math Handbook* to review the vocabulary.

Each person in your group should choose two Geoblocks. For each block, count and write down the number of faces, vertices, and edges. Then compare answers with the rest of your group. Did anyone get the same answers as you?

Have students compare the blocks and discuss how they counted the faces, vertices, and edges.

Does turning a 3-dimensional shape make it easier to count faces, edges, and vertices?

Students might say:

"I turned the shape so the triangles were on the top and bottom. Then I counted 3 vertices on the top and 3 on the bottom."

"No matter how I turn a cube, there are 4 edges around the top, 4 around the bottom, and 4 that connect top to bottom."

As a class, discuss why many answers are the same. Have students group the Geoblocks by their features. Have them describe each of the groups by the way the blocks in the group look.

Students might say:

"All the blocks in this group look like ramps."

"All the faces on blocks in this group are squares."

Distribute copies of Faces, Vertices, and Edges (R15).

ELL English Language Learners

Model Thinking Aloud Using a Geoblock, model how to count the edges as you share your thought process for solving the problem aloud. Then have volunteers share their thought processes. Listen for correct use of vocabulary.

When counting edges, I count the edges on the top first. The bottom might have the same number of edges as the top. Then I count the edges around the sides. I can turn a block to make counting easier.

Additional Resource

Student Math Handbook pages 124–125

Differentiation in Investigation 2

Mathematics in This Investigation

The mathematics focuses on identifying and describing attributes of 2-D shapes and using this information to compare, construct, and sort shapes. Quadrilaterals, specifically rectangles, are studied.

Understanding the Mathematics

Students identify and sort 2-D shapes by important geometric features, such as number of sides or number of angles. Students identify which shapes are rectangles and which are not. They describe, compare, and construct a variety of rectangles. They understand and can articulate that rectangles are shapes with four sides and four right angles. They use this knowledge to explain why some shapes are not rectangles.

Option: Assign the **Extension** activity.

Partially Understanding the Mathematics

Students describe and identify most 2-D shapes and can correctly identify and sort shapes that are or are not rectangles. They may occasionally misidentify some shapes. Students may not be certain that all shapes with four straight sides and four right angles are rectangles, regardless of position. For example, they may identify a tilted rectangle as a different shape. They may not always use the correct terms for the different attributes of a shape (e.g., they may say *corners* instead of *right angles*).

Option: Assign the **Practice** activity.

Not Understanding the Mathematics

Students are inconsistent in attending to important geometric features of shape and may describe and sort according to such physical properties as color or size. Students do not have a coherent understanding of what a rectangle is. Students may be able to identify and articulate some, but not all, of the attributes of a rectangle. They may know that opposite sides of a rectangle are equal, but then they may go on to think that any shape with this attribute is a rectangle.

Option: Assign the **Intervention** activity.

Investigation 2 Quiz

In addition to your observations and students' work in Investigation 2, the Quiz (R16) can be used to gather more information.

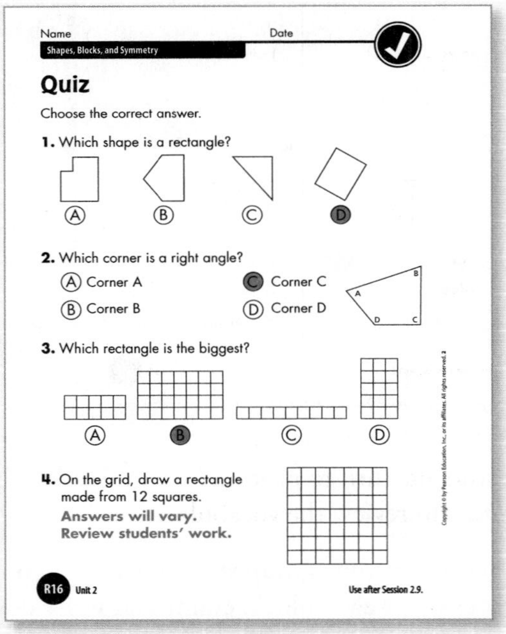
Name Date

Shapes, Blocks, and Symmetry

Quiz

Choose the correct answer.

1. Which shape is a rectangle?

Ⓐ Ⓑ Ⓒ Ⓓ

2. Which corner is a right angle?

Ⓐ Corner A Ⓒ Corner C

Ⓑ Corner B Ⓓ Corner D

3. Which rectangle is the biggest?

Ⓐ Ⓑ Ⓒ Ⓓ

4. On the grid, draw a rectangle made from 12 squares.

Answers will vary. Review students' work.

R16 Unit 2 Use after Session 2.9.

Copyright © by Pearson Education, Inc., or its affiliates. All rights reserved. 2

Intervention

20 MIN PAIRS

Rectangles and Squares

Use anytime after Session 2.2.

Math Focus Points

- Identifying rectangles as 4-sided shapes with 4 right angles

Vocabulary: rectangle, angle, right angle, square

Materials: color tiles or square pattern blocks (1 per pair), *Student Math Handbook* p. 121, M29, R17

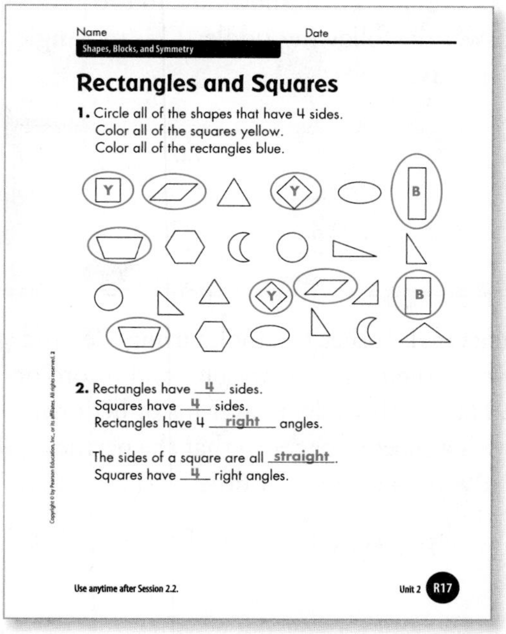
Name Date

Shapes, Blocks, and Symmetry

Rectangles and Squares

1. Circle all of the shapes that have 4 sides.
Color all of the squares yellow.
Color all of the rectangles blue.

2. Rectangles have 4 sides.
Squares have 4 sides.
Rectangles have 4 right angles.

The sides of a square are all straight.
Squares have 4 right angles.

Use anytime after Session 2.2.

Unit 2 R17

Distribute a color tile or pattern block square to each pair and ask them to turn to page 121 of the *Student Math Handbook.*

We have been talking about the features of different shapes. Information like the number of sides, and whether they are straight or curved, and the types of angles are some of things that make shapes different from each other.

Look at page 121 and read the text together. Ask students to count the number of sides on each rectangle.

Remind students that the place where two sides come together is called an angle. One special feature of a rectangle is that it has 4 right angles. Sometimes people call these square corners. Can you find the 4 right angles on each rectangle?

Show students how they can use a square tile to see if an angle is a right angle. Have them count and check the right angles on each rectangle.

Have the same discussion about the squares on page 121. Then compare the two shapes. First, ask students to describe how squares and rectangles are the same, and then how they are different. Record their responses on chart paper.

Now you are going to use Centimeter Grid Paper (M29) to draw examples of rectangles and squares. Remember the important information about squares and rectangles. Record the following on the board.

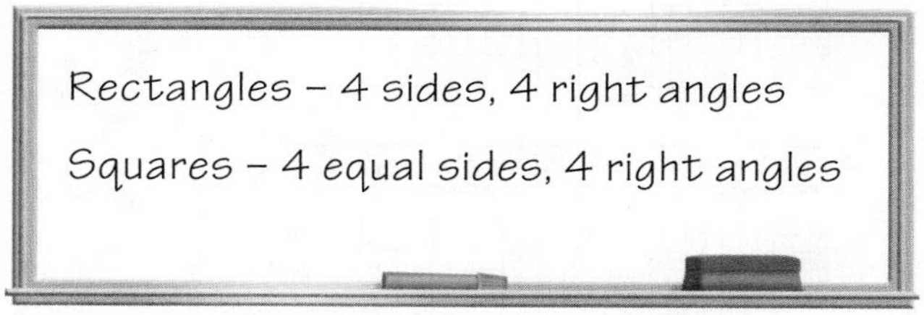

Students use M29 to draw at least three examples of each shape. Partners exchange papers and check each other's work.

Distribute copies of Rectangles and Squares (R17).

ELL English Language Learners

Partner Talk Have students describe similarities and differences between rectangles and squares to a partner. Encourage more proficient speakers to use words such as *rectangle, square, sides, angles,* and *right angles.* Less proficient speakers can point to the parts of the rectangles and squares as they explain.

Additional Resource

Student Math Handbook page 121

Practice

20 MIN PAIRS

More Rectangle Riddles

Use anytime after Session 2.5.

Math Focus Points

- Making different rectangular arrays using the same number of tiles
- Describing rectangular arrays of tiles

Vocabulary: row, column

Materials: color tiles, M29 (1 per pair), R18

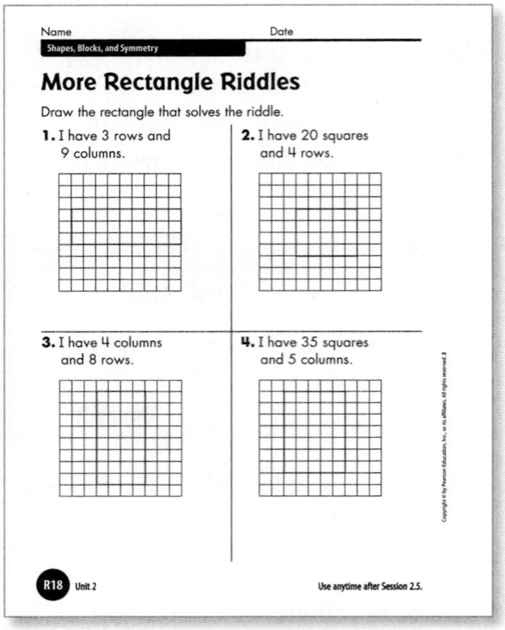

Name Date

Shapes, Blocks, and Symmetry

More Rectangle Riddles

Draw the rectangle that solves the riddle.

1. I have 3 rows and 9 columns.
2. I have 20 squares and 4 rows.
3. I have 4 columns and 8 rows.
4. I have 35 squares and 5 columns.

Copyright © by Pearson Education, Inc., or its affiliates. All rights reserved. 3

R18 Unit 2 Use anytime after Session 2.5.

Distribute color tiles and Centimeter Grid Paper (M29) to each pair of students. We will use the tiles to make and solve riddles about rectangles. Make a rectangle with 2 rows of 9 tiles.

Give students a few minutes to make the rectangle. Remind students that rows go across, columns go up and down, and that every row must have the same number of tiles. If you want to tell someone about this rectangle in a different way, what can you say? Tell enough information so someone else could make the rectangle.

Students might say:

"My rectangle has 18 tiles in 2 rows."

"My rectangle has 9 columns with 2 tiles in each column."

Discuss how the things we say about a rectangle can be written as a riddle. Then, show how to use grid paper to answer the following riddle: This rectangle has 18 squares in 2 rows.

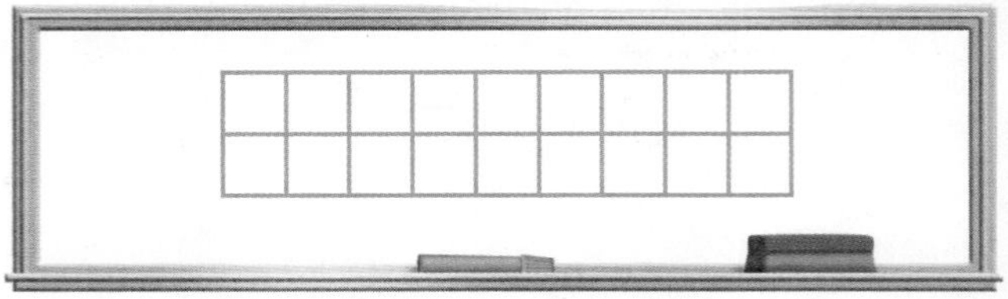

Have students make other rectangles using tiles and write riddles for their partners to solve and record on grid paper. Have each student cover his or her own rectangle with a sheet of paper so that the partner cannot see it while solving the riddle.

Distribute copies of More Rectangle Riddles (R18).

ELL English Language Learners

Provide a Word List Some English Language Learners may confuse the words *row* and *column*. Draw an array with 4 rows of 2 on the board. Trace a column in one color and write the word *column* by it. Trace a row in another color and write the word *row* by it.

Show students a photograph of an architectural column. Some buildings, like this one, have columns. How is this column and the column in my rectangle the same? Elicit that both columns are taller than they are wide and standing upright.

Additional Resource

Student Math Handbook page 126

Extension

20 MIN PAIRS

Finding Larger Rectangles

Use anytime after Session 2.6.

Math Focus Points

- Making different rectangular arrays using the same number of tiles

Vocabulary: congruent

Materials: color tiles (20 of the same color per pair), M29

Distribute color tiles to each pair of students. How many different rectangles do you think can be made from 20 tiles? Make as many rectangles as you can. Remember, each rectangle must have an equal number of tiles in each row. Each time you make a rectangle, outline or shade your rectangle on Centimeter Grid Paper (M29). Then rearrange the tiles to see whether you can make a different rectangle.

You may want to tell students that when they are drawing or shading on grid paper, they should start in a corner instead of the middle of the paper so they will have more space for other rectangles. They may need to tape two sheets of grid paper together if they need more space.

After about 5 minutes, have the class discuss the rectangles that everyone has made. How can you be sure to find all the rectangles that are possible with 20 square tiles?

Students might say:

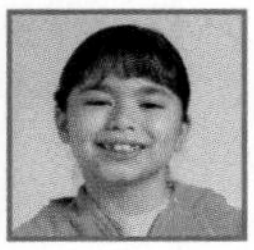

"I tried making different numbers of rows and saw whether the rows were equal. I listed each number that I tried until I had tried all numbers up to 10."

"First, I tried using 2 rows. Then, I tried 3 rows, 4 rows, and other numbers in order. After awhile, I saw that I was finding rectangles that were the same as ones I found before."

If no one makes a rectangle with either 1 row or 1 column, ask students if it is possible for a rectangle to be made with only 1 row or 1 column of tiles. List all the results on the board.

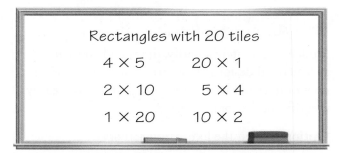

Rectangles with 20 tiles

4 × 5	20 × 1
2 × 10	5 × 4
1 × 20	10 × 2

Which of the rectangles that you described are congruent? That is, which ones are the same as another one but turned in a different way? Discuss why a 4 by 5 rectangle is congruent to a 5 by 4 rectangle.

Continue the activity by having students choose a different number of tiles between 21 and 36 and then find and record all the rectangles for that number. For the numbers 23, 29, and 31, only rectangles with 1 row or 1 column are possible. If students have more time, encourage them to try more numbers. Distribute additional copies of M29, as needed, so students can record their rectangles.

ELL English Language Learners

Rephrase Use other ways to ask if rows are *equal* when students are making their arrays, such as:

- Are the rows the *same length*?
- Does each row have the *same number of* tiles?
- Do the rows make a rectangle *without gaps* or open corners?

Additional Resource

Student Math Handbook page 126

Differentiation in Investigation 3

Mathematics in This Investigation

The mathematics focuses on identifying and constructing objects and designs with mirror symmetry.

Understanding the Mathematics

Students accurately identify, draw, and construct symmetrical designs. They articulate why a design does or does not have mirror symmetry. They easily identify the line of symmetry.

Option: Assign the **Extension** activity.

Partially Understanding the Mathematics

Students identify symmetrical designs in various contexts, and they identify the line of symmetry. They use Geoblocks or pattern blocks to construct symmetrical designs and may be able to produce symmetrical designs on paper. They may occasionally be slightly off in their construction or drawing.

Option: Assign the **Practice** activity.

Not Understanding the Mathematics

Students may not consistently identify designs with mirror symmetry. They cannot produce their own symmetrical designs using patterns blocks. They may also have difficulty either finishing an incomplete drawing of a symmetrical pattern or figuring out the total number of blocks or tiles when given one half of a symmetrical design.

Option: Assign the **Intervention** activity.

Investigation 3 Quiz

In addition to your observations and students' work in Investigation 3, the Quiz (R19) can be used to gather more information.

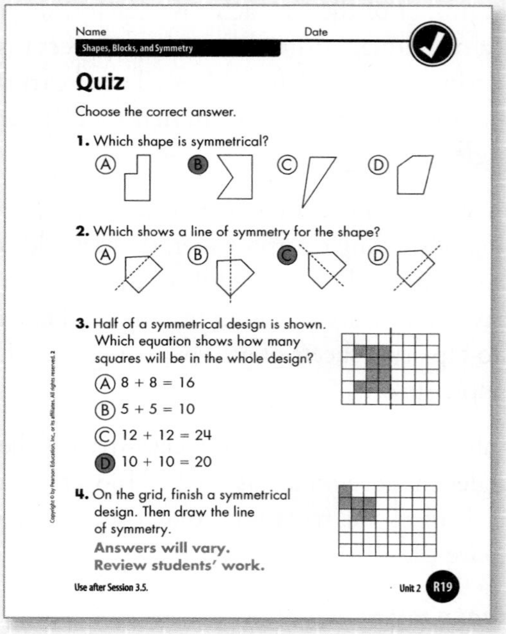
Name Date

Shapes, Blocks, and Symmetry

Quiz

Choose the correct answer.

1. Which shape is symmetrical?

Ⓐ Ⓑ Ⓒ Ⓓ

2. Which shows a line of symmetry for the shape?

Ⓐ Ⓑ Ⓒ Ⓓ

3. Half of a symmetrical design is shown. Which equation shows how many squares will be in the whole design?

Ⓐ 8 + 8 = 16

Ⓑ 5 + 5 = 10

Ⓒ 12 + 12 = 24

Ⓓ 10 + 10 = 20

4. On the grid, finish a symmetrical design. Then draw the line of symmetry.

Answers will vary. Review students' work.

Use after Session 3.5.

Unit 2 R19

Copyright © by Pearson Education, Inc., or its affiliates. All rights reserved. 2

Intervention

20 MIN INDIVIDUALS

Geoblock Symmetry

Use anytime after Session 3.1.

Math Focus Points

- Describing and identifying objects and designs that have mirror symmetry
- Constructing 2-D and 3-D symmetrical designs with mirror symmetry

Vocabulary: symmetry

Materials: Geoblocks (in subsets), cardstock

Materials to Prepare: Choose four Geoblocks of various shapes and sizes and then find four more that are identical to the first four.

Some students may have difficulty understanding how to build a symmetrical building. Work with these students individually to build together.

Place all eight Geoblocks on a table in no particular arrangement, within reach of you and the student but off to one side. Sit beside the student.

Today we will make a building with Geoblocks that is symmetrical. Our building is going to look the same on each side.

Ask the student to select a block and place it on the table. Put a piece of cardstock vertically against one side and then place the matching block on the opposite side so the card marks the line of symmetry. You may need to turn the student's block so that the cardstock is perpendicular to you and the student. The student should be able to see both the left and the right sides of the building at the same time.

Look how I have placed the block. The card is between the two blocks, and the two sides are like mirror images. Now it is your turn to place another block on your side of the building, and I'll put a matching block on my side.

Repeat a third time. This time, purposely place the block in the right place but turned the wrong way.

Ask the student what they notice and if they can fix your block so that both sides of the building are exactly the same.

Have the student place their last block. Then, place the final block to complete the symmetrical building.

What do you notice about our building? Can you show me how it is the same on both sides? Our building is symmetrical.

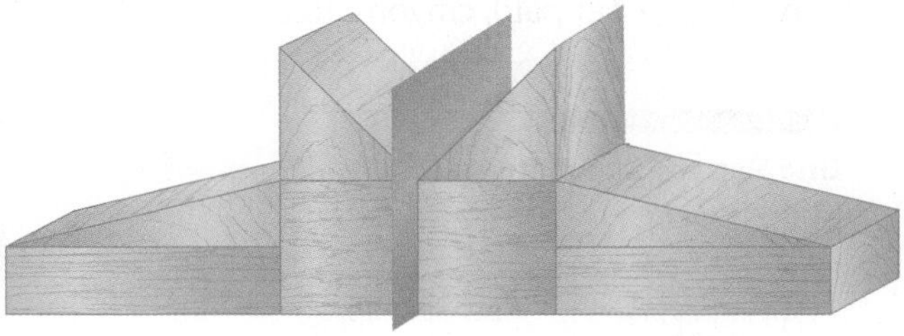

Repeat the activity but with the student matching blocks that you place. Now it is your turn to match the blocks that I place. Choose a different starting block. Hold the card against one side as the student chooses the block to match your first block. Continue taking turns as before. If the student makes a mistake, ask him or her to figure out and fix the mistake before you continue with the next block.

For more or less difficulty, choose four new pairs of matching blocks that are either simpler (such as cubes) or harder (such as triangular prisms).

Finally, ask the student to work independently to build a symmetrical building using the set of eight blocks.

ELL English Language Learners

Model Thinking Aloud As you place each block, model your thinking. This block matches the block on your side. Now I need to place my block so that it is a *mirror image* of your block.

Additional Resource

Student Math Handbook page 129

Practice

20 MIN PAIRS

Grid Pattern Symmetry

Use anytime after Session 3.2.

Math Focus Points

- Constructing 2-D and 3-D symmetrical designs with mirror symmetry
- Reflecting a shape across a line of symmetry

Vocabulary: symmetry

Materials: color tiles (20 of the same color per student), M15 (2 per pair), crayons, R20

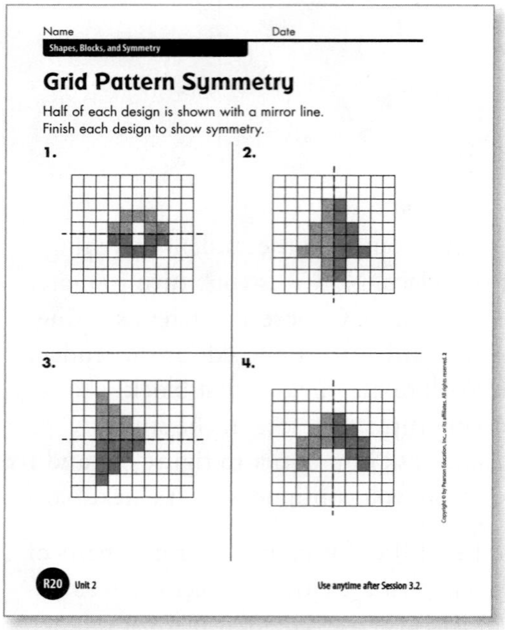
Name Date

Shapes, Blocks, and Symmetry

Grid Pattern Symmetry

Half of each design is shown with a mirror line.
Finish each design to show symmetry.

1.

2.

3.

4.

R20 Unit 2

Use anytime after Session 3.2.

Distribute color tiles and Inch Grid Paper (M15) to each pair of students.

We will use color tiles to make designs that have symmetry. Either you or your partner should first draw a line across the middle of your grid paper from left to right, tracing over a dashed line. We will call this line the "mirror line."

With your partner, take turns placing tiles over squares on the paper. One person should place a tile against one side of the line, and then the partner should place a tile on the other side to create a mirror image. Continue until you have placed 10 tiles each. Always place new tiles against the tiles already in place.

When students have finished the first design with their tiles, have them put the design off to one side. Direct them to repeat the activity by putting tiles over the second sheet of paper but to begin with a mirror line drawn from top to bottom through the center. Also, have the student who was the leader the first time become the follower.

When you finish your second design, you and your partner should each color in one of the designs on the grid paper. Explain to students that they can use different colors, however, their colored design must be symmetrical.

When students are finished ask them to look at their two designs. How do you know if a design is symmetrical? How can you check?

Students might say:

"If I fold the paper on the mirror line, the two sides will match."

Distribute copies of Grid Pattern Symmetry (R20).

ELL English Language Learners

Partner Talk Draw two shapes on the board, one that shows symmetry and one that doesn't. Have pairs answer the following questions. Which shape is *symmetrical*? How do you know? Less proficient students may only be able to respond with short phrases. More proficient students can add information to help create a more detailed response.

Additional Resource

Student Math Handbook page 129

Extension

20 MIN INDIVIDUALS

More Symmetry

Use anytime after Session 3.3.

Math Focus Points

- Exploring symmetry by folding and cutting paper patterns
- Reflecting a shape across a line of symmetry

Vocabulary: line of symmetry

Materials: Shape Cards (M1–M4), rulers, R21

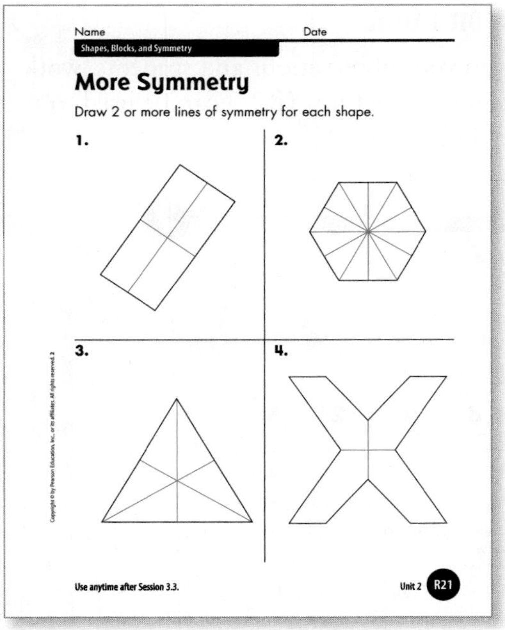

Name Date

Shapes, Blocks, and Symmetry

More Symmetry

Draw 2 or more lines of symmetry for each shape.

1. 2. 3. 4.

Use anytime after Session 3.3. Unit 2 R21

Materials to Prepare: Using Shape Cards (M1–M4), cut out shapes A, B, C, F, H, U, V, and X. Make a set of shapes for each student.

Distribute a set of paper shapes to each student.

Today you will be looking at shapes that are symmetrical. You will test shapes by folding them in different ways. Hold up a hexagon. How can folding a shape help you tell if it is symmetrical?

Students might say:

"If the two halves match, the shape is symmetrical."

As you try different shapes and notice the symmetry, mark the fold line, or the line of symmetry, and then use a ruler to draw a line of symmetry. Show an example with a hexagon.

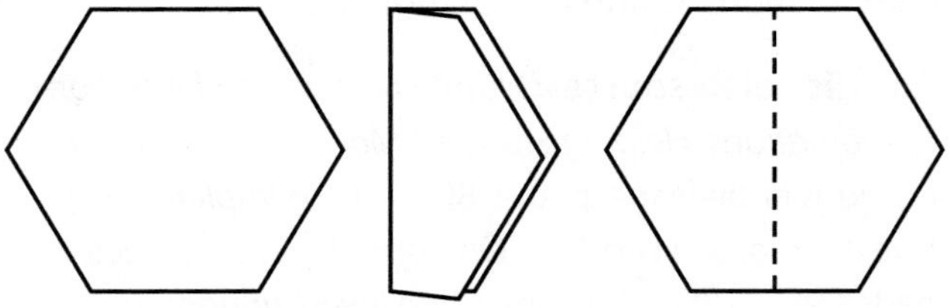

Some shapes have more than one line of symmetry. As you work with the shapes, draw as many lines of symmetry as you can. Always unfold the paper before testing another possible line of symmetry.

Tell students to find the lines of symmetry on each shape. Students should exchange shapes to check each other's work.

Distribute copies of More Symmetry (R21).

ELL English Language Learners

Rephrase If students have difficulty with the term *line of symmetry*, rephrase questions using words that may be more familiar to the student.

- Where can you fold the shape so that the two halves *match*? Draw a line there.
- Can you break the shape into two parts that have the *same shape and size*?

Additional Resource

Student Math Handbook page 129

Differentiation in Investigation 1

Mathematics in This Investigation

The mathematics focuses on investigating and using the commutative property of addition to solve problems with multiple addends and on using known combinations to add two or more numbers.

Additional Resources: *Number Strings and Addition Combinations: Helping Students Make Connections to Previous Knowledge*, pages 85–86 (See *Implementing Investigations in Grade 2*); *On Communicating Ideas*, pages 95–97 (See *Implementing Investigations in Grade 2*)

Understanding the Mathematics

Students recognize addition problems and solve them accurately and efficiently. They use combinations they know to help them solve a problem with several addends, and they are flexible in composing and decomposing numbers. Students understand that the order of addends does not matter in addition. They may make and prove generalizations about other properties of addition.

Option: Assign the **Extension** activity.

Partially Understanding the Mathematics

Students recognize addition problems and solve them accurately, though they may sometimes make a small computational error. They may not always recognize and use familiar combinations when solving a problem with several addends. Students may not yet be fully convinced that the order of addends does not matter in addition. They show less flexibility when composing, decomposing, and adding numbers.

Option: Assign the **Practice** activity.

Not Understanding the Mathematics

Students are challenged by problems with multiple addends. They may recognize and use some familiar combinations when these addends are consecutive numbers, but overall, they have difficulty keeping track of which numbers they have or have not added. These students may not add all the numbers or may add one number twice.

Option: Assign the **Intervention** activity.

Investigation 1 Quiz

In addition to your observations and students' work in Investigation 1, the Quiz (R22) can be used to gather more information.

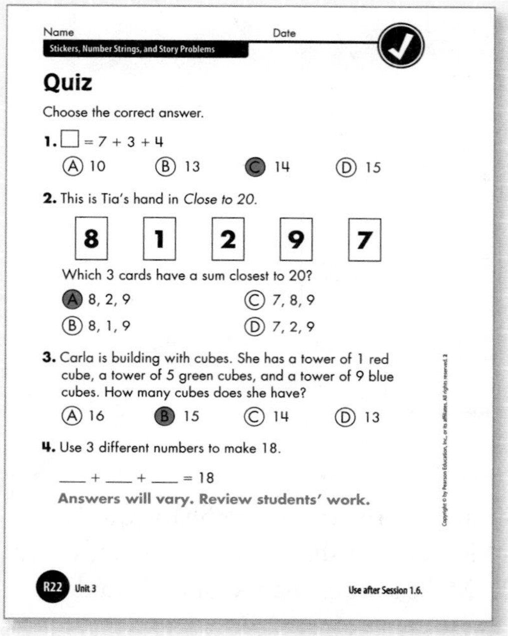

Name Date

Stickers, Number Strings, and Story Problems

Quiz

Choose the correct answer.

1. □ = 7 + 3 + 4

Ⓐ 10 Ⓑ 13 Ⓒ 14 Ⓓ 15

2. This is Tia's hand in *Close to 20*.

8 1 2 9 7

Which 3 cards have a sum closest to 20?

Ⓐ 8, 2, 9 Ⓒ 7, 8, 9

Ⓑ 8, 1, 9 Ⓓ 7, 2, 9

3. Carla is building with cubes. She has a tower of 1 red cube, a tower of 5 green cubes, and a tower of 9 blue cubes. How many cubes does she have?

Ⓐ 16 Ⓑ 15 Ⓒ 14 Ⓓ 13

4. Use 3 different numbers to make 18.

___ + ___ + ___ = 18

Answers will vary. Review students' work.

Copyright © by Pearson Education, Inc., or its affiliates. All rights reserved. 2

R22 Unit 3 Use after Session 1.6.

Intervention

25 MIN INDIVIDUALS

What's the Order?

Use anytime after Session 1.1.

Math Focus Points

- Considering whether reordering three addends results in the same total

Vocabulary: order, addend, total

Materials: connecting cubes (10 red, 10 green, 10 blue per student)

Tell students to listen to the following problem and to try and picture it in their minds. Ask them to remember as many of the details as possible. Juanita is building with cubes. She has a train of 4 red cubes, a train of 2 green cubes, and a train of 8 blue cubes. How many connecting cubes does she have?

Have students retell the story in their own words. What is happening in the story? Is Juanita putting groups of cubes together or taking some cubes away? How many groups is she putting together? How many cubes are in each group? What are you asked to find? Draw the cubes in each of the three groups on the board and write the numbers beneath.

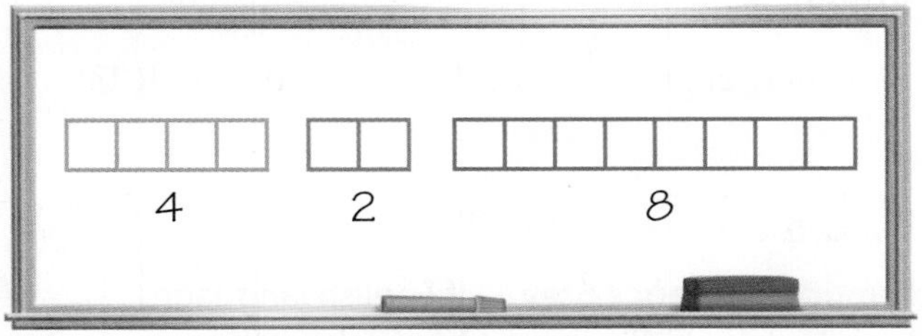

Ask a volunteer to demonstrate how to use cubes to solve the problem. Then ask the class for an equation that shows the order in which the cubes were added. Write the equation on the board.

This equation shows the order in which [Chen] added the cubes.

Remind students that the numbers 4, 2, and 8 in the problem are called *addends* because they are being *added* together. Do you think the order of the addends matters?

Ask another volunteer to add the cubes in a different order, and share his or her equation. Add the new equation to the board. In what order did [Jacy] add the numbers? Did [Jacy] get the same total as [Chen]? Remind students that the *total* is the sum of all three addends.

Are there other ways to change the order of the addends? Do you think we will get the same total? Why or why not? Test out different orders and confirm with students that the total is the same each time.

Provide students with a new problem to solve. Darren is building with cubes. He has a tower of 7 red cubes, a tower of 3 green cubes, and a tower of 1 blue cube. How many connecting cubes does he have?

Have students build cube towers to represent the problem and then solve the problem twice using a different order for the addends each time. They should record an equation for each solution.

Bring students together to share the different ways they found. Record all equations on the board and discuss why the total remains the same. Confirm that the total is the same each time.

ELL English Language Learners

Provide a Word List Review vocabulary and unfamiliar words used in this activity. Start the list with *order, addend,* and *total.* Use cubes to emphasize meanings. Add any unfamiliar words that surface to the list. These may include *group, equation, same, change, sum,* and *always.* Some English Language Learners may confuse the meanings for the words *order, change,* and *sum* with the meanings of their homophones.

Additional Resource

Student Math Handbook page 54

Practice

20 MIN PAIRS

More Than 2 Addends

Use anytime after Session 1.2.

Math Focus Points

- Using known combinations to add two or more numbers

Vocabulary: doubles

Materials: blank number cubes and labels (3 per pair), connecting cubes, R23

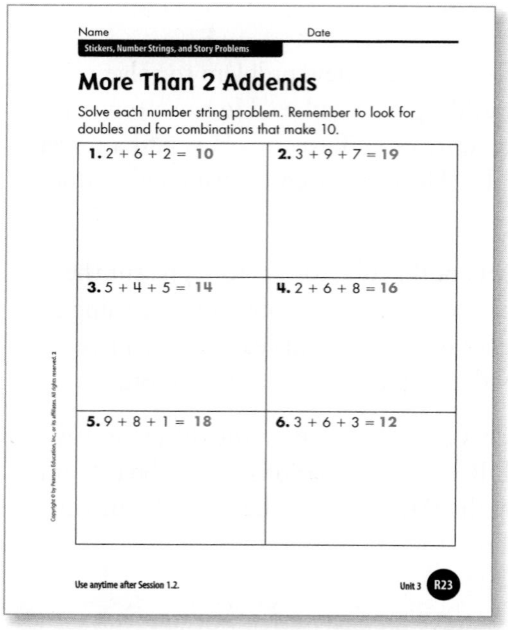

Name Date

Stickers, Number Strings, and Story Problems

More Than 2 Addends

Solve each number string problem. Remember to look for doubles and for combinations that make 10.

1. 2 + 6 + 2 = 10	**2.** 3 + 9 + 7 = 19
3. 5 + 4 + 5 = 14	**4.** 2 + 6 + 8 = 16
5. 9 + 8 + 1 = 18	**6.** 3 + 6 + 3 = 12

Use anytime after Session 1.2. Unit 3 R23

Materials to Prepare: Prepare a set of three number cubes for each pair of students. Label the first blank cube with the numbers 1–6, a second cube with the numbers 2–7, and a third cube with the numbers 4–9.

Display three cube trains: a yellow train with 4 cubes, a blue train with 6 cubes, and a red train with 4 cubes. Have students verify the number of cubes in each train. Connect the three trains together to make one long train. What number string can we write that matches our cube train? Write 4 + 6 + 4 on the board.

Have students solve the number string individually and then discuss their methods using the cubes to model each solution. How did you solve the problem?

Students might say:

"I know 4 + 6 is 10, so I added that first. Then I added 10 + 4 to get 14."

"I added 4 + 4. That equals 8. Then I added 8 + 6. 8, 9, 10, 11, 12, 13, 14."

Remind students to look for combinations that they know. [Alberto] added the combination that makes 10 first. [Rochelle] added the double 4s first.

Distribute a set of number cubes to each pair of students. Take turns rolling the three number cubes. Each person should record a number string with the numbers you get. Model this action.

Solve the problem and record how you solved it. Compare your solution with your partner's. Students roll, record, and solve at least 6 number strings.

Distribute copies of More Than 2 Addends (R23).

ELL English Language Learners

Provide Sentence Stems If English language learners have difficulty explaining how they solved the problems, provide the following sentence stems:

- I added ______ and ______ first because ______.
- Then I added ______ because ______.
- The answer is ______.

Additional Resource

Student Math Handbook page 54

Extension

25 MIN PAIRS

More Than 3 Addends and Larger Numbers

Use anytime after Session 1.1.

Math Focus Points

- Considering a generalization about reordering addends for all numbers

Vocabulary: total, order, addend

Materials: R24

Name Date

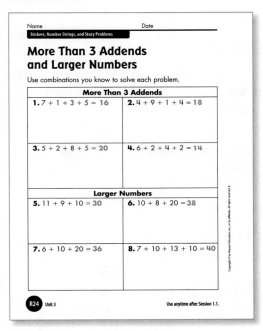

Stickers, Number Strings, and Story Problems

More Than 3 Addends and Larger Numbers

Use combinations you know to solve each problem.

More Than 3 Addends	
1. 7 + 1 + 3 + 5 = 16	**2.** 4 + 9 + 1 + 4 = 18
3. 5 + 2 + 8 + 5 = 20	**4.** 6 + 2 + 4 + 2 = 14
Larger Numbers	
5. 11 + 9 + 10 = 30	**6.** 10 + 8 + 20 = 38
7. 6 + 10 + 20 = 36	**8.** 7 + 10 + 13 + 10 = 40

R24 Unit 3 Use anytime after Session 1.1.

Copyright © by Pearson Education, Inc., or its affiliates. All rights reserved. 2

Write 3 + 8 + 7 on the board. Review adding three numbers. What is the total? In what order did you add the addends? Why? Will the total be the same if we change the order? Why or why not?

Ask students to consider the order of addends in different situations. When you add four or five numbers together, will the total be the same if you change the order of the addends? What about when you add larger numbers?

Discuss students' ideas briefly. Then write the following problems on the board.

More Than 3 Addends	Larger Numbers
2 + 5 + 1 + 2 =	20 + 9 + 10 =
3 + 6 + 7 + 4 =	10 + 18 + 2
4 + 3 + 5 + 3 + 1 =	10 + 15 + 10 + 5 =

Students work in pairs. They should select one set of problems to investigate. Their task is to find a way to prove that in addition, the order of the addends does not affect the sum.

You and your partner can use cubes, sketches, equations or words to explain why you think this is true or not true when adding a set of numbers.

End the activity by having students share their work.

Distribute copies of More Than 3 Addends and Larger Numbers (R24).

ELL English Language Learners

Use Repetition Post the word *order*. Write a number from 1 to 6 on each of three pieces of paper. Make 2 plus signs and 1 equal sign. Arrange the numbers and symbols to form an equation with three addends. Have a student find the total and write it after the equal sign. Then rearrange the addends several times and repeat, I am changing the *order*. Have students rearrange the addends and say, "I am changing the *order*."

Additional Resource

Student Math Handbook

Game: *Beat the Calculator* SMH G1

Materials: calculator, *Beat the Calculator* Cards

Variation: Play alone. First solve the problem mentally, then check with a calculator.

Differentiation in Investigation 2

Mathematics in This Investigation

The mathematics focuses on developing strategies for understanding and solving addition and subtraction story problems.

Understanding the Mathematics

Students correctly interpret addition and subtraction story problems. They visualize the action, solve the problem accurately, and record their work. Students may have several strategies for solving a subtraction problem, such as counting on or back, subtracting in chunks, using combinations that they know, or reasoning about the relationship between addition and subtraction. They can write their own story problem to match a given expression.

Option: Assign the **Extension** activity.

Partially Understanding the Mathematics

Students correctly interpret and solve story problems, but they may need to model each situation directly. To solve a subtraction problem, they may show all and remove some to get the answer. They may have difficulty keeping track when using less familiar strategies, such as counting on or back or subtracting in chunks. These students may also make minor computational errors.

Option: Assign the **Practice** activity.

Not Understanding the Mathematics

Students have difficulty interpreting the action of a story problem. They may be unable to begin on their own or to model a problem correctly. They may only have one strategy, counting all, to solve an addition problem. For a subtraction problem, students may not be able to identify what parts of the problem the numbers represent, and they may not be able to tell whether the answer will have more than or less than the total number of objects given in the story.

Option: Assign the **Intervention** activity.

Investigation 2 Quiz

In addition to your observations and students' work in Investigation 2, the Quiz (R25) can be used to gather more information.

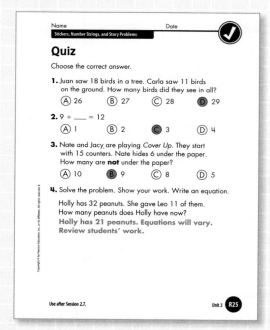

Name Date

Stickers, Number Strings, and Story Problems

Quiz

Choose the correct answer.

1. Juan saw 18 birds in a tree. Carla saw 11 birds on the ground. How many birds did they see in all?
   Ⓐ 26 Ⓑ 27 Ⓒ 28 Ⓓ 29

2. 9 + ___ = 12
   Ⓐ 1 Ⓑ 2 Ⓒ 3 Ⓓ 4

3. Nate and Jacy are playing *Cover Up*. They start with 15 counters. Nate hides 6 under the paper. How many are **not** under the paper?
   Ⓐ 10 Ⓑ 9 Ⓒ 8 Ⓓ 5

4. Solve the problem. Show your work. Write an equation.

   Holly has 32 peanuts. She gave Leo 11 of them. How many peanuts does Holly have now?

   Holly has 21 peanuts. Equations will vary. Review students' work.

Copyright © by Pearson Education, Inc., or its affiliates. All rights reserved. 2

Use after Session 2.7. Unit 3 R25

Intervention

25 MIN PAIRS

Solving and Recording Addition Problems

Use anytime after Session 2.1.

Math Focus Points

- Visualizing, retelling, and modeling the action of a variety of addition situations

Vocabulary: count all, count on

Materials: connecting cubes (30 cubes of one color, 30 cubes of another color per pair), blank paper

Tell students you will read a story problem to them. Ask them to close their eyes and picture what is happening. Amaya and Lonzell collect stamps. Amaya has 23 stamps in her collection. Lonzell has 15 stamps in his collection. How many stamps do they have altogether?

Have students work in pairs. Ask one partner to retell the story. Have the other partner confirm or correct the information given. Bring students back together and discuss the information given in the problem. What do you know? What is the problem asking you to find? Make a list of this information on the board. Will the answer be more or less than 23 stamps? How do you know?

Distribute connecting cubes to pairs. Work with your partner to show the two groups of stamps. Use one color to show Amaya's stamps and the other color to show Lonzell's stamps.

Next, have pairs use the connecting cubes to solve the problem. As pairs work, ask them to explain their thinking. Why are you putting those cubes together? How will you figure out how many there are in all?

Then have pairs record their work on paper. Show how you solved the problem. Be sure that anyone looking at your paper can tell what you did.

As a group, discuss the strategies the various pairs used and how they were recorded. [Carolina] showed Amaya's stamps with the blue cubes and Lonzell's stamps with the red cubes. Then she put both groups together and *counted all* the cubes. Look how she drew each cube and wrote a number beneath it. [Malcolm] wrote the number 23 and then drew 15 cubes. Below the cubes he wrote 24, 25, 26, . . . , 38. I can see from his drawing that he *counted on* from 23.

Have pairs repeat the process to solve another problem: Roshaun and Monisha are collecting stamps. Roshaun has 16 stamps in his collection. Monisha has 21 stamps in her collection. How many stamps do they have altogether?

ELL English Language Learners

Suggest a Sequence Support students in verbalizing and recording their steps. What did you do *first*? What did you do *next*? What did you do *last*? Give students time between each question to record each step.

Additional Resource

Student Math Handbook pages 59–60

Practice

30 MIN PAIRS

Unknown Change

Use anytime after Session 2.4.

Math Focus Points

- Solving problems with an unknown change

Vocabulary: equation

Materials: connecting cubes, R26

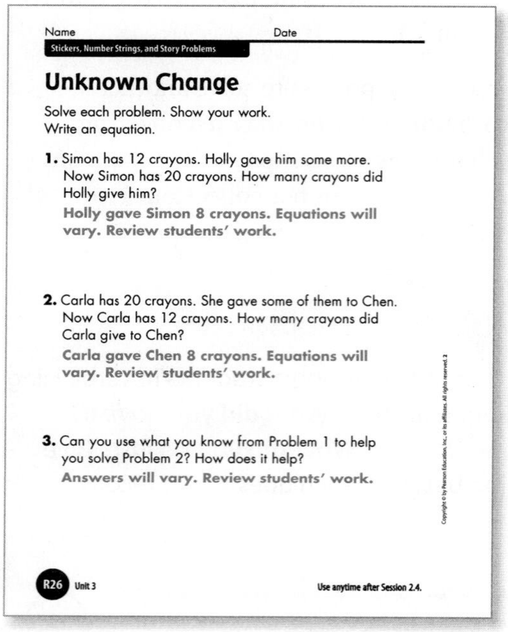

Name Date

Stickers, Number Strings, and Story Problems

Unknown Change

Solve each problem. Show your work.
Write an equation.

1. Simon has 12 crayons. Holly gave him some more. Now Simon has 20 crayons. How many crayons did Holly give him?
Holly gave Simon 8 crayons. Equations will vary. Review students' work.

2. Carla has 20 crayons. She gave some of them to Chen. Now Carla has 12 crayons. How many crayons did Carla give to Chen?
Carla gave Chen 8 crayons. Equations will vary. Review students' work.

3. Can you use what you know from Problem 1 to help you solve Problem 2? How does it help?
Answers will vary. Review students' work.

Copyright © by Pearson Education, Inc., or its affiliates. All rights reserved. 2

R26 Unit 3 Use anytime after Session 2.4.

Read the following problem aloud. Gregory has 16 markers. Katrina gave him some more. Now Gregory has 25 markers. How many markers did Katrina give him?

Have students work in pairs. Talk with your partner about the story problem. What do you know? What are you trying to find? Do you think the answer to this problem will be more than 25 markers or fewer than 25? Why?

Distribute connecting cubes to each pair. How can you use connecting cubes to model the problem? Allow pairs time to agree on a model. Ask a volunteer to share their model with the class. [Nate] started with 16 cubes of one color. Then, he added cubes of another color until he reached 25. Then, he counted the number of cubes he added.

What might [Nate's] equation look like? Write $16 + \underline{9} = 25$ on the board.

Did anyone use cubes to solve the problem in a different way? Have another volunteer share their model. [Paige] started with a train of 25 cubes. Then, she broke off a train of 16 cubes. Then, she counted the number of cubes left. What might [Paige's] equation look like? Write $25 - 16 = \underline{9}$ below the first equation on the board.

$$16 + \underline{9} = 25$$
$$25 - 16 = \underline{9}$$

Discuss the relationship between the problems. How could you use the first problem to help solve the second problem? Point out that the parts *(16 and 9)* and the whole *(25)* are the same in both problems. If time allows, discuss how to show both problems using a number line.

Distribute copies of Unknown Change (R26).

ELL English Language Learners

Suggest a Sequence These types of story problems can be especially challenging for English Language Learners. Help them by suggesting a sequence of questions to answer, such as:

1. What information do you know?
2. What do you need to find?
3. How can you use cubes or a number line to show the problem?
4. What equation can you write?

Additional Resource

Student Math Handbook pages 76–77

Extension

20 MIN PAIRS

Adding Tens and Ones

Use anytime after Session 2.1.

Math Focus Points

- Developing strategies for solving a variety of addition story problems with totals up to 45 and recording work

Vocabulary: add tens and ones

Materials: connecting cubes (as needed), number lines (as needed), R27

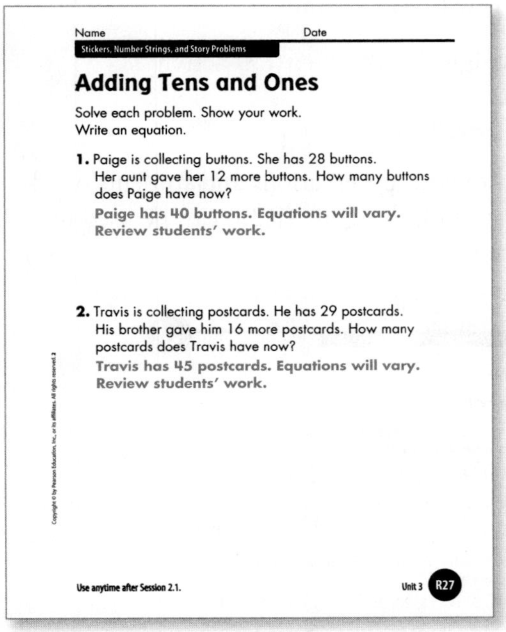

Name Date

Stickers, Number Strings, and Story Problems

Adding Tens and Ones

Solve each problem. Show your work.
Write an equation.

1. Paige is collecting buttons. She has 28 buttons. Her aunt gave her 12 more buttons. How many buttons does Paige have now?
Paige has 40 buttons. Equations will vary. Review students' work.

2. Travis is collecting postcards. He has 29 postcards. His brother gave him 16 more postcards. How many postcards does Travis have now?
Travis has 45 postcards. Equations will vary. Review students' work.

Use anytime after Session 2.1. Unit 3 R27

Read the following problem aloud. Tia has 21 acorns. Her sister gave her 19 more. How many acorns does Tia now have?

Have students work in pairs. As they work together to solve the problem, have them follow the "Story Problem Routine" from Session 2.1 (page 73).

- One partner retells the story.
- The other partner tells if the result will be more or less than the starting amount and then writes an equation that represents the problem.
- One partner decides on a strategy, solves the problem, and completes the equation.
- The other partner records how they solved it.

Have partners display the record they made and see if others can determine how they solved the problem. What can you tell from [Alberto] and [Jeffrey's] picture? How did they solve the problem? Allow pairs to clarify their strategies and confirm or correct information, as needed.

If no one suggests it, discuss adding tens and ones. I can add tens and ones to solve the problem. I know that 2 tens plus 1 ten equals 3 tens, or 30. I added the ones, 1 and 9, to make another 10. So, 30 + 10 = 40.

$$21 + 19 = 20 + 1 + 10 + 9$$
$$20 + 10 = 30$$
$$1 + 9 = 10$$
$$30 + 10 = 40$$

Have partners switch roles and solve another problem. Darren has 28 acorns. His brother gave him 13 more. How many acorns does Darren now have? Encourage students to try solving the problem by adding tens and ones.

Distribute copies of Adding Tens and Ones (R27).

ELL English Language Learners

Provide Sentence Stems To help students add tens and ones, provide sentence stems such as the following. First, I add the ________ *(tens)*. Then, I add the ________ *(ones)*. Next, I add the ________ *(tens)* and the ________ *(ones)* together.

Additional Resource

Student Math Handbook pages 59–61

Differentiation in Investigation 3

Mathematics in This Investigation

The mathematics focuses on developing strategies for accurately counting by 1s and by groups (2s, 5s, and 10s) and on developing an understanding of even and odd numbers.

Understanding the Mathematics

Students know the pattern of counting by 2s, 5s, and 10s up to 100 or above and accurately use skip counting to solve problems. They know that the total number in a set of objects remains the same no matter how it is counted. Students know that even numbers make groups of two (e.g., partners) or two equal groups (e.g., teams), while odd numbers do not make groups of two or two equal groups. These students may be able to make and prove generalizations about these numbers.

Option: Assign the **Extension** activity.

Partially Understanding the Mathematics

Students may be able to count by 2s, 5s, and 10s to solve some problems, but they occasionally lose track of their count or are unsure of the rote counting sequence beyond a certain number. These students may be unsure as to whether the total will always be the same no matter how it is counted. They can articulate that even numbers make groups of two or two equal groups, while odd numbers do not. However, these students sometimes may make minor errors identifying even and odd numbers due to inaccurate counting or an incomplete representation.

Option: Assign the **Practice** activity.

Not Understanding the Mathematics

Students may sometimes be able to count a small set using skip counting. They may quickly lose track as the numbers increase and not know the rote counting sequence. They do not yet understand that the total will remain the same no matter how it is counted, and they are surprised to see that happen when they count the same set of objects in different ways. They do not solve problems about even and odd numbers based on any understanding of these numbers, and they may have difficulty recognizing any patterns with these numbers.

Option: Assign the **Intervention** activity.

Investigation 3 Quiz

In addition to your observations and students' work in Investigation 3, the Quiz (R28) can be used to gather more information.

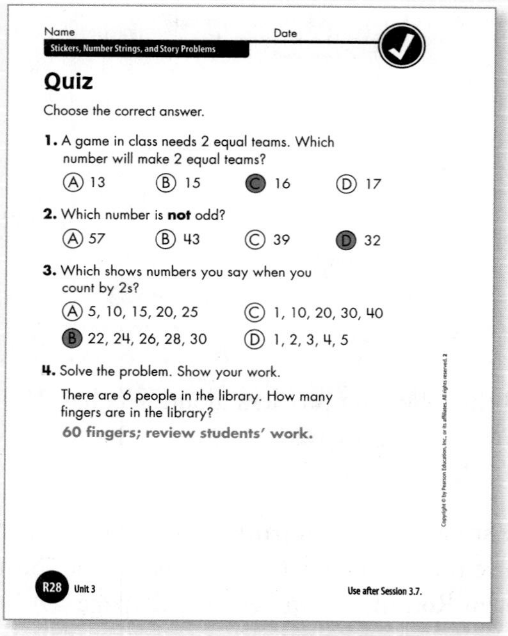

Name Date

Stickers, Number Strings, and Story Problems

Quiz

Choose the correct answer.

1. A game in class needs 2 equal teams. Which number will make 2 equal teams?
   (A) 13 (B) 15 (C) 16 (D) 17
2. Which number is **not** odd?
   (A) 57 (B) 43 (C) 39 (D) 32
3. Which shows numbers you say when you count by 2s?
   (A) 5, 10, 15, 20, 25 (C) 1, 10, 20, 30, 40
   (B) 22, 24, 26, 28, 30 (D) 1, 2, 3, 4, 5
4. Solve the problem. Show your work.
   There are 6 people in the library. How many fingers are in the library?
   60 fingers; review students' work.

Copyright © by Pearson Education, Inc., or its affiliates. All rights reserved. 2

R28 Unit 3 Use after Session 3.7.

Intervention

35 MIN PAIRS

Groups of 2, 5, and 10

Use anytime after Session 3.6.

Math Focus Points

- Developing fluency with skip counting by 2s, 5s, and 10s

Materials: small objects (20–60 per pair), bags (1 per pair), self-stick notes, R88

Materials to Prepare: Write each decade number 10–60 on a self-stick note, plus 61 and 62. Write each count-by-5 number 5–60 on a self-stick note, plus 61 and 62. Prepare bags of 20–60 small objects, such as beans or cubes, 1 bag per pair. Make an extra bag with exactly 62 objects.

Display a copy of Blank Ten-Frames (R88) and the extra bag with 62 objects. There are some [beans] in my bag. I'm going to use these ten-frames to help me count how many there are. Pour the objects onto the table. Have a student move them one-at-a-time onto the ten-frames as everyone counts the objects by 1s.

How many beans are in each ten-frame? Have students verify that there are 10 objects in every ten-frame. Now let's count the [beans] by 10s. Place the self-stick note for 10 next to the first ten-frame. Point to the second ten-frame. Another 10 makes 20. Place the self-stick note for 20 next to the second filled ten-frame.

Continue in this way until 60 objects have been counted and the self-stick note for 60 is next to the last filled ten-frame. For the last 2 objects, count on by 1s: 61, 62. With students, recount by 10s, pointing to each number as you do, and then counting on by 1s for the last 2 objects. Place the self-stick notes for these counting numbers in a row on the board, but leave the beans on the ten-frames. How many beans are in each row of the ten-frames? We can also use the ten-frames to count by 5s.

Count the objects by 5s, placing the self-stick note with the appropriate number next to each row. For the last 2 objects, count on by 1s: 61, 62.

Place these self-stick notes on the board under the numbers you counted by 10s. Compare the two sets of numbers. What do you notice about the numbers you counted by 5s and the numbers you counted by 10s?

Students might say:

"When you count by 10, the numbers all end in 0."

"When you count by 5, you say all the numbers you count by 10, too."

Next, have students count the objects by 2s as a volunteer moves 2 objects at a time off the ten-frames. Write the numbers on the board. Verify with students that for all the ways they counted, the total remained the same.

Distribute 1 bag of objects and another copy of R88 to each pair. Have partners count the objects in their bag, first by 1s, then by 10s, 5s, and 2s, recording the numbers on paper as they do.

ELL English Language Learners

Model Thinking Aloud English Language Learners having difficulty counting sets of objects by 5s or 10s may benefit from seeing a model. Demonstrate counting a set of 62 objects by 10s. As you switch from counting by 10s to counting on by 1s, talk about why you have to make that change. There are some [beans] left over. There are less than 10 [beans] left, so I can't count on another 10. I will have to count the last [beans] by 1s: 61, 62.

Additional Resource

Student Math Handbook pages 37–39

Practice

25 MIN PAIRS

Counting by 5s and 10s

Use anytime after Session 3.4.

Math Focus Points

- Looking at patterns and developing fluency with skip counting by 5s and 10s

Vocabulary: counting by 5s, counting by 10s

Materials: connecting cubes, index cards (1 per pair), R29

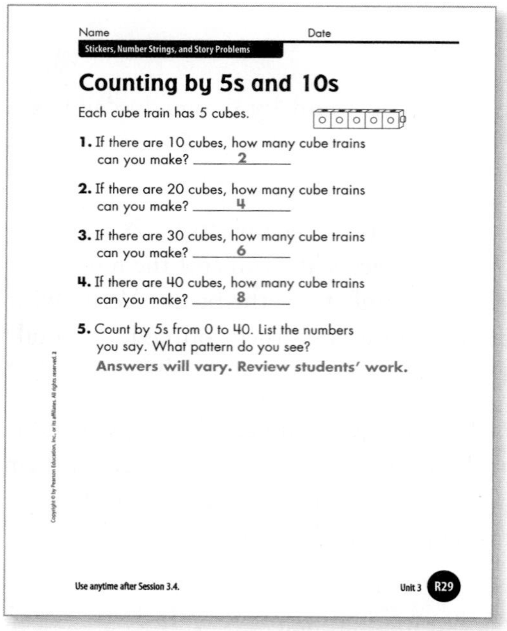

Name Date

Stickers, Number Strings, and Story Problems

Counting by 5s and 10s

Each cube train has 5 cubes.

1. If there are 10 cubes, how many cube trains can you make? 2
2. If there are 20 cubes, how many cube trains can you make? 4
3. If there are 30 cubes, how many cube trains can you make? 6
4. If there are 40 cubes, how many cube trains can you make? 8
5. Count by 5s from 0 to 40. List the numbers you say. What pattern do you see?
Answers will vary. Review students' work.

Use anytime after Session 3.4. Unit 3 R29

Materials to Prepare: Write the numbers between 15 and 30 on index cards, one number per card.

Write the following problem on the board, using the number of students in another class.

> There are [26] students in [Mrs. Baker's] class. How many fingers are there on all of their hands?

Ask students to think about the information given in the problem. What do we know? What do we need to find out? How could we solve it?

Students might say:

"Draw 26 people and count their hands by 5s."

"There are 10 fingers on each person, so count the people by 10s."

Discuss all the strategies presented. Include an example of using cubes to count by 5s and 10s. Then distribute a number card to each pair. Explain to students that they will solve problems about people at a library. The number card tells the number of people at *your* library.

Write the following questions on the board.

> - How many hands are there?
> - How many fingers are on all of their hands?

Partners work together to solve both problems, recording their work. Have pairs share their solution strategies.

Distribute copies of Counting by 5s and 10s (R29).

ELL English Language Learners

Provide a Word List Review unfamiliar words that occur in these problems, such as *fingers, hands, toes,* and *feet.* Write the words on chart paper and ask students to illustrate each one. Post the list and have students refer to it as needed.

Additional Resource

Student Math Handbook pages 38–39

Extension

25 MIN PAIRS

More Counting Bags

Use anytime after Session 3.6.

Math Focus Points

- Developing fluency with skip counting by 2s, 5s, and 10s

Vocabulary: tally marks

Materials: small objects (50–70 per pair), bags (1 per pair), R30

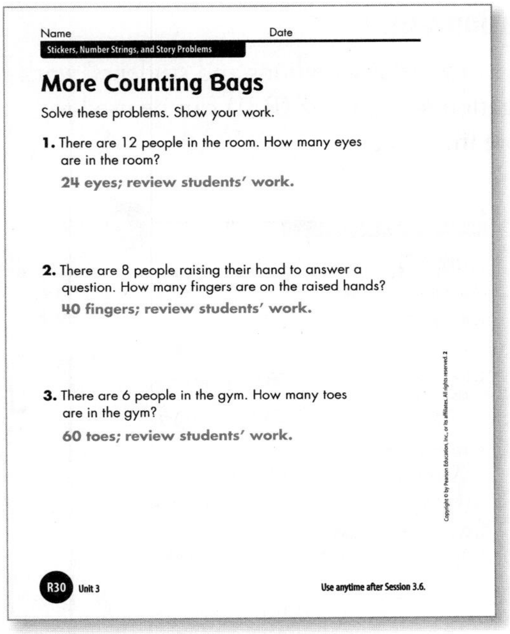

Name Date

Stickers, Number Strings, and Story Problems

More Counting Bags

Solve these problems. Show your work.

1. There are 12 people in the room. How many eyes are in the room?
   24 eyes; review students' work.

2. There are 8 people raising their hand to answer a question. How many fingers are on the raised hands?
   40 fingers; review students' work.

3. There are 6 people in the gym. How many toes are in the gym?
   60 toes; review students' work.

Copyright © by Pearson Education, Inc., or its affiliates. All rights reserved. 2

R30 Unit 3 Use anytime after Session 3.6.

Materials to Prepare: Fill each bag with an even number of 50–70 small objects, such as beans, pennies, or cubes. Prepare 1 bag per pair of students plus 1 extra bag for demonstration.

Pour the contents of the demonstration bag onto the table. Today we will find different ways of counting these [beans] *without* counting by 1s. Who can show us one way?

Have volunteers model the strategies they suggest. When there are not enough objects left to group in 5s or 10s, encourage students to count on by 2s instead of 1s. Discuss methods of recording their work, including using pictures, numbers, words, and tally marks.

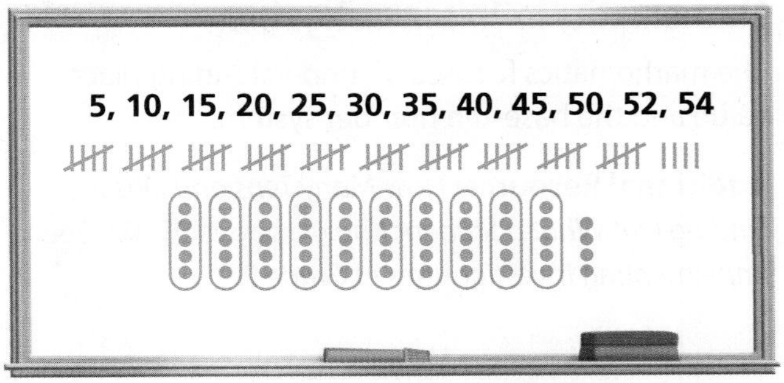

Have students work in pairs. Distribute 1 bag of objects to each pair. Have partners work together to find two ways of counting the objects without counting by 1s. Each partner should make his or her own record of how they both counted.

As a class, students share their work and their strategies for counting by groups.

Distribute copies of More Counting Bags (R30).

ELL English Language Learners

Suggest a Sequence Clarify instructions by sequencing the steps for students. Model each step for Beginner ELLs who need more support.

1. Count the objects by 2s, 5s, or 10s. Do not count by 1s.
2. Record the way you counted.
3. Count the objects again, in another way. Do not count by 1s.
4. Record the way you counted.

Additional Resource

Student Math Handbook

Game: *Collect 50¢* SMH G4

Materials: dot cubes or number cubes, coins

Variation: Players try to have the fewest coins possible at the end of each round.

Differentiation in Investigation 4

Mathematics in This Investigation

The mathematics focuses on understanding place value and the base-ten number system.

Additional Resource: *How Many Tens and Ones? Finding Out What a Student Knows*, pages 91–92 (See *Implementing Investigations in Grade 2*)

Understanding the Mathematics

Students understand that one 10 is equal to ten 1s and use a "sticker" context to represent this relationship. They recognize that the first digit of a 2-digit number designates the number of groups of 10, and the second digit designates the number of 1s. They interpret story problems about 10s and 1s and solve them accurately and efficiently either by counting on or by breaking numbers into 10s and 1s and adding like groups.

Option: Assign the **Extension** activity.

Partially Understanding the Mathematics

Students are beginning to use 10s and 1s models with understanding, to represent and identify 2-digit numbers. Students interpret and solve addition problems with 2-digit addends but may make minor errors in their computation. They sometimes use their knowledge of 10s and 1s to help them solve a problem, though they may revert to counting by 1s for harder problems.

Option: Assign the **Practice** activity.

Not Understanding the Mathematics

Students may represent 1- and smaller 2-digit numbers using stickers or cubes, but they may not use the 10 to 1 relationship with understanding. Instead, students count by 1s to confirm the number of stickers or cubes. They may use the strategies of counting all or counting on to solve any addition problem.

Option: Assign the **Intervention** activity.

Investigation 4 Quiz

In addition to your observations and students' work in Investigation 4, the Quiz (R31) can be used to gather more information

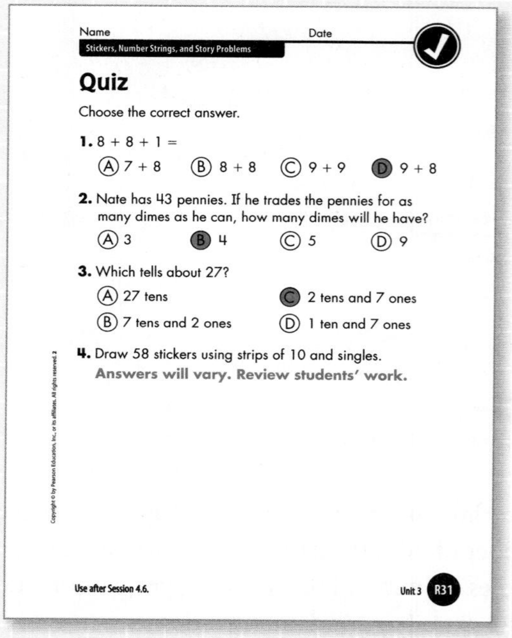

Name Date

Stickers, Number Strings, and Story Problems

Quiz

Choose the correct answer.

1. 8 + 8 + 1 =

(A) 7 + 8 (B) 8 + 8 (C) 9 + 9 (D) 9 + 8

2. Nate has 43 pennies. If he trades the pennies for as many dimes as he can, how many dimes will he have?

(A) 3 (B) 4 (C) 5 (D) 9

3. Which tells about 27?

(A) 27 tens (C) 2 tens and 7 ones

(B) 7 tens and 2 ones (D) 1 ten and 7 ones

4. Draw 58 stickers using strips of 10 and singles.

Answers will vary. Review students' work.

Copyright © by Pearson Education, Inc., or its affiliates. All rights reserved. 2

Use after Session 4.6. Unit 3 R31

Intervention

35 MIN PAIRS

Modeling Tens and Ones

Use anytime after Session 4.4.

Math Focus Points

- Using a place-value model to represent a number as 10s and 1s

Materials: connecting cubes (60 per student), blank paper, R88

Students count 10 cubes of one color and place them on the ten-frame. Then they count 8 cubes of another color and place those on a ten-frame. How many full frames? How many leftovers? How many cubes in all? Record this information on the board. Discuss with students how they can tell there are 18 cubes without counting each cube by ones. Emphasize the group of 10.

Have students add 1 cube and discuss how many (19). Then add 1 more cube (20). Reinforce the number of full frames and the number of extra cubes. Now you have 20 cubes.

Full ten-frames (10s)	Extra (1s)	Total
1	8	18
1	9	19
2	0	20

Tell students to snap together the 10 cubes in the first frame and place the tower across the ten-frame. Now how many cubes do you have? Have students snap together the cubes on the second frame and place that tower across the ten-frame. Now how many cubes do you have? Reinforce that two groups of 10 is the same as 20. Can you show 25 cubes? What about 28 cubes? I noticed that most of you just added 3 cubes. How do you know that you have 28 cubes? Ask students to build 32. Record 25, 28, and 32 on the board, noting the number of full ten-frames and the number of extras, and discuss.

Pairs of students work together to choose a number between 20 and 60 and build that on the ten-frame. Tell them to snap together a tower of 10 when they have a full frame. Students should make a list of the numbers they build.

As a whole group, discuss various numbers and add information about tens and ones to the chart posted on the board.

ELL English Language Learners

Use Repetition Focus on words that give students difficulty. Some students may need extra help understanding *tens* and *ones*. They may benefit from more work relating pictures of tens and ones to their numerical representatives. Point to the tens in a picture of tens and ones. Then point to the tens place in the number. Have students repeat several times with you: The 2 in the tens place means that there are two tens. Do the same for the ones place.

Additional Resource

Student Math Handbook page 29

Practice

20 MIN INDIVIDUALS

Strips and Singles

Use anytime after Session 4.5.

Math Focus Points

- Using a place-value model to represent a number as 10s and 1s
- Recognizing that different combinations of 10s and 1s for the same number are equivalent (e.g., 4 tens and 6 ones = 3 tens and 16 ones, etc.)

Materials: connecting cubes (organized in single color towers of 10), R32

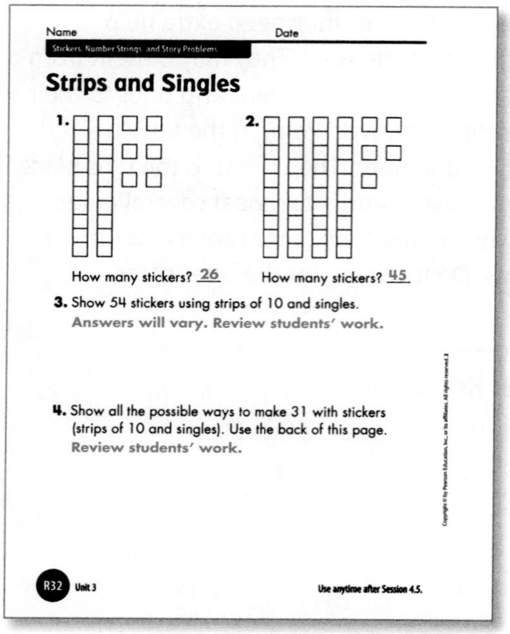

Name Date

Stickers, Number Strings, and Story Problems

Strips and Singles

1\. How many stickers? 26

2\. How many stickers? 45

3\. Show 54 stickers using strips of 10 and singles.
Answers will vary. Review students' work.

4\. Show all the possible ways to make 31 with stickers (strips of 10 and singles). Use the back of this page.
Review students' work.

R32 Unit 3 Use anytime after Session 4.5.

Write this problem on the board and read it aloud. Esteban has 53 stickers. Some are strips of ten and some are singles. How many of each kind could he have?

Students might say:

"5 strips of 10 and 3 singles."

"3 strips of 10 plus 23 singles."

Have students use cubes to model each way they suggest. How many tens and ones is that? List the numbers of strips and singles, tens and ones, and the number combination on the board.

53

5 strips 3 singles	5 tens 3 ones	50 + 3
4 strips 13 singles	4 tens 13 ones	40 + 13

Now write this problem on the board and read it aloud. Holly has 49 stickers. How many strips of ten and how many singles could she have? Can you find all the combinations? Students work individually to solve the problem and record their work. Have them write the number of strips and singles, tens and ones, and a number combination for each way they find.

Bring students together and list all the ways of making 49 that they found. Do you think we found all the ways? How do you know?

Distribute copies of Strips and Singles (R32).

ELL English Language Learners

Rephrase Some students may confuse strips and singles when describing numbers. Review the tens place and the ones place. Strips have 10 stickers. Strips describe the number in the tens place. Singles describe the number in the ones place. If students have difficulty, guide them in describing the number in *strips* and *singles* or *tens* and *ones*.

Additional Resource

Student Math Handbook page 28

Extension

25 MIN PAIRS

Combinations of Tens and Ones

Use anytime after Session 4.4.

Math Focus Points

- Using a place-value model to represent a number as 10s and 1s

Vocabulary: tens place, ones place

Materials: connecting cubes, R33

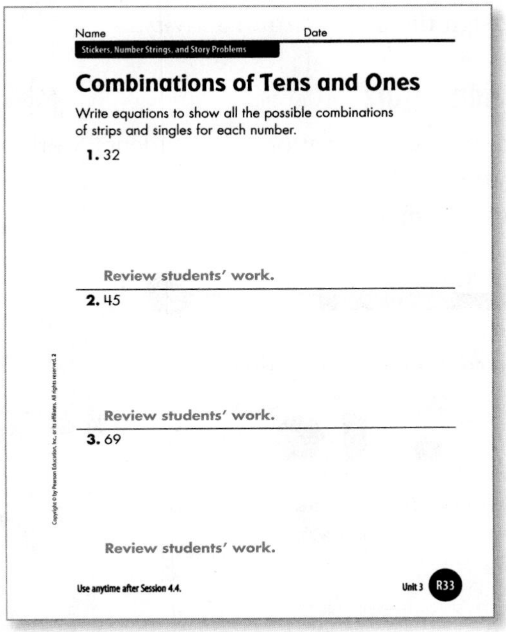

Name Date

Stickers, Number Strings, and Story Problems

Combinations of Tens and Ones

Write equations to show all the possible combinations of strips and singles for each number.

1. 32

Review students' work.

2. 45

Review students' work.

3. 69

Review students' work.

Use anytime after Session 4.4. Unit 3 R33

Display 6 cube towers of 10 and 5 single cubes. How many cubes do I have? Write 65 on the board. How many tens are there? What number is in the tens place? How many ones are there? What number is in the ones place? What combination can we write? Record the tens and ones and the combination on the board.

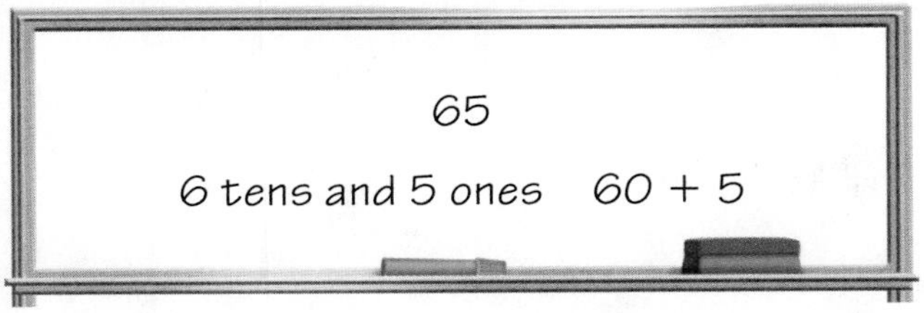

Suppose I broke up one tower of 10 into 10 single cubes. How many cubes would I have? Reinforce that the total doesn't change *(65)* but the number of tens and ones changes. Record 5 tens and 15 ones on the board. What equation represents this? *(50 + 15)* As a group, list the other equations for 65 if you were to break up each tower of 10 (e.g., 40 + 25, 30 + 35) and record this information on the board.

Have students work in pairs to find all the combinations of tens and ones for 73. They should record an equation for each combination.

End the activity with a discussion. List students' equations for 73. Discuss the patterns that students notice.

Students might say:

"There is a number pattern in the ones. The ones number stayed the same but the tens number went up by 1s: 3, 13, 23, 33, ...73."

"The tens number went down by 10 but the ones number went up by 10."

Distribute copies of Combinations of Tens and Ones (R33).

ELL English Language Learners

Provide Sentence Stems If students need support recording the tens and ones, the combinations, and the numbers, provide them with these sentence stems to help:

________ tens and ________ ones

________ + ________

____

Additional Resource

Student Math Handbook pages 28–29

Differentiation in Investigation 1

Mathematics in This Investigation

The mathematics focuses on sorting, classifying, and representing categorical data.

Understanding the Mathematics

Students sort and organize data into clear categories, and are able to reorganize the data in multiple ways using different categories. Students use pictures, tables, graphs, and Venn diagrams to effectively organize and represent their data, and they extract important information from their representations. They understand and use Venn diagrams to show overlapping categories.

Option: Assign the **Extension** activity.

Partially Understanding the Mathematics

Students sort and organize data into clear categories that may not always be consistent in theme or subject matter. They make clear representations of their data, but they may make some minor errors in their tables or graphs or have some difficulty classifying and representing data in overlapping categories. They can represent and interpret data using a Venn diagram but may not be confident about what the intersection represents and/or how to interpret data placed outside of the two circles.

Option: Assign the **Practice** activity.

Not Understanding the Mathematics

Students may still be working on what it means to organize data into categories. They sort each piece of data into a separate category or only put pieces of identical data together in categories. They do not yet understand the purpose of representing data to communicate information to others, and they are unsure how to make a picture, table, or graph to represent their data.

Option: Assign the **Intervention** activity.

Investigation 1 Quiz

In addition to your observations and students' work in Investigation 1, the Quiz (R34) can be used to gather more information.

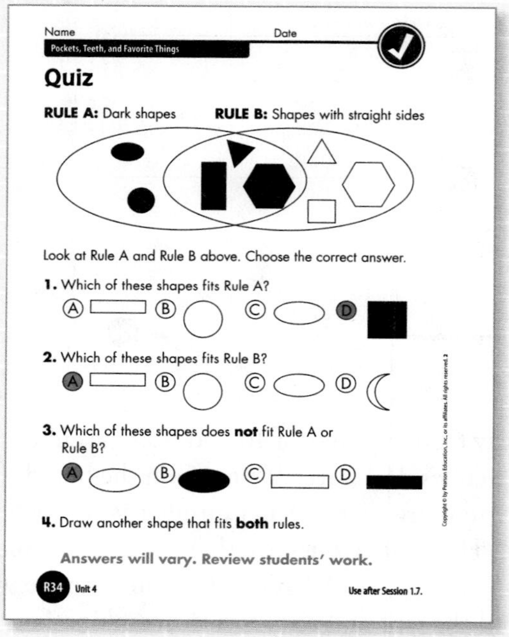
Name Date

Pockets, Teeth, and Favorite Things

Quiz

RULE A: Dark shapes **RULE B:** Shapes with straight sides

Look at Rule A and Rule B above. Choose the correct answer.

1. Which of these shapes fits Rule A?
(A) (B) (C) (D)

2. Which of these shapes fits Rule B?
(A) (B) (C) (D)

3. Which of these shapes does **not** fit Rule A or Rule B?
(A) (B) (C) (D)

4. Draw another shape that fits **both** rules.

Answers will vary. Review students' work.

R34 Unit 4 Use after Session 1.7.

Copyright © by Pearson Education, Inc., or its affiliates. All rights reserved. 2

Intervention

20 MIN INDIVIDUALS

Different Representations

Use anytime after Session 1.1.

Math Focus Points

- Representing a set of data sorted into categories
- Comparing representations of a set of data

Vocabulary: data, representation

Materials: blank paper or M15 (from Unit 2), stick-on dots (as needed), self-stick notes (as needed)

Select a set of *Guess My Rule* data that the class collected in Session 1.1. For example, are you wearing sneakers? Record the data on the board.

14 people are wearing sneakers.

10 people are not wearing sneakers.

Today we will think of different ways to show data. If I was going to show that 14 people were wearing sneakers it would take me a really long time to draw all of those people. What is an easier and quicker way to show this information?

Students might say:

"I can draw one smiley face for each person."

"I would use sticky dots, one for each person."

Suppose I wanted to use a line. How many lines would I make to show the number of people wearing sneakers? Not wearing sneakers? What if I used cubes? How could I show the data?

Discuss ideas for representing the data. Students might suggest using dots, tiles, tally marks, or self-stick notes.

Select one idea and, as a group, make a representation of the data set. As you are recording each piece of data, point out to students that it is easier to understand a representation if the data are organized in a row or in a column.

Explain to students that they will now choose a way to represent this same set of data.

As students are working, remind them to line up their symbols clearly. If they are showing too many details, encourage them to draw circles or simple symbols first and add more details if they have extra time. They should also include the number of pieces of data in each group.

Discuss students' representations, highlighting the way each student represented the information.

ELL English Language Learners

Rephrase Use other ways to ask about representing data in different ways, such as:

- Is there an easier way to show the same thing?
- What is a simpler way to show the data?

Additional Resource

Student Math Handbook page 104

Practice

20 MIN GROUPS

Sorting Flower Data

Use anytime after Session 1.5.

Math Focus Points

- Grouping data into categories based on similar attributes
- Representing a set of data sorted into categories

Materials: index cards (3 per student plus extras), red and yellow crayons, 2 yarn loops (optional), tape (as needed), blank paper, R35

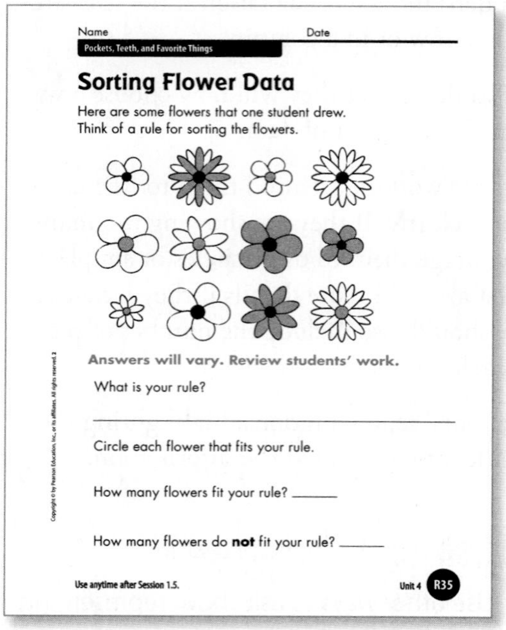
Name Date

Pockets, Teeth, and Favorite Things

Sorting Flower Data

Here are some flowers that one student drew.
Think of a rule for sorting the flowers.

Answers will vary. Review students' work.

What is your rule?

Circle each flower that fits your rule.

How many flowers fit your rule? ______

How many flowers do **not** fit your rule? ______

Use anytime after Session 1.5. Unit 4 R35

Distribute 3 index cards to each student. Record the following information on the board.

Flower Data

center - ○ ●

petals - ∩ ∧

number of petals - 4, 5, 6, 7

color of petals - red, yellow, plain

Today we are going to make a set of flower data. Draw one flower on each index card. Demonstrate how to make a simple flower using the criteria on the board. I made a flower with a black center and 6 rounded petals. My flower has plain petals. Explain that each student should make 2–3 different flowers. Review the flower attributes. Give students time to draw the flowers.

Gather the group in a circle and place each index card in the center or tape each card to the board so that everyone can see the set of flower data. How can we sort the flowers? Talk with your neighbor about different ways to sort them. Record students' ideas on the board. Select 2 rules to use in a Venn diagram.

Draw a large Venn diagram on the board or use the yarn loops to make one on the floor or table. I have chosen 2 rules from our list. One rule is Red Flowers and the other is Black Centers. Write these rules on index cards and place them on the Venn. Students take turns placing their flowers in the Venn. [James] has a yellow flower with a plain center. Where should he put that piece of data?

Once all the flowers have been placed, ask students to describe each group as you point to each section of the Venn. Be sure to discuss the cards outside. Distribute blank paper. Students record information about the data representation. For example: 5 flowers are red. 12 flowers have black centers. 3 flowers are red with black centers.

Distribute copies of Sorting Flower Data (R35).

ELL English Language Learners

Provide Sentence Stems Some students may be confused by using phrases for rules. Provide a sentence stem. For example, RULE: The flowers that go inside this circle are the flowers with ________.
Students should complete the sentence with one or two words, such as *yellow petals* or *black centers*.

Additional Resource

Student Math Handbook page 108

Extension

20 MIN PAIRS

Two Rules for Data

Use anytime after Session 1.7.

Math Focus Points

- Grouping data into categories based on similar attributes
- Sorting a set of data by two attributes at one time
- Using a Venn diagram to represent a sorted set of data

Materials: yarn loops (2 per group), various buttons or Geoblocks (12–15 per group), index cards (2 per group), R36

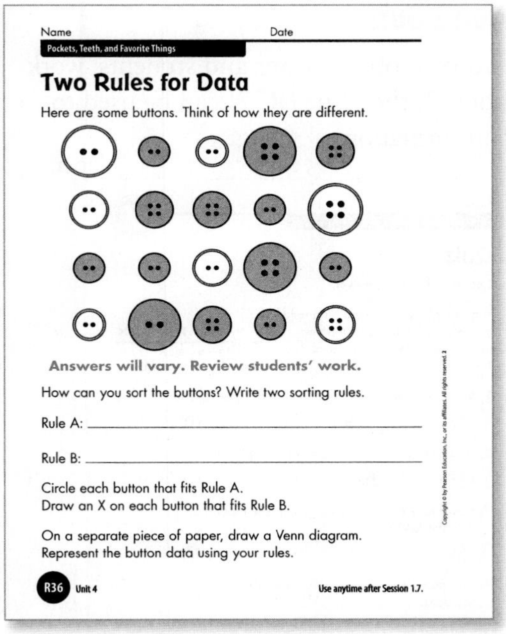
Name Date

Pockets, Teeth, and Favorite Things

Two Rules for Data

Here are some buttons. Think of how they are different.

Answers will vary. Review students' work.

How can you sort the buttons? Write two sorting rules.

Rule A: ____________________

Rule B: ____________________

Circle each button that fits Rule A.
Draw an X on each button that fits Rule B.

On a separate piece of paper, draw a Venn diagram.
Represent the button data using your rules.

R36 Unit 4 Use anytime after Session 1.7.

Distribute yarn loops, index cards, and buttons or Geoblocks to each group of students.

Today you will sort objects by two rules and make a Venn diagram with yarn loops. With your partner, look at the objects and think of ways to describe or sort them.

Briefly discuss students' ideas for sorting the objects. Each person should secretly choose two rules and write the rules on the index cards. It is okay for an object to fit both rules.

Students might say:

"I can sort the buttons by the number of holes they have or by color."

"I can sort them by their shapes."

After you each write down your rules, arrange your yarn as two loops that overlap. Take turns playing *Guess My Rule.* Player 1 puts an index card facedown above each loop. Player 2 places an object in the circle. Player 1 decides whether it is correctly placed. Once all the objects have been placed, Player 2 can guess the rules based on how the objects have been sorted.

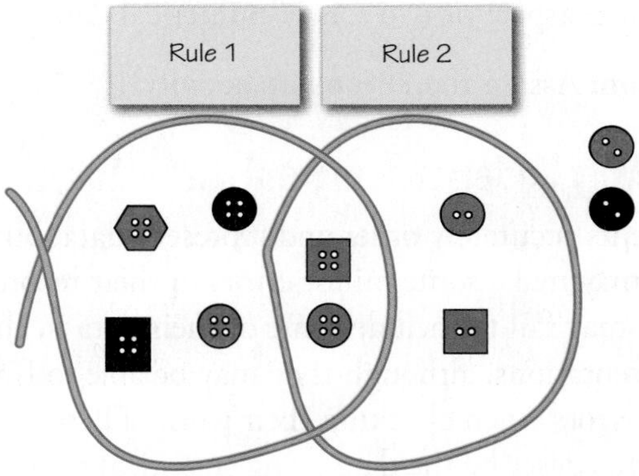

As pairs finish suggest that they switch partners and play again.

Distribute copies of Two Rules for Data (R36).

ELL English Language Learners

Rephrase Some students may need help understanding the meaning of *both* and/or *neither.* If a button fits *both* rules, it fits Rule A and Rule B. If it fits *neither* rule, the button does not fit Rule A or Rule B.

Additional Resource

Student Math Handbook page 108

Differentiation in Investigation 2

Mathematics in This Investigation

The mathematics focuses on ordering numerical data, describing important features of numerical data (e.g., mode, outlier, range), and representing numerical data in various ways. This information is used to compare two data sets and to interpret or make predictions about what the data show.

Understanding the Mathematics

Students accurately order and represent data using bar graphs and line plots. They understand that data representations are ways to communicate information to others, and students achieve that in their own representations. They describe and interpret data on a line plot using statistical language, and they accurately answer questions about the data. Students make comparisons about the same aspect of two sets of numerical data.

Option: Assign the **Extension** activity.

Partially Understanding the Mathematics

Students accurately order and represent data, but they may make some minor errors in their recording. They may fail to include some of their data in their representations, although they may be able to find their errors when checking their work. These students describe the data using statistical terms. They may not easily interpret the data, although they can usually answer questions about the representations when asked.

Option: Assign the **Practice** activity.

Not Understanding the Mathematics

Students may represent numerical data but not in a numerically ordered way. Their representation may not include the entire data set. Students make statements about the data that may or may not be accurate or specific. They may have difficulty knowing what information to look for in a set of data, so they may focus on less important aspects of the data, rather than describing features such as the range, mode, or outliers. Comparing two data sets is challenging.

Option: Assign the **Intervention** activity.

Investigation 2 Quiz

In addition to your observations and students' work in Investigation 2, the Quiz (R37) can be used to gather more information.

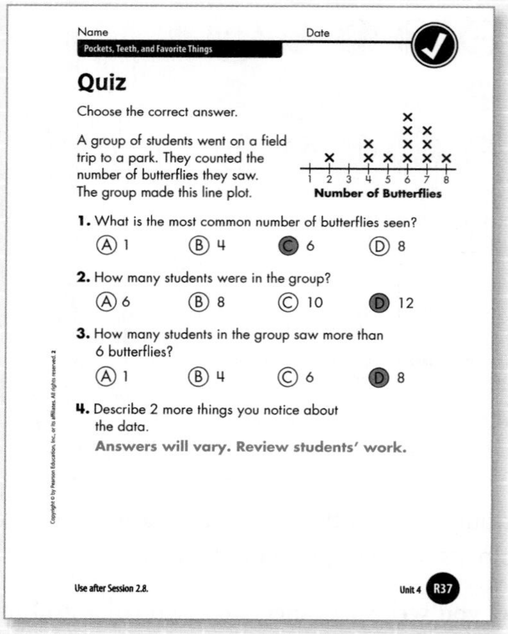

Name Date

Pockets, Teeth, and Favorite Things

Quiz

Choose the correct answer.

A group of students went on a field trip to a park. They counted the number of butterflies they saw. The group made this line plot.

1. What is the most common number of butterflies seen?
   Ⓐ 1 Ⓑ 4 Ⓒ 6 Ⓓ 8
2. How many students were in the group?
   Ⓐ 6 Ⓑ 8 Ⓒ 10 Ⓓ 12
3. How many students in the group saw more than 6 butterflies?
   Ⓐ 1 Ⓑ 4 Ⓒ 6 Ⓓ 8
4. Describe 2 more things you notice about the data.
   Answers will vary. Review students' work.

Use after Session 2.8. Unit 4 R37

Intervention

20 MIN PAIRS

Reading and Comparing Line Plots

Use anytime after Session 2.6.

Math Focus Points

- Comparing two sets of data

Materials: self-stick notes or small 2 × 2 paper squares (12 of one color, 12 of another color per pair)

Write the following data on the board.

> How many birds did you see?
>
> BOYS: 4, 2, 1, 4, 8, 8, 7, 4, 6, 2, 6, 8
>
> GIRLS: 5, 4, 7, 8, 3, 2, 2, 3, 7, 7, 5, 2

A class put a bird feeder outside a window. One morning, students counted how many birds they saw. The data written on the board are the data collected by the boys and girls in the class.

Work with your partner. Copy the girls' data onto the [yellow] squares. Write one number on each square. Copy the boys' data using the [blue] paper squares.

Demonstrate and make a data set for yourself. After students have recorded each data set have them put each set in order from least to greatest.

Now you have the bird data in two long lines: one for girls and one for boys. Put your data into a stack or a tower so that all the 2s are in a stack, then the 3s, and so on.

Draw two line plots on the board. Discuss why it is important to include all of the numbers between the greatest and the least numbers on the line plot, even if there are no data for some of the numbers. Using the set of squares you made, stack the squares above the corresponding number.

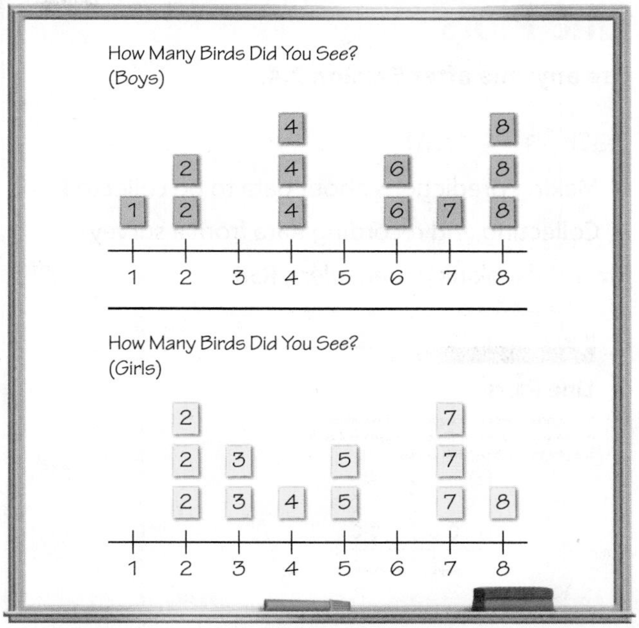

Describe the features of the data for the boys and the data for the girls. What do you notice? Then ask students to compare the same aspect of the data. How many girls saw two birds? How many boys?

After students have answered several questions about the data, remove one number square at a time and replace them with Xs. Then discuss what the Xs stand for. Look at the line plot. Each X stands for one person. How many girls saw 8 birds? How can you tell? Look at your girl data. How many 8s do you have?

ELL English Language Learners

Partner Talk Have pairs answer the following questions. How are the two line plots the same? How are they different? Encourage more proficient speakers to use words such as *line plot, data,* and *mode* in their explanations. Less proficient speakers should point to each and then summarize the similarities and differences described with short phrases.

Additional Resource

Student Math Handbook page 110

Practice

20 MIN INDIVIDUALS

Line Plots

Use anytime after Session 2.4.

Math Focus Points

- Making predictions about data to be collected
- Collecting and recording data from a survey

Materials: blank paper, rulers, R38

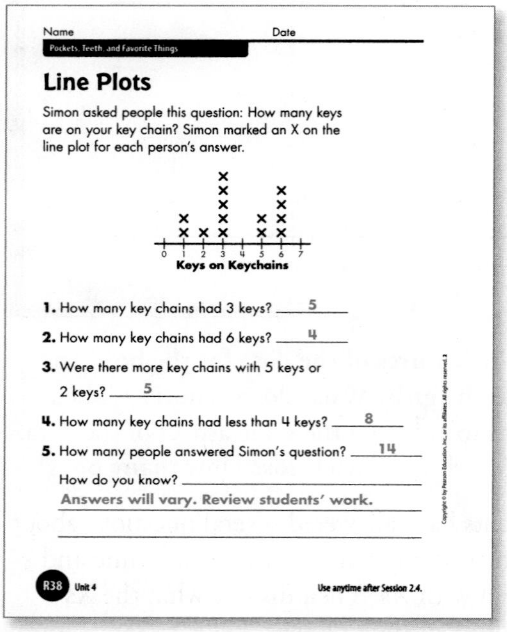

Name Date

Pockets, Teeth, and Favorite Things

Line Plots

Simon asked people this question: How many keys are on your key chain? Simon marked an X on the line plot for each person's answer.

1. How many key chains had 3 keys? 5
2. How many key chains had 6 keys? 4
3. Were there more key chains with 5 keys or 2 keys? 5
4. How many key chains had less than 4 keys? 8
5. How many people answered Simon's question? 14

How do you know?
Answers will vary. Review students' work.

R38 Unit 4 Use anytime after Session 2.4.

Ask the class a question with a numerical answer and record their responses in an organized list. The board below shows a sample question and data.

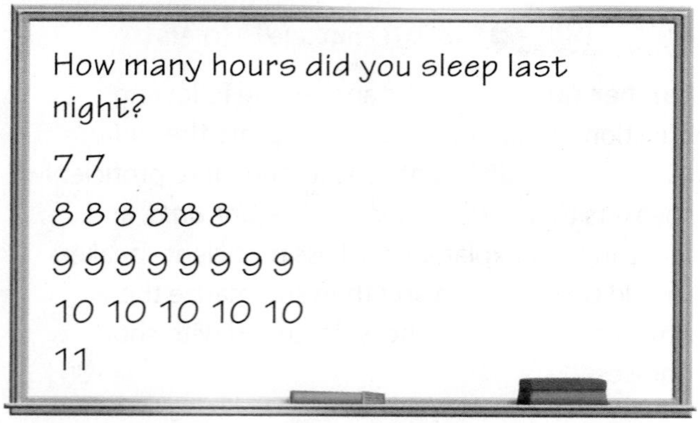

What do you notice about how long people in our class sleep? What is the least number of hours? The most?

Tell students they are going to represent the data on a line plot. Distribute a sheet of blank paper and a ruler to each student. Have them fold the paper in half horizontally. Copy the data on the top half of your paper. Draw a line near the bottom edge. Model on the board while students make a line plot on their paper. What is the first thing you need to know when you make a line plot?

Students might say:

"I need to know the smallest and largest numbers that will be on the line plot."

After we label the line plot, what should we do? Remember, there should be an X for each piece of data. Discuss how many Xs should be above each value and what each X means. How many Xs should be on the finished line plot? What do the Xs show?

Have students discuss the important features of the completed line plot, such as the highest number, the lowest number, and the mode. Talk about the number of responses above or below a specific number. How many people slept more than 9 hours? Less than 9 hours? How can you tell?

Finally, ask students to make a prediction based on the data. If we went to another 2nd grade classroom and asked the same question, do you think the data would be the same or different? Why? What if we asked a 6th grade class? Then distribute copies of Line Plots (R38).

ELL English Language Learners

Rephrase You may need to rephrase questions using different words. For example, instead of *lowest* you might say *least* or *smallest*. Instead of *highest* you might say *greatest* or *largest*. *Mode* is the *most common number* or the number that *appears the most*.

Additional Resource

Student Math Handbook pages 110–111

Extension

20 MIN PAIRS

Representing Age Data

Use anytime after Session 2.7.

Math Focus Points

- Representing data on a line plot
- Describing important features of a data set

Materials: blank paper, R39

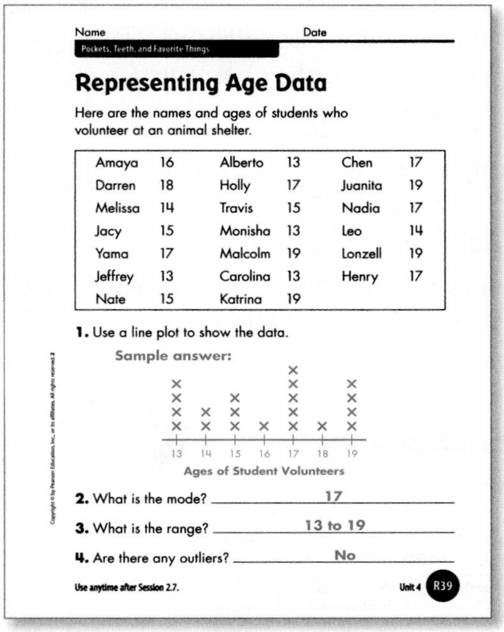

Name Date

Pockets, Teeth, and Favorite Things

Representing Age Data

Here are the names and ages of students who volunteer at an animal shelter.

Amaya	16	Alberto	13	Chen	17
Darren	18	Holly	17	Juanita	19
Melissa	14	Travis	15	Nadia	17
Jacy	15	Monisha	13	Leo	14
Yama	17	Malcolm	19	Lonzell	19
Jeffrey	13	Carolina	13	Henry	17
Nate	15	Katrina	19		

1. Use a line plot to show the data.

Sample answer:

13 14 15 16 17 18 19

Ages of Student Volunteers

2. What is the mode? 17

3. What is the range? 13 to 19

4. Are there any outliers? No

Use anytime after Session 2.7. Unit 4 R39

Write the following data sample on the board:

Ages of Students in a Chess Club

12, 10, 10, 11, 13, 14, 7, 14, 15, 11, 13, 14, 10, 16, 14, 12, 11, 10, 11, 14

Copy the data onto your paper. You will represent the data on a line plot. How can you make sure that you don't plot the same number twice?

Students might say:

"Cross off each number as you put an X on the line plot."

"Count the number of each age and put that many Xs on the line plot."

When you finish your line plot, find a partner and take turns asking each other about important features of the data set. Ask questions such as:

- Are there any outliers?
- What is the mode? The range?
- How many students in the club are 10 years old?
- How many students are older than 12 years old?

When students are finished discussing the data, they should answer these questions on their paper:

- What does the data tell you about this chess club?
- Do you think the data is representative of the ages of people in all chess clubs? Why or why not?

Distribute copies of Representing Age Data (R39).

ELL English Language Learners

Use Repetition Some students may confuse the words *mode, outlier,* and *range.* Discuss the meaning of each word, then have students retell each meaning in their own words. Some students may also benefit from illustrating each word. Emphasize the use of these words throughout the activity.

Additional Resource

Student Math Handbook pages 110–111

Differentiation in Investigation 1

Mathematics in This Investigation

The mathematics focuses on developing an understanding of ratio as a relationship between two quantities and on using tables to organize and represent the relationship between these quantities.

Additional Resource: *Using and Interpreting Tables,* pages 107–108 (See Curriculum Unit 5)

Understanding the Mathematics

Students understand and describe ratio relationships. They know what the numbers in a table represent in a constant ratio situation involving ratios of 1:2, 1:3, 1:4, 1:5, 1:6, and more. They use the ratio relationship of two variables to complete and extend tables involving a constant ratio. They are able to use the ratio relationship to determine the value of a quantity when only one value is known.

Option: Assign the **Extension** activity.

Partially Understanding the Mathematics

Students may be able to complete and extend tables involving a constant ratio; however, they may still be unsure how the variables are related. While they may be able to identify and describe the pattern that exists in a table which represents constant change, they may have difficulty understanding how the pattern can be used to predict a future outcome. These students may have trouble completing a table unless every value in the table is given. Some students may get a wrong answer by making a minor calculation or counting error when working on extending the pattern.

Option: Assign the **Practice** activity.

Not Understanding the Mathematics

Students may understand a ratio situation using classroom objects (e.g., adding pennies to a penny jar at a constant rate), however, they may not understand how this can be represented in a table. They do not make sense of what the numbers in the table mean or how they show a relationship between two changing quantities. They may or may not be able to identify and describe the patterns that exist in a table which represents constant change. They typically are unable to use the pattern to determine future outcomes.

Option: Assign the **Intervention** activity.

Investigation 1 Quiz

In addition to your observations and students' work in Investigation 1, the Quiz (R40) can be used to gather more information.

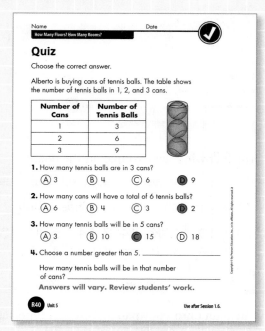

Name Date

How Many Floors? How Many Rooms?

Quiz

Choose the correct answer.

Alberto is buying cans of tennis balls. The table shows the number of tennis balls in 1, 2, and 3 cans.

Number of Cans	Number of Tennis Balls
1	3
2	6
3	9

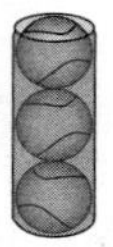

1. How many tennis balls are in 3 cans?
   (A) 3 (B) 4 (C) 6 (D) 9
2. How many cans will have a total of 6 tennis balls?
   (A) 6 (B) 4 (C) 3 (D) 2
3. How many tennis balls will be in 5 cans?
   (A) 3 (B) 10 (C) 15 (D) 18
4. Choose a number greater than 5. ______

   How many tennis balls will be in that number of cans? ______

   Answers will vary. Review students' work.

Copyright © by Pearson Education, Inc., or its affiliates. All rights reserved. 2

R40 Unit 5 Use after Session 1.6.

Intervention

20 MIN INDIVIDUALS

Colorful Cube Buildings

Use anytime after Session 1.2.

Math Focus Points

- Using tables to represent the ratio relationship between two quantities
- Connecting numbers in a table to the situation they represent
- Using conventional language for a table and its parts: rows, columns

Vocabulary: table, row, column

Materials: connecting cubes in various colors (20 per student)

Draw the following on the board. Explain to students that they will be making a building using cubes.

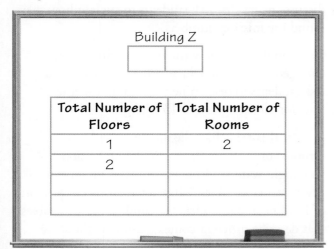

Building Z

Total Number of Floors	Total Number of Rooms
1	2
2	

Choose two connecting cubes of the same color to make a building that matches the floor plan for Building Z. Each cube is a room. How many rooms are on 1 floor? Help students get started, as needed.

Next, choose two connecting cubes of a different color to make the rooms on the second floor. Stack these cubes on top of the ones for the first floor. How many rooms are on 2 floors? Encourage students who count the rooms by 1s to apply what they know about counting by 2s to determine the total number of rooms.

Direct students' attention to the table. This table shows the number of floors and the total number of rooms in Building Z. The first column tells the total number of floors in Building Z and the second column shows the total number of rooms. Remind students that the rows go across, whereas the columns go up and down. We know there are 4 rooms on 2 floors. Where do you write the number 4?

Choose two connecting cubes of a color that you have not used yet. Connect them to make a third floor. What is the total number of rooms on 3 floors? In the table, where do we write this new information? Have students add the fourth floor in a different color. How can you find the total number of rooms on 4 floors?

Students might say:

"Since there are 6 in 3 floors, add two more, 7, 8."

Suppose a row in our table had an 8 in the left column and a 16 in the right column. What does that mean? Discuss the answer, making sure that students understand that the title of each column applies to any row. To verify the answer, extend the table and have students help you complete it by modeling the floors for each row.

ELL English Language Learners

Rephrase Some English Language Learners may confuse *table* with the type of table used for furniture. Explain how a mathematical table has rows and columns, and is used to organize information. Students may better understand *chart.* Rephrase questions as needed to prevent misunderstandings.

Additional Resource

Student Math Handbook page 96

Practice

20 MIN PAIRS

Polygons and Stars

Use anytime after Session 1.3.

Math Focus Points

- Using information in a table to determine the relationship between two quantities
- Using tables to represent the ratio relationship between two quantities
- Describing what is the same about situations that look different but can be represented by the same table

Vocabulary: row, column

Materials: R41

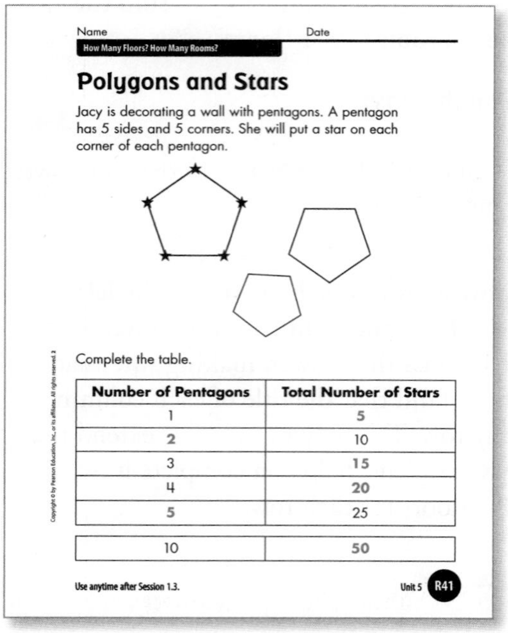

Name Date

How Many Floors? How Many Rooms?

Polygons and Stars

Jacy is decorating a wall with pentagons. A pentagon has 5 sides and 5 corners. She will put a star on each corner of each pentagon.

Complete the table.

Number of Pentagons	Total Number of Stars
1	5
2	10
3	15
4	20
5	25
10	50

Use anytime after Session 1.3. Unit 5 R41

Copyright © by Pearson Education, Inc., or its affiliates. All rights reserved. 3

Draw the following on the board.

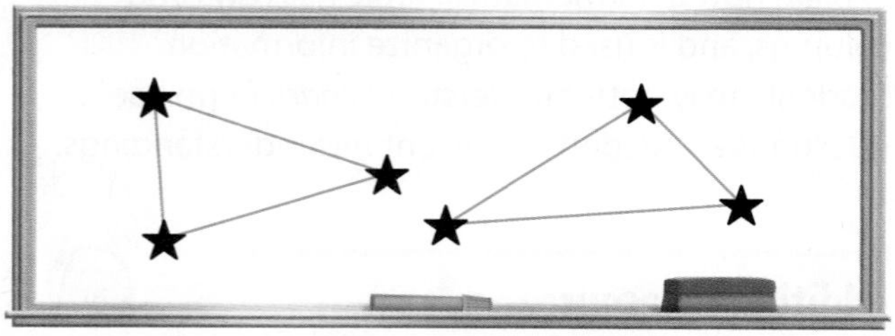

Write the following table on the board.

Number of Triangles	Total Number of Stars
1	3
2	
	9
4	
5	

Chen likes to draw triangles. One day he drew several triangles and then drew a star at each corner or vertex. Direct students' attention to the table. Ask them what they think this table represents. Discuss the information given in the rows and columns. Work with your partner. Copy the table and write the missing numbers. After pairs complete the table, discuss the results. Ask students to explain how they found the missing numbers.

Can you describe how the total number of stars changed every time you added another triangle? Ask students to determine the total number of stars for 10 triangles and 13 triangles.

How is this table like the one for a building with 3 rooms on a floor? After completing Session 1.5, you might want students to compare this table to Mystery Shape Tables 2 and 4, which also have a ratio of 1:3. Encourage students to think about why tables that describe different contexts can look the same.

Distribute copies of Polygons and Stars (R41).

ELL English Language Learners

Provide a Word List Write the words *row* and *column* on the board. Review their meanings with students. As pairs work together on the table, encourage them to use *row* and *column* in their explanations.

Additional Resource

Student Math Handbook pages 94–95

Extension

20 MIN GROUPS

Floor Plans and Tables

Use anytime after Session 1.5.

Math Focus Points

- Describing how the two numbers in the row of a table are connected to the situation the table represents
- Describing what is the same about situations that look different but can be represented by the same table

Materials: *Student Activity Book* p. 29, connecting cubes (60 per group), pattern blocks, M8 (1 per group), R42

Name Date

How Many Floors? How Many Rooms?

Floor Plans and Tables

Draw a floor plan for a cube building with 9 rooms on a floor. Then fill in the table with the missing information.

Review students' work.

Total Number of Floors	Total Number of Rooms
1	9
2	18
3	27
4	36
5	45
10	90
20	180

As the total number of floors increases, what happens to the total number of rooms? What pattern do you notice in the table?
Explanations will vary. Review students' work.

Copyright © by Pearson Education, Inc., or its affiliates. All rights reserved. 2

R42 Unit 5 Use anytime after Session 1.5.

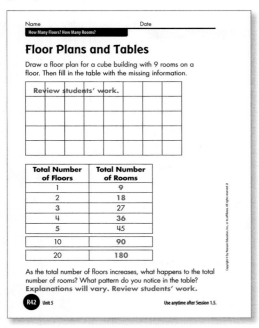

Discuss the pattern block situation and table on *Student Activity Book* page 29. Challenge groups to think about a cube building that can be represented by the same table. Have them record several possible floor plans for that building on Creating a Building (M8). How many rooms do you need to have on 1 floor? Why do you think so? Ask volunteers to share their floor plans.

Imagine stacking several floors to make a building. Let's make the table for that. Write the following table on the board.

Total Number of Floors	Total Number of Rooms
1	6
8	
	60

How can you find the total number of rooms on 8 floors?

Students might say:

"I can build 8 floors using cubes and then count the cubes."

"I would add four 6s and then four more 6s. This makes 24 and 24, which is 48 rooms."

How many floors are in a building with 60 rooms? Talk in your group about how you can figure that out. Some students may realize that 60 has two more 6s than 48, so 60 is 10 floors. Suppose this building were a skyscraper. How many rooms would be on the 20th floor? The 25th floor?

Distribute copies of Floor Plans and Tables (R42).

ELL English Language Learners

Provide Sentence Stems Students may benefit from completing sentences to describe the information shown in rows of the table. For example: 1 floor has 6 rooms. 8 floors have a total of ________ *(48)* rooms. ________ *(10)* floors have a total of 60 rooms.

Additional Resource

Student Math Handbook pages 97–98

Differentiation in Investigation 2

Mathematics in This Investigation

The mathematics focuses on understanding repeating patterns and number sequences—constructing, describing and extending number sequences with constant increments.

Understanding the Mathematics

Students extend repeating patterns with a variety of units (e.g., AB, AAB, ABCD) and use the quantity and structure of the unit to determine the element of the pattern at different numbered positions (e.g., the color of the 10th or 16th cube, or the number of the next red cube). They use the structure of the repeating pattern to determine how the pattern continues.

Option: Assign the **Extension** activity.

Partially Understanding the Mathematics

Students extend an AB pattern and determine the element of the pattern at different positions. They may not yet be using the structure of the pattern (e.g., the unit) to determine how it continues. Rather, they need to add on to the pattern one element at a time. They may recognize the unit of a 3- or 4-element pattern, but they may not necessarily see a pattern as a series of repeated units and be able to use that information to determine a specified element of a number sequence.

Option: Assign the **Practice** activity.

Not Understanding the Mathematics

Students recognize the unit of a repeating pattern and construct repeating patterns by adding on one element at a time but cannot extend an AB or ABC pattern to determine what is in a numbered position (e.g., the 10th or 16th). They do not see that repeating patterns are made up of repetitions of a single unit.

Option: Assign the **Intervention** activity.

Investigation 2 Quiz

In addition to your observations and students' work in Investigation 2, the Quiz (R43) can be used to gather more information.

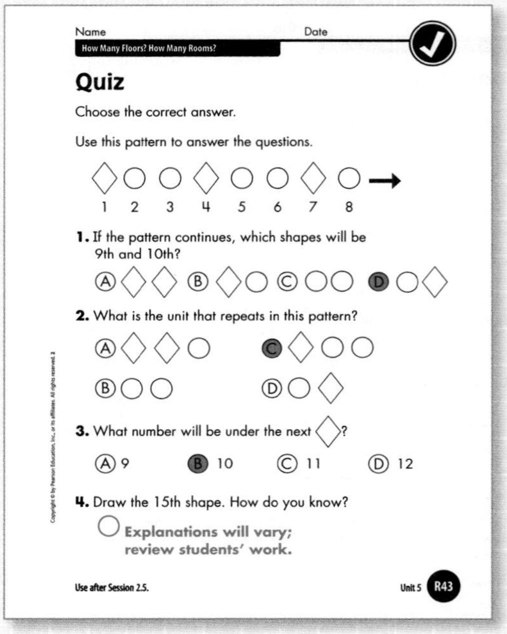

Name Date

How Many Floors? How Many Rooms?

Quiz

Choose the correct answer.

Use this pattern to answer the questions.

◇ ○ ○ ◇ ○ ○ ◇ ○ →
1 2 3 4 5 6 7 8

1. If the pattern continues, which shapes will be 9th and 10th?

Ⓐ ◇◇ Ⓑ ◇○ Ⓒ ○○ Ⓓ ○◇

2. What is the unit that repeats in this pattern?

Ⓐ ◇◇○ Ⓒ ◇○○
Ⓑ ○○ Ⓓ ○◇

3. What number will be under the next ◇?

Ⓐ 9 Ⓑ 10 Ⓒ 11 Ⓓ 12

4. Draw the 15th shape. How do you know?

○ **Explanations will vary; review students' work.**

Use after Session 2.5. Unit 5 R43

Intervention

20 MIN INDIVIDUALS

Orange-Yellow-Red Cube Train

Use anytime after Session 2.3.

Math Focus Points

- Determining and describing the number sequence associated with one of the elements in an ABC repeating pattern (3, 6, 9, . . . ; 1, 4, 7, . . . ; 2, 5, 8, . . .)
- Determining the element of a repeating pattern associated with a particular counting number in ABC and AABBC patterns

Vocabulary: repeating pattern, unit

Materials: connecting cubes, colored pencils, M29 (from Unit 2)

Students who are not easily generating number sequences that go with a particular color may benefit from working on more ABC patterns. Today we will work with more repeating patterns. Let's start with a tapping pattern. I'll start the pattern, and you can join in. Demonstrate this pattern: tap head–tap shoulder–tap knee, tap head–tap shoulder–tap knee, and so on. Record H, S, K, H, S, K on the board and explain to students that the letters each stand for a body part. What is the *unit* of this pattern? What is the part of the pattern that repeats?

Let's do this pattern again and count as we tap. As you count, emphasize each multiple of 3, corresponding to tapping a knee. Repeat the pattern again but this time record the numbers below each letter, as students count. What numbers did we say as we tapped our knees?

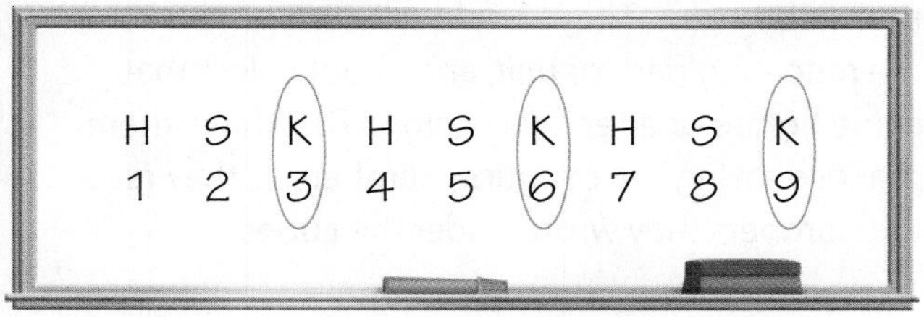

We can also use cubes to show this kind of pattern. Draw 3 squares on the board and label Orange, Yellow, and Red. Use your connecting cubes to make a cube train with 12 cubes, using the pattern unit shown on the board.

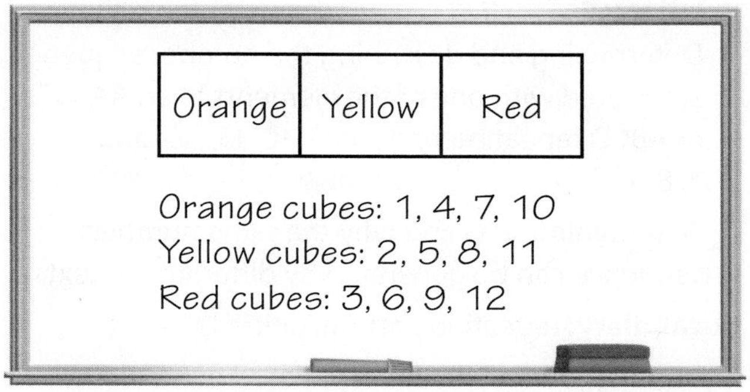

Ask students to draw the cube train pattern on Centimeter Grid Paper (M29). Remind them to start with an orange cube. Have them number the cubes 1 through 12. What numbers go with the orange cubes? What numbers go with the yellow cubes? What numbers go with the red cubes? As students respond, record the numerical patterns on the board.

Ask about cubes beyond the 12th cube. What color will the 13th cube be? What color will the 19th cube be? How do you know? Have students extend their cube trains and their recorded pattern to double-check.

Add onto the number patterns for each cube. Focus specifically on the number pattern for the red cubes. Point out to students that in each pattern they are counting by groups of 3.

ELL English Language Learners

Rephrase The word *unit* may be confusing to some students because it may imply a single cube. You might want to ask about the *smallest part* of the pattern, or the *chunk*, that repeats.

Additional Resource

Student Math Handbook pages 101–102

Practice

25 MIN INDIVIDUALS

Working with 5-Element Patterns

Use anytime after Session 2.4.

Math Focus Points

- Determining and describing the number sequence associated with one of the elements in an AABBC or ABCD repeating pattern (5, 10, 15, . . . , and 4, 8, 12, . . .)
- Determining how and why the same number sequence can be generated by different contexts

Vocabulary: repeating pattern, unit

Materials: connecting cubes, colored pencils, M29 (from Unit 2), R44

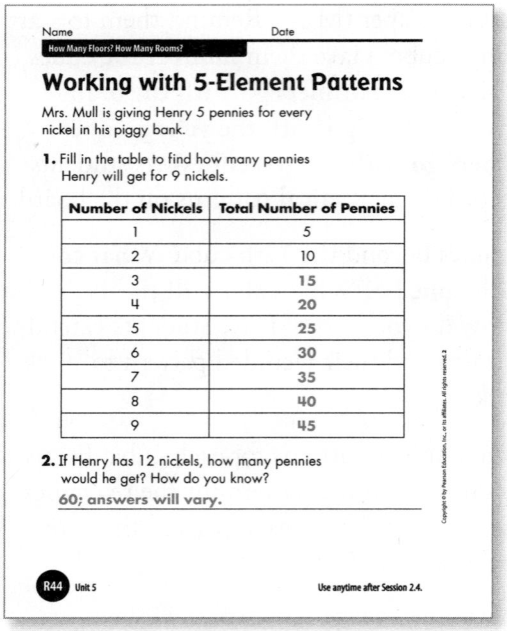
Name Date

How Many Floors? How Many Rooms?

Working with 5-Element Patterns

Mrs. Mull is giving Henry 5 pennies for every nickel in his piggy bank.

1. Fill in the table to find how many pennies Henry will get for 9 nickels.

Number of Nickels	Total Number of Pennies
1	5
2	10
3	15
4	20
5	25
6	30
7	35
8	40
9	45

2. If Henry has 12 nickels, how many pennies would he get? How do you know?
60; answers will vary.

R44 Unit 5 Use anytime after Session 2.4.

Show students a white-white-red-red-blue cube train. Use your connecting cubes to make a cube train with 20 cubes. It should show a repeating pattern using this unit. Ask students to draw their cube train on Centimeter Grid Paper (M29). Have them number the cubes 1 through 20. Ask students to write the number sequence shown by the blue cubes. What are the numbers for the blue cubes? Have a volunteer write the sequence 5, 10, 15, 20, on the board.

How would you describe these numbers? Do you remember seeing them in some of the tables when we built cube buildings?

Students might say:

"Those are numbers you get when you count by 5s."

"We got those numbers when we made buildings with 5 rooms on a floor."

Imagine that you keep making the train longer and longer. What number would the next blue cube be? How about the one after that? How did you figure it out?

Students might say:

"All the blue numbers are 5 apart. So the next blue cube would be 25, and the one after that would be 30."

Some students may need to extend the cube train or continue their drawing on paper to verify these answers. If our cube train was made of 50 cubes, how many blue cubes would there be?

Distribute copies of Working with 5-Element Patterns (R44).

ELL English Language Learners

Partner Talk Have students work in pairs to discuss their cube trains. They should tell each other about the repeating part, or *unit*, and about colors that come before or after other colors. Then have them practice saying the counting numbers as they read the numbers they wrote under the cubes.

Additional Resource

Student Math Handbook page 103

Extension

20 MIN PAIRS

More Cube Trains

Use anytime after Session 2.4.

Math Focus Points

- Determining and describing the number sequence associated with one of the elements in an AABBC or ABCD repeating pattern (5, 10, 15, . . . , and 4, 8, 12, . . .)
- Determining the element of a repeating pattern associated with a particular counting number in AABBC or ABCD patterns

Vocabulary: repeating pattern, unit

Materials: connecting cubes, R45

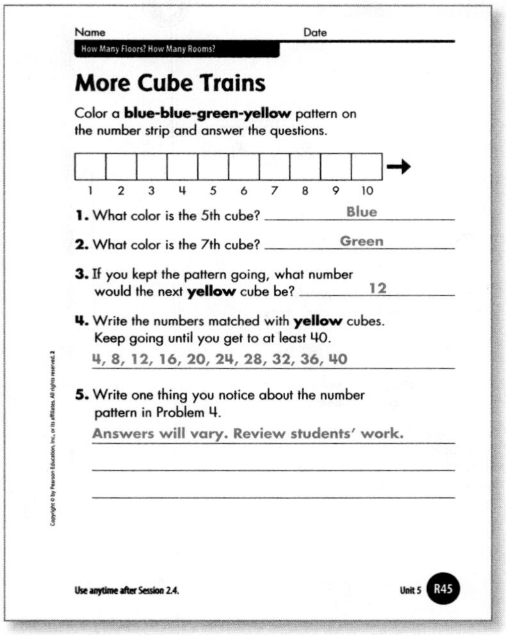

Name Date

How Many Floors? How Many Rooms?

More Cube Trains

Color a **blue-blue-green-yellow** pattern on the number strip and answer the questions.

1 2 3 4 5 6 7 8 9 10

1. What color is the 5th cube? Blue
2. What color is the 7th cube? Green
3. If you kept the pattern going, what number would the next **yellow** cube be? 12
4. Write the numbers matched with **yellow** cubes. Keep going until you get to at least 40.
   4, 8, 12, 16, 20, 24, 28, 32, 36, 40
5. Write one thing you notice about the number pattern in Problem 4.
   Answers will vary. Review students' work.

Use anytime after Session 2.4. Unit 5 R45

Demonstrate this repeating pattern: tap–clap–tap–snap, tap–clap–tap–snap, and so on. Listen to the sound pattern and identify the unit.

Show 4 squares on the board with color names.

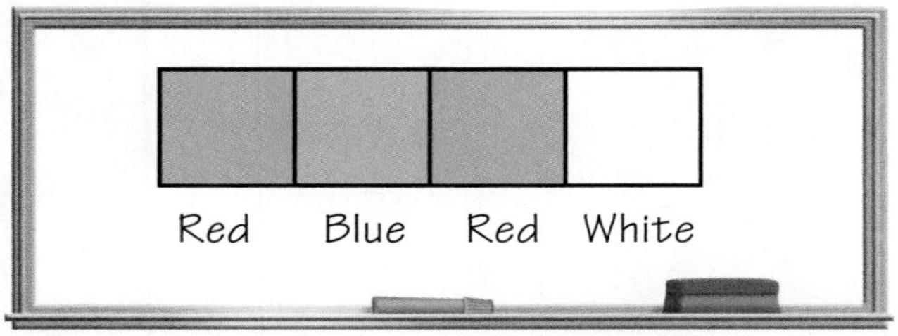

How is the color pattern like the sound pattern? Students should see that both are 4-element patterns with the first and third parts alike.

Use your connecting cubes to make a cube train with 20 cubes, using the pattern unit shown on the board. Have students draw their cube train and number the cubes 1 through 20. Ask students to identify the color for several numbers between 21 and 30. What color will the 23rd cube be? How do you know?

Students might say:

"The last cube is 20 and it's white. The pattern starts over after white. So the next cube is red; that's 21. Then it's blue; that's 22. And then it's red; that's 23."

Next, have students work in pairs and write the number sequence shown by each of the following:

- red cube that comes before blue
- blue cube
- red cube that comes after blue
- white cube

Challenge pairs to extend each sequence to at least 40. Have students share their answers and explain their thinking.

Distribute copies of More Cube Trains (R45).

ELL English Language Learners

Provide a Word List Write the words *before* and *after* on the board. Review the meanings of each. Have students draw a picture to help them remember each word.

Additional Resource

Student Math Handbook page 103

Differentiation in Investigation 1

Mathematics in This Investigation

The mathematics focuses on understanding place value and developing strategies for solving addition problems with totals to 100.

Additional Resource: *How Many Tens and Ones? Finding Out What a Student Knows*, pages 91–92 (See *Implementing Investigations in Grade 2*)

Understanding the Mathematics

Students accurately and efficiently solve 2-digit addition problems. They record equations to represent the problem and use a variety of strategies in their work, including adding by place and keeping one number whole and adding the second number in chunks.

Option: Assign the **Extension** activity.

Partially Understanding the Mathematics

Students understand what is being asked in an addition story problem but may not always represent the problem with an equation. They have at least one strategy for solving 2-digit addition but may make minor computational errors.

Option: Assign the **Practice** activity.

Not Understanding the Mathematics

Students solve addition problems by counting all or counting on by 1s or in small chunks. They may have difficulty visualizing what is happening in a story problem. They lose track of the values in 2-digit numbers.

Option: Assign the **Intervention** activity.

Investigation 1 Quiz

In addition to your observations and students' work in Investigation 1, the Quiz (R46) can be used to gather more information.

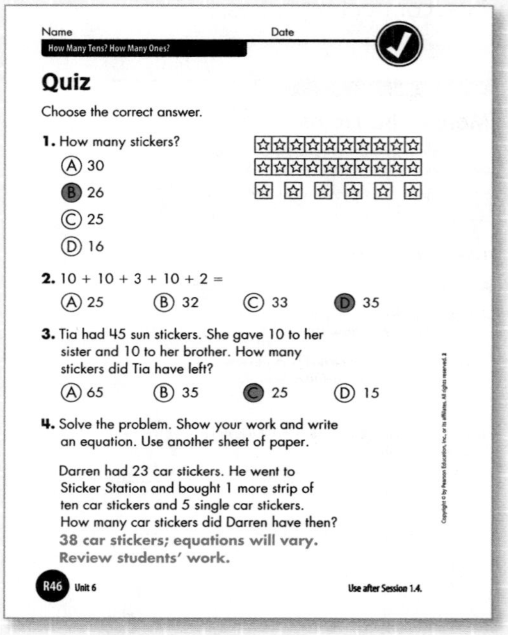

Name Date

How Many Tens? How Many Ones?

Quiz

Choose the correct answer.

1. How many stickers?
   - (A) 30
   - (B) 26
   - (C) 25
   - (D) 16
2. 10 + 10 + 3 + 10 + 2 =
   (A) 25 (B) 32 (C) 33 (D) 35
3. Tia had 45 sun stickers. She gave 10 to her sister and 10 to her brother. How many stickers did Tia have left?
   (A) 65 (B) 35 (C) 25 (D) 15
4. Solve the problem. Show your work and write an equation. Use another sheet of paper.

   Darren had 23 car stickers. He went to Sticker Station and bought 1 more strip of ten car stickers and 5 single car stickers. How many car stickers did Darren have then?
   38 car stickers; equations will vary. Review students' work.

R46 Unit 6 Use after Session 1.4.

Intervention

30 MIN INDIVIDUALS

Combining Stickers

Use anytime after Session 1.1.

Math Focus Points

- Adding tens and ones to combine 2-digit numbers

Vocabulary: tens, ones

Materials: connecting cubes organized into single-color towers of 10 (60 per student), R47

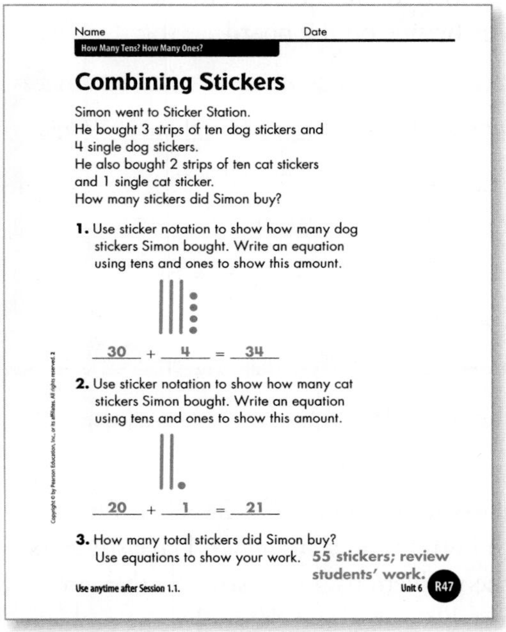
Name Date

How Many Tens? How Many Ones?

Combining Stickers

Simon went to Sticker Station.
He bought 3 strips of ten dog stickers and 4 single dog stickers.
He also bought 2 strips of ten cat stickers and 1 single cat sticker.
How many stickers did Simon buy?

1. Use sticker notation to show how many dog stickers Simon bought. Write an equation using tens and ones to show this amount.

30 + 4 = 34

2. Use sticker notation to show how many cat stickers Simon bought. Write an equation using tens and ones to show this amount.

20 + 1 = 21

3. How many total stickers did Simon buy? Use equations to show your work. 55 stickers; review students' work.

Use anytime after Session 1.1. Unit 6 R47

Write the following problem on the board.

> Roshaun went to Sticker Station. He bought 2 strips of ten dog stickers and 3 single dog stickers. He also bought 1 strip of ten cat stickers and 2 single cat stickers. How many stickers did Roshaun buy?

Distribute connecting cubes to students. How many dog stickers did Roshaun buy? Show this amount using cubes. Record this on the board using sticker notation. The 2 strips of ten is how many stickers? Right, 20 stickers. And the singles, or ones? Record 20 + 3 under the sticker notation. How many dog stickers does he have in all? Record 23 above the sticker notation. Repeat these steps for the cat stickers.

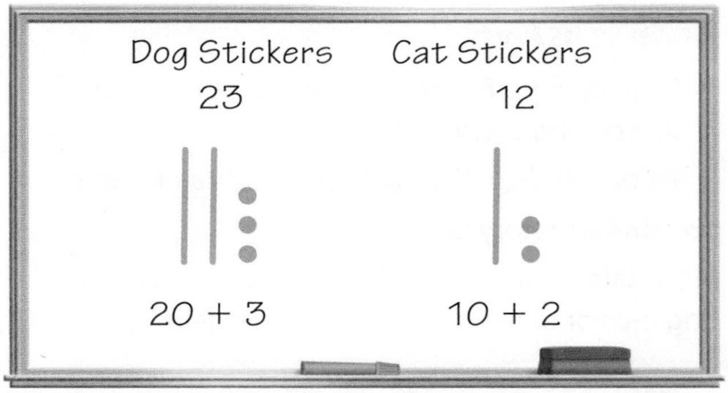

What are we trying to find out? What two numbers will we be adding? Record 23 + 12 = ___ at the top of the board. Let's add the strips of ten. Have students do this with their cubes. What equation would I write? How many total stickers is that? Record 20 + 10 = 30. Now, group the singles. What equation shows this? How many in all? Record 3 + 2 = 5 under 20 + 10 = 30. If we add the total number of tens and the total number of singles, how many cubes would Roshaun have in all? Record 30 + 5 = 35. Reread the problem and connect each part of the problem to the notation and equations you have written on the board. Finally complete the equation that you wrote at the top of the board.

Distribute Combining Stickers (R47). Encourage them to use cubes to represent the problems.

ELL English Language Learners

Rephrase Some students may have difficulty with detailed story problems. Break the problem into smaller pieces. First, focus on the dog stickers, and then focus on the cat stickers. Have students combine the two groups of stickers to find the total amount.

Additional Resource

Student Math Handbook page 62

Practice

25 MIN INDIVIDUALS

Using Strategies to Solve Problems

Use anytime after Session 1.3.

Math Focus Points

- Developing efficient methods for adding and subtracting 2-digit numbers
- Writing an equation that represents a problem

Vocabulary: story problem

Materials: connecting cubes organized into single-color towers of 10, blank paper, R48

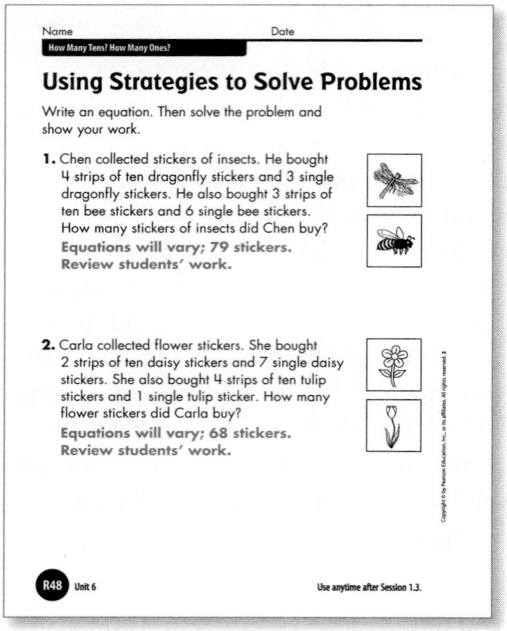

Name Date

How Many Tens? How Many Ones?

Using Strategies to Solve Problems

Write an equation. Then solve the problem and show your work.

1. Chen collected stickers of insects. He bought 4 strips of ten dragonfly stickers and 3 single dragonfly stickers. He also bought 3 strips of ten bee stickers and 6 single bee stickers. How many stickers of insects did Chen buy?
Equations will vary; 79 stickers. Review students' work.

2. Carla collected flower stickers. She bought 2 strips of ten daisy stickers and 7 single daisy stickers. She also bought 4 strips of ten tulip stickers and 1 single tulip sticker. How many flower stickers did Carla buy?
Equations will vary; 68 stickers. Review students' work.

Copyright © by Pearson Education, Inc., or its affiliates. All rights reserved. 2

R48 Unit 6 Use anytime after Session 1.3.

Read the following story problem aloud: Carolina collected stickers of fruits. She bought 3 strips of ten apple stickers and 3 single apple stickers. She also bought 2 strips of ten banana stickers and 6 single banana stickers. How many fruit stickers did Carolina buy?

Discuss and record the information given in the problem. How many apple stickers did Carolina buy? How many banana stickers? Will Carolina have more than 33 stickers or fewer? What action is taking place? Should we add or subtract?

Ask students to help you write an equation. What equation can we write to show the problem? What does the 33 stand for? What does the 26 stand for? Distribute blank paper and have students record the equations, then solve the problem. As students are working, note the strategy that each student is using. Have one student use cubes to model adding by 10s and 1s. Have another student use cubes to add by keeping one addend whole and breaking apart the other number. Write equations to show these strategies side by side on the board.

Add Tens and Ones	Keep One Number Whole
$33 + 26 = \_\_\_\_$	$33 + 26 = \_\_\_\_$
$30 + 20 = 50$	$33 + 20 = 53$
$3 + 6 = 9$	$53 + 6 = 59$
$50 + 9 = 59$	

Compare the strategies. Why are the sums the same?

Present a new sticker problem for 24 + 31. Discuss solving with both number strategies. Have students first solve the problem using the strategy they are most comfortable using, and then solve the problem using the other strategy. Then, distribute copies of Using Strategies to Solve Problems (R48).

ELL English Language Learners

Provide a Word List Make a list of words and phrases used to describe strategies. Include *adding 10s and 1s* and *keeping one number whole.* Add to the list as new strategies are introduced. Read the list with students and have them model or explain each one using 2-digit numbers.

Additional Resource

Student Math Handbook pages 63–66

Extension

20 MIN INDIVIDUALS

Reordering Addends

Use anytime after Session 1.3.

Math Focus Points

- Developing efficient methods for adding and subtracting 2-digit numbers

Materials: connecting cubes

In this activity, students will explore the commutative property of addition and its role in addition strategies. On the board, write 32 + 14 = ______. Suppose we wanted to add these two numbers by breaking them apart into 10s and 1s and then combining the 10s and the 1s from both numbers. What equations would we write?

Record one set of equations and then write 14 + 32 = ______. Students may recognize that this is the same combination but with the addends in a different order. Ask for another volunteer to add this combination by 10s and 1s. Write the equations that match.

32 + 14 = ____	14 + 32 = ____
30 + 10 = 40	10 + 30 = 40
2 + 4 = 6	4 + 2 = 6
40 + 6 = 46	40 + 6 = 46

Compare the equations for the two combinations. What do you notice about these two combinations and the two sets of equations? How are they alike? How are they different?

Students might say:

"Each way uses the same numbers, but they are in a different order."

"The answers in each step are the same for both combinations."

So the sum of 32 + 14 is the same as the sum of 14 + 32. The order of the addends doesn't matter for this pair of numbers. Do you think this is true for this combination only or for all combinations of 2-digit numbers? Discuss students' ideas.

Explain to students that their next task is to test their ideas. If you think the order of the addends *doesn't* matter for *any* addition combination, show why you think so. If you think the order *does* matter for *some* combinations, show why you think so. Either way, find examples of numbers to support your idea.

Provide connecting cubes as needed and have students record their work. Remind them that someone else should be able to look at their papers and follow their strategies.

When students have finished, gather them together to share their work. How did you test your idea? Were you able to prove that your idea was true? What examples did you find?

ELL English Language Learners

Partner Talk Have students work in pairs to discuss their ideas. Students with limited language may only be able to respond with short phrases like "different order" and "same number." More proficient speakers should be encouraged to use the following words: *order, addends, combination, equation, test,* and *prove.*

Additional Resource

Student Math Handbook pages 63–66

Differentiation in Investigation 2

Mathematics in This Investigation

The mathematics focuses on developing an understanding of place value with specific emphasis on the structure of 100 and using this understanding to determine the difference between any 2-digit number and 100.

Additional Resource: *Moving to Bigger Numbers*, pages 81–82 (See *Implementing Investigations in Grade 2*)

Understanding the Mathematics

Students are familiar with numbers to 100 and beyond. They can articulate the value of each place in a 2-digit number and easily locate numbers on a mostly blank 100 chart. Students accurately and efficiently determine the difference between a number and any multiple of 10 up to 100 or beyond. They solve problems by adding on 10s or a multiple of 10 first and then ones to find the total or may jump to the closest multiple of 10 and then continue adding 10s or a multiple of 10.

Option: Assign the **Extension** activity.

Partially Understanding the Mathematics

Students are familiar with numbers to 100 and easily locate numbers on the 100 chart. They are able to compose and decompose numbers into tens and ones. They solve 2-digit addition problems with totals to 100 but may make minor errors in their computation. They may use a strategy of counting on by ones when solving missing-part problems or use tools such as tallies, a 100 chart, or their fingers to help them solve the problem.

Option: Assign the **Practice** activity.

Not Understanding the Mathematics

Students are thinking and working primarily in ones and have not shifted to thinking about 2-digit numbers in terms of groups of tens and ones. They have difficulty placing or finding numbers on the 100 chart. They cannot readily articulate the value of each place in a 2-digit number.

Option: Assign the **Intervention** activity.

Investigation 2 Quiz

In addition to your observations and students' work in Investigation 2, the Quiz (R49) can be used to gather more information.

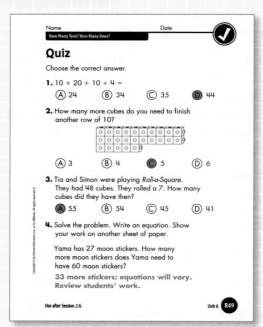

Name Date

How Many Tens? How Many Ones?

Quiz

Choose the correct answer.

1. 10 + 20 + 10 + 4 =

Ⓐ 24 Ⓑ 34 Ⓒ 35 Ⓓ 44

2. How many more cubes do you need to finish another row of 10?

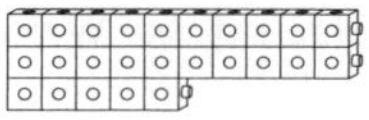

Ⓐ 3 Ⓑ 4 Ⓒ 5 Ⓓ 6

3. Tia and Simon were playing *Roll-a-Square*. They had 48 cubes. They rolled a 7. How many cubes did they have then?

Ⓐ 55 Ⓑ 54 Ⓒ 45 Ⓓ 41

4. Solve the problem. Write an equation. Show your work on another sheet of paper.

Yama has 27 moon stickers. How many more moon stickers does Yama need to have 60 moon stickers?

33 more stickers; equations will vary. Review students' work.

Copyright © by Pearson Education, Inc., or its affiliates. All rights reserved. 2

Use after Session 2.6. Unit 6 R49

Intervention

30 MIN INDIVIDUALS

Solving Sticker Book Problems

Use anytime after Session 2.4.

Math Focus Points

- Using a place-value model to represent a number as 10s and 1s
- Determining the difference between a number and a multiple of 10 up to 100

Materials: connecting cubes organized into single-color towers of 10 (50 per pair), 100 charts (as needed), T58, M14–M15

In this activity, students will use cubes to model sticker problems. Display Pages in a Sticker Book (T58) on an overhead projector. Cover all but the first grid. Review the story from Sticker Books (M14). Why did Kira buy a sticker book? How many rows of stickers are there on each page? How many stickers fit in each row?

Read the following problem aloud. Rochelle also bought a sticker book for her stickers. On the first page, she put 27 star stickers. How can we show 27 with cubes? Ask a volunteer to build the cube model. Relate the model to the stickers in the story. How many towers of 10 and single cubes make 27? How many strips of 10 stickers and single stickers make 27?

Have another student shade the grid on the overhead projector to show Rochelle's stickers. Label this area 27. [Leo], how did you know what to shade?

Read the next problem aloud. Rochelle's goal is to have 40 star stickers. How can we find the number of stickers she still needs?

Students might say:

"Use a 100 chart. Count all the boxes after 27 until you get to 40."

Have students use cubes, a grid, or a 100 chart to demonstrate their strategies. Once students agree that Rochelle would need 13 additional stickers, ask a volunteer to add 13 cubes to the group of 27. Ask another student to shade and label 13 additional squares on the overhead transparency grid.

Distribute Pages in a Sticker Book (M15) and connecting cubes to each student. Write the following problem on the board.

> Rochelle put 31 sun stickers on another page of her book. She wants to have 50 sun stickers. How many more does she need to have 50 sun stickers?

Each student should model the problem with cubes, shade and label a grid, then solve the problem. Discuss students' strategies as a group and then give students two more problems similar to the previous ones to solve.

ELL English Language Learners

Partner Talk Students may benefit from more practice explaining their strategies. Pair ELLs of different language proficiencies to give them practice with English. Give each student a number between 11 and 30. Have partners explain to each other how to show that many stickers on a grid. Ask them to use the following words and phrases in their explanations: *tens, ones, strips of ten stickers,* and *single stickers.*

Additional Resource

Student Math Handbook pages 78–80

Practice

25 MIN INDIVIDUALS

Problems on a Grid

Use anytime after Session 2.5.

Math Focus Points

- Determining the difference between a number and a multiple of 10 up to 100
- Writing an equation that represents a problem

Materials: 100 charts, connecting cubes organized into single-color towers of 10, T58, M15, R50

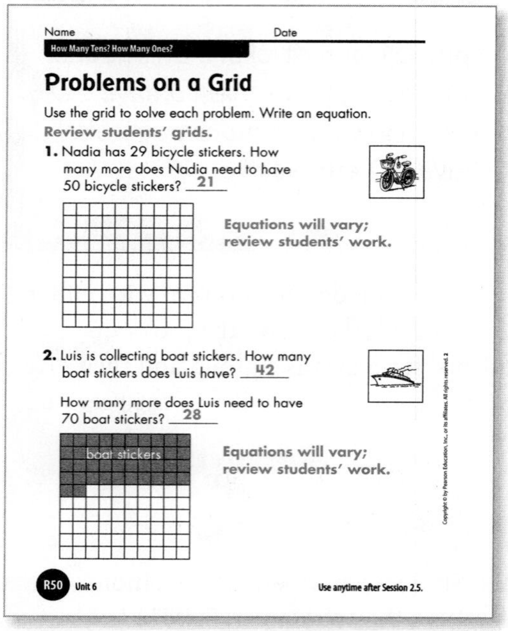

Name Date

How Many Tens? How Many Ones?

Problems on a Grid

Use the grid to solve each problem. Write an equation.

Review students' grids.

1. Nadia has 29 bicycle stickers. How many more does Nadia need to have 50 bicycle stickers? 21

Equations will vary; review students' work.

2. Luis is collecting boat stickers. How many boat stickers does Luis have? 42

How many more does Luis need to have 70 boat stickers? 28

boat stickers

Equations will vary; review students' work.

Copyright © by Pearson Education, Inc., or its affiliates. All rights reserved. 2

R50 Unit 6 Use anytime after Session 2.5.

Display Pages in a Sticker Book (T58, M15) and distribute copies to students. Henry has 34 baseball stickers. He wants to put them on 1 page of his sticker book. Have students shade and label the first grid on their papers to show 34 stickers. Ask a student to shade the grid on the overhead.

Henry wants to have 60 baseball stickers. How many more stickers does Henry need to make 60? Write 34 + ______ = 60 on the board. Students should write the equation under the grid. 34 plus *what* equals 60? How could we find out?

Students might say:

"We could use the grid to count up from 34 to 60. That's 6 to get to 40 and 2 more tens to get to 60: 6 + 20 = 26."

Have students solve the problem, shading the number of cubes on the grid and completing the equation. As students share strategies, record the equations that match their strategies.

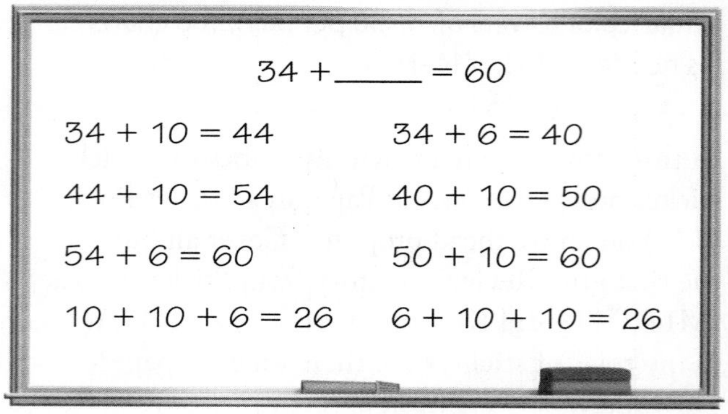

Discuss ways of recording the work. Then present several more similar problems for students to solve on their own. Keep totals under 100.

Distribute copies of Problems on a Grid (R50).

ELL English Language Learners

Model Thinking Aloud Some students may benefit from seeing you work through the problem as you model your thinking aloud. Henry has 34 stickers. First, I shaded 34 on the grid. Then, I counted 6 more to get to 40. Write 34 + 6 = 40. I added a ten to get to 50. Write 40 + 10 = 50. I needed 1 more ten to get to 60. Write 50 + 10 = 60. Since 6 + 10 + 10 = 26, I added 26 to 34 to get 60.

Additional Resource

Student Math Handbook

Game: *Roll-a-Square* SMH G12

Materials: number cubes, connecting cubes, M11– M12

Extension

20 MIN GROUPS

More Than 100 Stickers

Use anytime after Session 2.4.

Math Focus Points

- Using a place-value model to represent a number as 10s and 1s
- Determining the difference between a number and a multiple of 10 up to 100

Materials: connecting cubes (as needed), 100 charts (as needed), T57, M14–M15, R51

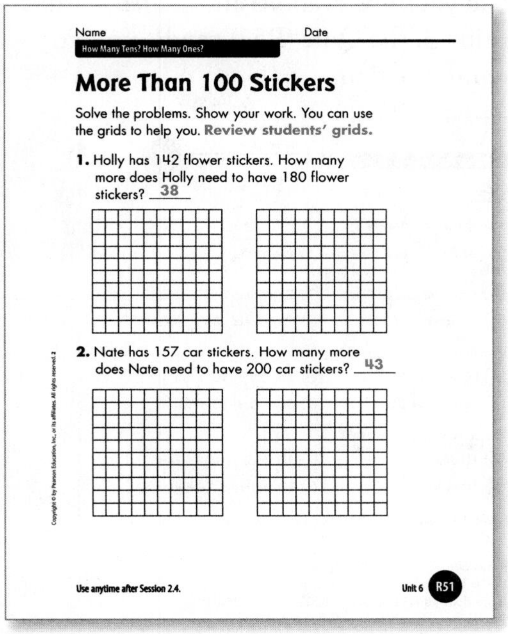
Name Date

How Many Tens? How Many Ones?

More Than 100 Stickers

Solve the problems. Show your work. You can use the grids to help you. **Review students' grids.**

1. Holly has 142 flower stickers. How many more does Holly need to have 180 flower stickers? 38

2. Nate has 157 car stickers. How many more does Nate need to have 200 car stickers? 43

Use anytime after Session 2.4. Unit 6 R51

This activity introduces sticker problems for numbers above 100. Display Sticker Books (M14 or T57). Briefly review the sticker book concept. Each book has 10 pages. Each page holds 10 rows of 10 stickers either in strips of 10 or as single stickers.

Read the following problem to students. Travis has 115 car stickers. Could he put these in his sticker book? If so, how would it look?

Students might say:

"One page holds only 10 rows of 10 stickers. That's 100. You need more rows to show 115."

"You could use 2 pages. You can show 115 on 2 grids."

Ask a volunteer to shade the grids on M14 to show Travis's car stickers. Then continue the problem: Travis wants to have 150 car stickers. How many more car stickers does he need to have 150?

Ask students to solve the problem using the top 2 grids on Pages in a Sticker Book (M15). Provide connecting cubes and 100 charts, as needed. They should shade in the answer on the grid, label each amount on the grid, and write an equation. When they are finished, have them share their strategies. Write the equations that match their strategies on the board.

Present another 3-digit problem. Have students use the lower 2 grids on their papers to solve it.

Distribute copies of More Than 100 Stickers (R51).

ELL English Language Learners

Suggest a Sequence If students need support explaining their strategies, provide them with a sequence of steps such as the following.

1. Shade the grids.
2. Use connecting cubes or a 100 chart to solve the problem.
3. Write equations for your steps.

Additional Resource

Student Math Handbook

Game: *Guess My Number on the 100 Chart* SMH G8

Materials: 200 charts

Variation: Use the 200 chart for the gameboard.

Differentiation in Investigation 3

Mathematics in This Investigation

The mathematics continues to focus on place value and on developing strategies for solving addition and subtraction problems with totals to 100.

Additional Resource: *What to Do With the Seven,* pages 97–99 (See *Implementing Investigations in Grade 2*)

Understanding the Mathematics

Students accurately and efficiently solve 2-digit addition and subtraction problems by using various strategies. They may add on or count back by 10s or a multiple of 10 first and then ones to find the answer, or they may jump forward or back to the closest multiple of 10 and then continue adding or subtracting 10s or multiples of 10.

Option: Assign the **Extension** activity.

Partially Understanding the Mathematics

Students solve 2-digit addition and subtraction problems with totals up to 100 but may make minor errors in their computation. They may use a strategy of counting on or back by ones when solving subtraction problems or use tools such as tallies, a 100 chart, or their fingers to help them solve the problem.

Option: Assign the **Practice** activity.

Not Understanding the Mathematics

Students are thinking and working primarily in ones and are not yet fluent with the equivalence of ten 1s equaling one 10. They solve addition problems by counting all or counting on by ones. They may solve subtraction problems by counting all and removing some.

Option: Assign the **Intervention** activity.

Investigation 3 Quiz

In addition to your observations and students' work in Investigation 3, the Quiz (R52) can be used to gather more information.

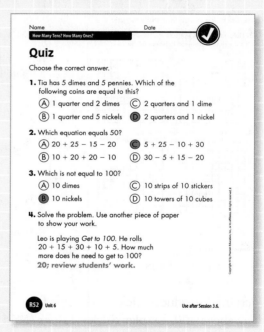

Name Date

How Many Tens? How Many Ones?

Quiz

Choose the correct answer.

1. Tia has 5 dimes and 5 pennies. Which of the following coins are equal to this?

Ⓐ 1 quarter and 2 dimes
Ⓒ 2 quarters and 1 dime
Ⓑ 1 quarter and 5 nickels
Ⓓ 2 quarters and 1 nickel

2. Which equation equals 50?

Ⓐ 20 + 25 − 15 − 20
Ⓒ 5 + 25 − 10 + 30
Ⓑ 10 + 20 + 20 − 10
Ⓓ 30 − 5 + 15 − 20

3. Which is not equal to 100?

Ⓐ 10 dimes
Ⓒ 10 strips of 10 stickers
Ⓑ 10 nickels
Ⓓ 10 towers of 10 cubes

4. Solve the problem. Use another piece of paper to show your work.

Leo is playing *Get to 100.* He rolls 20 + 15 + 30 + 10 + 5. How much more does he need to get to 100?

20; review students' work.

Copyright © by Pearson Education, Inc., or its affiliates. All rights reserved. 2

R52 Unit 6 Use after Session 3.6.

Intervention

30 MIN INDIVIDUALS

Adding and Subtracting on a 100 Chart

Use anytime after Session 3.3.

Math Focus Points

- Adding and subtracting 10 and multiples of 10 to/from any number

Materials: pocket 100 chart, pocket 100 chart numbers, M5

Place the following numbers in a pocket 100 chart: 4, 16, 23, 38, 41, 55, 67, 72, 90, and 99. Our first task today is to complete the 100 chart. I'll show a number, and you raise your hand if you know where it goes. Display number cards one at a time and have volunteers place them in their correct positions on the 100 chart. How did you decide where to put [52]?

Students might say:

"The number [55] is showing, so I counted backward to [52]."

When the 100 chart has been completed, write the following equation on the board: 38 + 10 + 10 = ______. Who can show how to solve this equation using the 100 chart? Have volunteers demonstrate their strategies and explain their thinking.

Distribute a 100 Chart (M5) to each student. Repeat the process for 46 + 10 + 10 + 10 = ______. Use your 100 chart to figure out the answer to this problem. Have students share their strategies. How do the numbers on the 100 chart change when you add 10? Repeat the process for the equation 69 + 10 + 20 = ______.

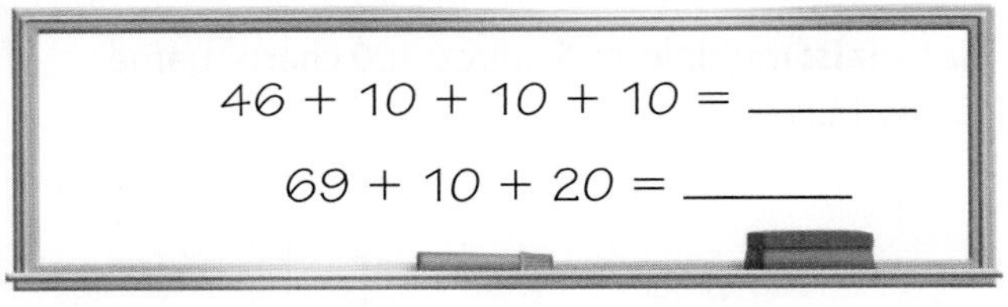

Next write the following subtraction problem on the board: 62 − 10 − 10 − 10 = ______. How can you use the 100 chart to solve this problem? How is subtracting on the 100 chart different from adding on the 100 chart? Ask students to look at the numbers 62, 52, 42, 32 and discuss what part of the number changes and what part stays the same.

Students might say:

"Start on 62 and move up one row to 52. Then move up another row to 42 and then up another row to 32."

Display 73 − 20 = ______ and 94 − 10 − 10 − 20 = ______ on the board. Have students solve them individually using their own 100 chart and then discuss each solution as a group.

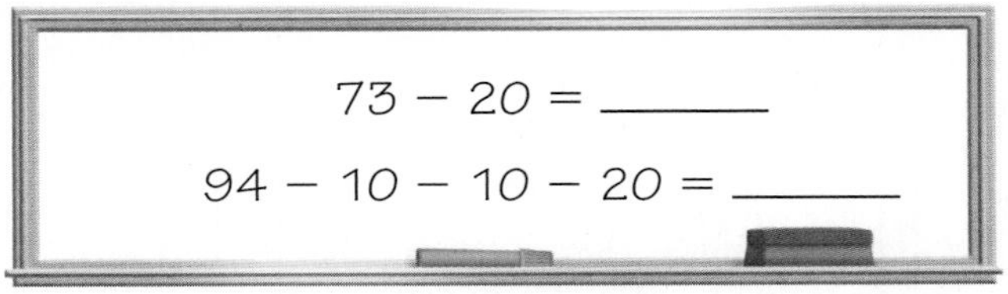

ELL English Language Learners

Provide Sentence Stems Provide sentence stems, such as the following, to support students who have difficulty explaining their thinking.

I started on ________.
I [added] ________.
I landed on ________.

Additional Resource

Student Math Handbook

Game: *Guess My Number on the 100 Chart* SMH G8

Materials: 100 chart

Variation: Students play on teams. Turns pass from team to team.

Practice

20 MIN PAIRS

Addition and Subtraction Equations

Use anytime after Session 3.3.

Math Focus Points

- Adding and subtracting 10 and multiples of 10 to/from any number

Materials: envelopes or resealable bags, 2 × 2 pieces of paper, R53, R89

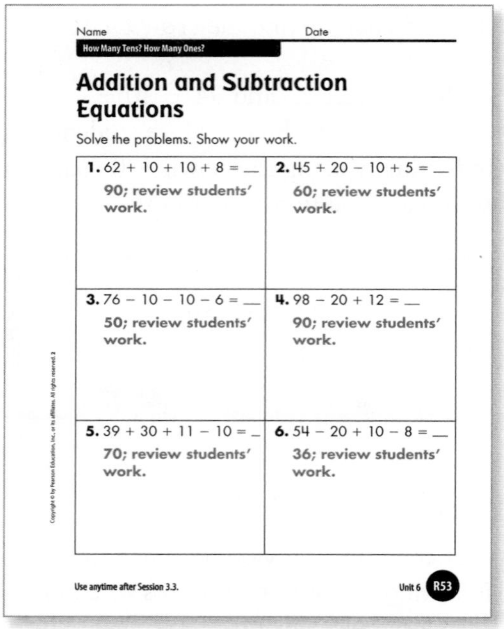

Name Date

How Many Tens? How Many Ones?

Addition and Subtraction Equations

Solve the problems. Show your work.

1. 62 + 10 + 10 + 8 = __ **90; review students' work.**	**2.** 45 + 20 − 10 + 5 = __ **60; review students' work.**
3. 76 − 10 − 10 − 6 = __ **50; review students' work.**	**4.** 98 − 20 + 12 = __ **90; review students' work.**
5. 39 + 30 + 11 − 10 = __ **70; review students' work.**	**6.** 54 − 20 + 10 − 8 = __ **36; review students' work.**

Use anytime after Session 3.3. Unit 6 R53

Materials to Prepare: Make a deck of Addition and Subtraction Equation Cards (R89) for each student. Place each deck in an envelope or resealable bag.

Distribute a deck of cards and several 2 × 2 pieces of paper to each student. Explain the following steps:

1. On 2 × 2 paper, Player 1 secretly writes a start number and Player 2 secretly writes a target number. Numbers should be between 10 and 99.
2. Players use number and symbol cards to make an equation that equals their target number, adding and subtracting numbers. Partners check each other's work, then record their equations.
3. Players switch roles, secretly record new start and target numbers, and then make a new equation.

Demonstrate how to play using 43 as your start number and 50 as the target number. Use cards to display 43 + 10 + 7 − 10 =.

This is my equation. How can we solve it to make sure it equals my target number?

Students might say:

"Count up 10 to 53. Add 7: 3 + 7 = 10, so that's 60. Then count back by 10. That's 50."

"It's like Today's Number. Plus 10 and minus 10 equals 0, so don't count them. Just add the 7: 43 + 7 = 50."

As students work on the activity, circulate to listen to explanations and check equations.

This game can be made easier by using only addition (or only subtraction) and selecting a start number that is between 10 and 49 and a target number that is between 50 and 99. A more difficult variation is to limit the number of number cards used for each equation (e.g., use only 5 number cards).

Distribute copies of Addition and Subtraction Equations (R53).

ELL English Language Learners

Model Thinking Aloud Model your thinking for finding the solution to the equation. For example: First, I added 43 and 10: 43 + 10 = 53. Then, I added on 7 more: 53 + 7 = 60. Finally, I subtracted 10: 60 − 10 = 50.

Additional Resource

Student Math Handbook

Game: *Get to 100* SMH G7

Materials: multiple-of-5 cubes, 100 charts, game pieces, M24

Extension

30 MIN PAIRS

Get to 0

Use anytime after Session 3.5.

Math Focus Points

- Subtracting amounts from 100 or $1.00, down to 0

Materials: chart paper, 100 charts, multiple-of-5 number cubes (2 per pair), game pieces, blank paper, M5 (1 per pair), R54

Name Date

How Many Tens? How Many Ones?

Get to 0

Anita and Darren are playing *Get to 0*. Below are the numbers they rolled. Write an equation for each problem. Show your work.

1. Anita's game piece is on 50. She rolls 20 and 15. On what number should she put her game piece now? 15

Equations will vary; review students' work.

What numbers does Anita need to roll to get exactly to 0? 5 and 10

Equations will vary; review students' work.

2. Darren's game piece is on 65. He rolls 20 and 25. On what number should he put his game piece now? 20

Equations will vary; review students' work.

What numbers does Darren need to roll to get exactly to 0? 10 or 5 and 10 or 15

Equations will vary; review students' work.

Copyright © by Pearson Education, Inc., or its affiliates. All rights reserved.

R54 Unit 6 Use anytime after Session 3.5.

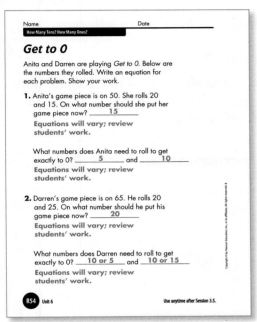

Students play *Get to 0*, a variation of *Get to 100*. Explain that in this version of the game, they start on 100 and subtract down to 0.

Post the game rules on chart paper so that students can refer to them if needed.

Display a 100 chart and model a few rounds of the game with a student partner. I'll go first. I rolled a 5 and a 10. On what number should I put my game piece? How do you know?

Students might say:

"You could subtract 100 − 10; that's 90. Then 90 − 5 = 85."

Get to 0 Rules

1. Both players place a game piece on the number 100 on the 100 chart.
2. Player 1 rolls 2 multiple-of-5 cubes, subtracts that many from 100, and records the equation. Player 1 moves his or her game piece to the square showing the difference.
3. Now player 2 takes a turn and repeats step 2.
4. On the next turn, players subtract from the number on which their game pieces are sitting.
5. The game is over when one player reaches 0 or goes past it off the 100 chart.

Have pairs of students play *Get to 0*. Check with each pair to be sure that they understand the rules. Remind them to record an equation after each turn to show how they moved.

Distribute copies of *Get to 0* (R54).

ELL English Language Learners

Use Repetition Review the rules of the game. Have students act out each step. If students seem confused, simplify the language and model the steps for them. First, roll the cubes. Then, subtract the 2 numbers that come up. I rolled a [10] and a [5]: [100 − 10 = 90; 90 − 5 = 85.] Now move the game piece to [85].

Additional Resource

Student Math Handbook

Game: *Spend $1.00* SMH G13

Materials: dot cubes or number cubes, coin sets, M36

Variation: At the end of each turn, try to make trades so that you have the fewest possible coins.

Differentiation in Investigation 4

Mathematics in This Investigation

The mathematics focuses on understanding the structure of 100 as being composed of equal groups of 2, 5, and 10.

Understanding the Mathematics

Students count fluently by 2s, 5s, and 10s to 100 and beyond. They accurately and legibly record number sequences for skip counting by 2s, 5s, and 10s. They understand the multiplicative structure of 100 and reason numerically to solve problems about 5s and 10s (e.g., There are 10 groups of 10 in 100, therefore there are 20 groups of 5 in 100). Students know and use coin equivalencies to solve problems about money.

Option: Assign the **Extension** activity.

Partially Understanding the Mathematics

Students count by 2s, 5s, and 10s to 100 but pause as they count to think of the next number. They may make some minor errors when recording their work. They may skip count and list the numbers to fill in a 100 chart by 5s or 10s rather than use what they know about 10s to reason about the number of 5s in 100. Students know coin equivalencies but may not apply this knowledge consistently when calculating with multiple coins.

Option: Assign the **Practice** activity.

Not Understanding the Mathematics

Students skip count by 2s, 5s, or 10s but may not be able to use that information to correctly fill in numbers on a 100 chart. They may not recognize the patterns of 5s and 10s on the 100 chart or see any connections between numbers, the skip counting sequence, and counting by groups of objects, which might help them in their work. Students are not yet fluent with coin equivalencies.

Option: Assign the **Intervention** activity.

Investigation 4 Quiz

In addition to your observations and students' work in Investigation 4, the Quiz (R55) can be used to gather more information.

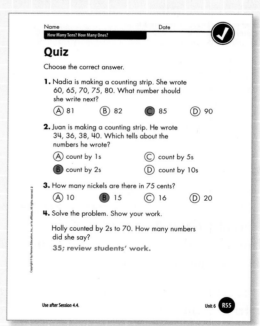

Name Date

How Many Tens? How Many Ones?

Quiz

Choose the correct answer.

1. Nadia is making a counting strip. She wrote 60, 65, 70, 75, 80. What number should she write next?
   Ⓐ 81 Ⓑ 82 Ⓒ 85 Ⓓ 90
2. Juan is making a counting strip. He wrote 34, 36, 38, 40. Which tells about the numbers he wrote?
   Ⓐ count by 1s Ⓒ count by 5s
   Ⓑ count by 2s Ⓓ count by 10s
3. How many nickels are there in 75 cents?
   Ⓐ 10 Ⓑ 15 Ⓒ 16 Ⓓ 20
4. Solve the problem. Show your work.
   Holly counted by 2s to 70. How many numbers did she say?
   35; review students' work.

Copyright © by Pearson Education, Inc., or its affiliates. All rights reserved. 2

Use after Session 4.4. Unit 6 R55

Intervention

20 MIN PAIRS

Multiples of 5 and 10

Use anytime after Session 4.1.

Math Focus Points

- Skip counting by 5s and 10s
- Thinking about the structure of 100 in terms of groups of 5 and 10

Vocabulary: skip counting, multiple

Materials: connecting cubes (100 per pair), pocket 100 chart, color transparent inserts for the pocket chart, M18–M19 (as needed), M30

Distribute connecting cubes to pairs of students. Explain to students that they will use the cubes to explore the number 100. Today we will build a model of 100 using cubes. Your model should have 10 rows with 10 cubes in each row.

Partners work together to build a 10 × 10 square with 100 cubes. If students need more support to complete this task, give them a copy of Make Your Own *Roll-a-Square* Gameboard (M18–M19) to use as a guide. Ten rows of 10 connecting cubes will cover this gameboard exactly.

Display a copy of Blank 100 Chart (M30). Have students count the cubes in their first row aloud as you point to the numbers in the first row of the pocket 100 chart. Review that 1 tower of 10 cubes is the same as 10 single cubes or 10 ones. Highlight the number 10 on the pocket 100 chart. Continue counting each row of cubes aloud with students and pointing to the corresponding numbers on the 100 chart. Highlight each multiple of 10.

Then have students use their cubes to skip count by 10s, touching the 10th cube in each row as they say the corresponding number. Point to the count-by-10s numbers on the 100 chart as students say them. Explain that the count-by-10s numbers are called multiples of 10. Then discuss the model and compare it to a 100 chart. How many towers of 10 did it take to make 100? How many tens are in 100? How is the cubes square similar to a 100 chart?

Present the following problem to students.

> We found out that there are 10 groups of 10 in 100. How could we find out how many groups of 5 there are in 100?

Students might say:

"Make towers of 5 cubes each and then count how many towers there are."

"Count the cubes by 5s. Write down the numbers we say. Then count how many numbers we wrote."

Model the methods that students suggest. Be sure to include highlighting all the multiples of 5 on the 100 chart and then counting them. Confirm that the number of 5s in 100 remains the same, regardless of the strategy used to find the answer.

Distribute copies of M30 and have students fill in the multiples of 5 and 10.

ELL English Language Learners

Model Thinking Aloud While counting the cubes and writing numbers on the 100 chart, talk about the different number patterns. I see that starting with 11, the numbers in the *ones place* repeat the 1–9 sequence. All the *multiples* of 10 have a 0 in the ones place, and the number in the *tens place* increases by 1 each time. When I *skip count* by 5s, the numbers end in either 0 or 5. As students work, ask questions that encourage them to explain their thinking.

Additional Resource

Student Math Handbook pages 38–39

Practice

25 MIN INDIVIDUALS

Skip Counting from Any Multiple

Use anytime after Session 4.2.

Math Focus Points

- Skip counting by 2s, 5s, and 10s

Materials: strips of adding machine tape, M5, R56

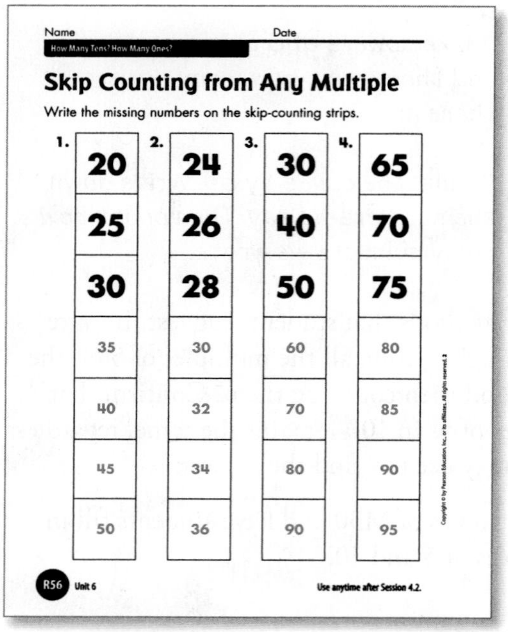

Name Date

How Many Tens? How Many Ones?

Skip Counting from Any Multiple

Write the missing numbers on the skip-counting strips.

1.	2.	3.	4.
20	24	30	65
25	26	40	70
30	28	50	75
35	30	60	80
40	32	70	85
45	34	80	90
50	36	90	95

R56 Unit 6 Use anytime after Session 4.2.

This activity provides additional practice with skip counting by 2s, 5s, and 10s. Briefly review making skip-counting strips. Display the 100 Chart (M5) as a reference for students.

Write the following sequence in a column on the board: 0, 5, 10, 15. Henry is making a skip-counting strip. He wrote these numbers. How is he counting? Is he counting by 1s, 2s, 5s, or 10s? How do you know? What will be the next number he should write?

Continue with the following sequence in another column on the board: 40, 45, 50, 55. Henry wrote these numbers on another skip-counting strip. By what number is he skip counting? How do you know? What will be the next number he writes?

Students might say:

"He is counting by 5s because 40 + 5 = 45. If you add 5 to 45, that's 50. If you add 5 to 50, it's 55."

"He is counting by 5s because Henry writes every fifth number from the 100 chart. The next number will be 60."

Write a new sequence on the board: 62, 64, 66, 68. Have students continue the sequence, writing on strips of adding machine tape. Give them a few minutes to work and then have them share their skip-counting sequences. By what number did you skip count? How high did you go? What do you notice about the numbers you wrote? What pattern do they make?

Repeat the activity for another series, counting by 2s, 5s, and 10s. Begin each sequence on 0 or on a multiple of the counting-by number.

Distribute copies of Skip Counting from Any Multiple (R56).

ELL English Language Learners

Rephrase Ask each question again using a simpler, shorter form. For example: Are you counting by 1s? Are you counting by 2s? Are you counting by 5s? Are you counting by 10s? What number comes next?

Additional Resource

Student Math Handbook pages 37–39

Extension

25 MIN GROUPS

How Many 5s in Larger Numbers

Use anytime after Session 4.1.

Math Focus Points

- Skip counting by 5s and 10s
- Thinking about the structure of 100 in terms of groups of 5 and 10

Materials: tape, M30 (3 per student), R57

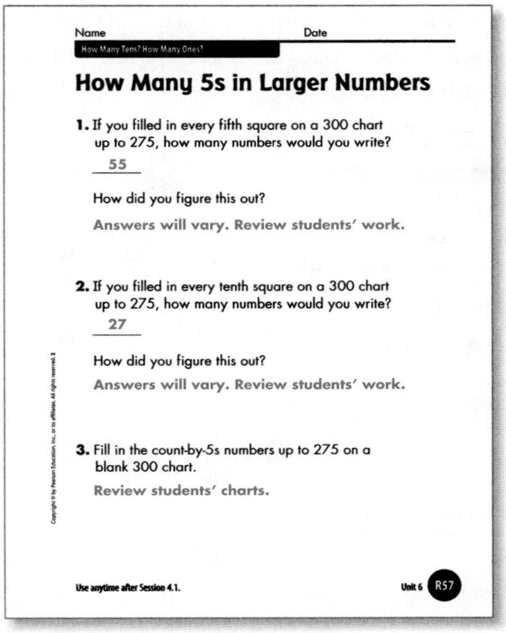

Name Date

How Many Tens? How Many Ones?

How Many 5s in Larger Numbers

1. If you filled in every fifth square on a 300 chart up to 275, how many numbers would you write?
   55

   How did you figure this out?

   Answers will vary. Review students' work.

2. If you filled in every tenth square on a 300 chart up to 275, how many numbers would you write?
   27

   How did you figure this out?

   Answers will vary. Review students' work.

3. Fill in the count-by-5s numbers up to 275 on a blank 300 chart.

   Review students' charts.

Use anytime after Session 4.1. Unit 6 R57

Materials to Prepare: Make a blank 200 chart, by taping 2 copies of the Blank 100 Chart (M30) together, one above the other.

Explain to students that in this activity, they will investigate how many 5s are in numbers that are larger than 100. Display the blank 200 chart. If we filled in every fifth square on a blank 200 chart, how many numbers would we write? How could we find out?

Students might say:

"Write every fifth number on the blank 200 chart. Then count the numbers we wrote."

"Since you fill in 2 numbers in each row, count the rows by 2s."

Have students model their strategies. Include a discussion of using information they already know to help solve the current problem. We know there are 10 tens in 100. How many 5s are in 100? How could knowing there are twenty 5s in 100 help us find how many 5s are in 200?

Distribute 3 copies of M30 to each student. Have them make a blank 300 chart by taping the 3 pages together. Read the following problem aloud. If you filled in every fifth square through 250, how many numbers would you write?

Ask students to solve the problem and record their work. When they have finished, bring them together to discuss their strategies. How did you solve the problem? How did you record your work? Did anyone use what they know about 200 to solve this problem?

Distribute copies of How Many 5s in Larger Numbers (R57).

ELL English Language Learners

Provide a Word List Students may need support with verbalizing their strategies. Write *skip counting, multiples, fifth, and tenth* on the board. Discuss the meaning of each with students. Point to the words on the list as you use them in discussion. Encourage students to refer to the list as needed.

Additional Resource

Student Math Handbook pages 37–39

Differentiation in Investigation 1

Mathematics in This Investigation

The mathematics focuses on understanding fractions as equal parts of a whole or of a group, with emphasis on one half.

Understanding the Mathematics

Students understand that one half indicates two equal parts of a whole. They correctly identify and accurately color halves of an area (e.g., a rectangle). They can show which Geoblock is half of a given Geoblock. They reason numerically to solve problems about finding one half of a set of objects, such as a bunch of balloons, and they identify which groups of objects can or cannot be divided in half. Students use fraction notation to describe one half.

Option: Assign the **Extension** activity.

Partially Understanding the Mathematics

Students correctly identify halves of rectangles, but they may be inaccurate when asked to color in the halves. They solve problems about finding one half of a set of objects often by counting out the objects by ones, rather than reasoning numerically. They may sometimes lose track when working with larger numbers.

Option: Assign the **Practice** activity.

Not Understanding the Mathematics

Students may know that one half is part of a whole, but they do not show halves as equal parts of a whole. They are unsure how to proceed when asked to solve a problem involving finding one half of a set of objects, and they may solve it by dividing the set into unequal portions.

Option: Assign the **Intervention** activity.

Investigation 1 Quiz

In addition to your observations and students' work in Investigation 1, the Quiz (R58) can be used to gather more information.

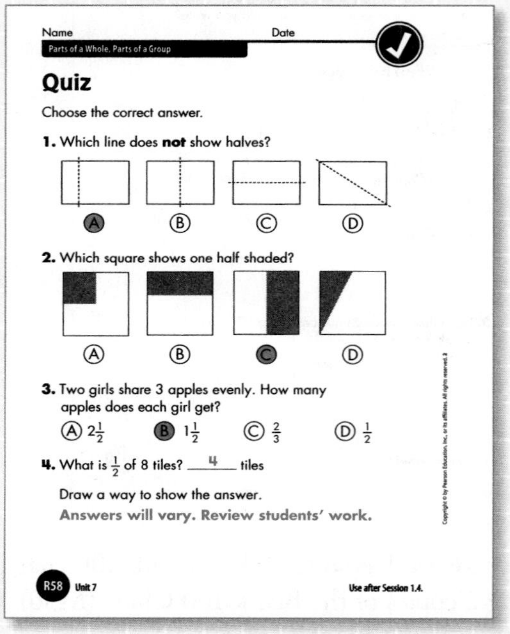
Name Date

Parts of a Whole, Parts of a Group

Quiz

Choose the correct answer.

1. Which line does **not** show halves?

(A) (B) (C) (D)

2. Which square shows one half shaded?

(A) (B) (C) (D)

3. Two girls share 3 apples evenly. How many apples does each girl get?

(A) $2\frac{1}{2}$ (B) $1\frac{1}{2}$ (C) $\frac{2}{3}$ (D) $\frac{1}{2}$

4. What is $\frac{1}{2}$ of 8 tiles? 4 tiles

Draw a way to show the answer.

Answers will vary. Review students' work.

Copyright © by Pearson Education, Inc., or its affiliates. All rights reserved. 2

R58 Unit 7 Use after Session 1.4.

Intervention

20 MIN INDIVIDUALS

Sharing to Find a Half

Use anytime after Session 1.1.

Math Focus Points

- Finding one half of a set

Vocabulary: half

Materials: color tiles (14 per student), M3 (from Unit 6)

Materials to Prepare: Cut strips of 8 star stickers from Stickers: Strips and Singles (M3). There should be 1 strip for every student.

Some students may have difficulty finding half of a set. In this activity, students find $\frac{1}{2}$ of 8 objects in different ways.

Give each student a strip of 8 star stickers. Draw the strip of 8 star stickers on the board.

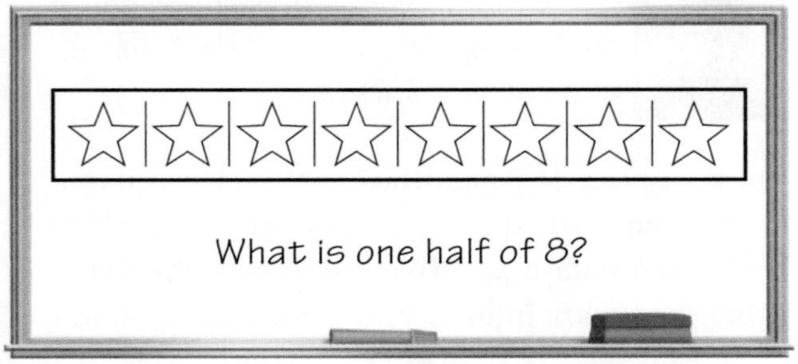

Two students, Simon and Paige, are sharing 8 star stickers. Each student gets half the stickers. How can I divide the stickers evenly?

Students might say:

"I can mark one for Simon, the next for Paige, the next for Simon, and so on, until all the stickers are marked."

"I can draw a line between 2 groups that have the same number of stickers. Look. If I fold the strip in half, I know where to draw the line."

So, what is one half of 8? How many stickers does each student get?

Another way to solve the problem is to use tiles. We'll pretend that each tile is a star sticker. This time, Simon and Paige are sharing 10 star stickers. Have each student take 10 tiles. How many stickers will each child get? After students have solved the problem, ask them to share their solution strategies. Emphasize that each child must get exactly the same number of stickers. Repeat using 12 or 14 stickers.

ELL English Language Learners

Rephrase You may need to rephrase the questions using different vocabulary. For example, instead of *evenly*, you might say *equally*, or *so each part is exactly the same amount*. Instead of *split* the rectangle, you might say *divide* or *separate* the rectangle.

Additional Resource

Student Math Handbook page 86

Practice

20 MIN GROUPS

Halves or Not?

Use anytime after Session 1.2.

Math Focus Points

- Determining whether a block is half of another block
- Showing one half of an object

Vocabulary: half

Materials: pattern blocks, colored pencils, R59

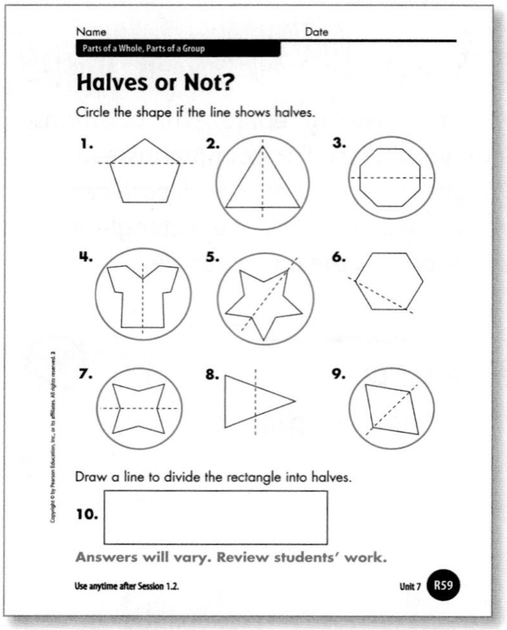
Name Date

Parts of a Whole, Parts of a Group

Halves or Not?

Circle the shape if the line shows halves.

1. 2. 3.

4. 5. 6.

7. 8. 9.

Draw a line to divide the rectangle into halves.

10.

Answers will vary. Review students' work.

Use anytime after Session 1.2. Unit 7 R59

Review the names of the shapes of the pattern blocks. Ask students to take a yellow hexagon. Look for a pattern block that is one half of the hexagon. What pattern block did you choose? How do you know it is half as big as the hexagon?

Students might say:

"The red trapezoid is half as big. When I put two of them together, they fit exactly on top of the hexagon."

That's right. On a piece of paper, trace around the hexagon. Then use the trapezoid to figure out where you can draw a line to split the hexagon in half. Then color in one half of the hexagon.

Look at the other pattern blocks. Work together in your groups. Can you find a pattern block that is half of another pattern block? Ask volunteers to share their findings.

On your piece of paper, trace around the blue rhombus. Then use the triangle to show where to draw a line that splits the rhombus in half. Color in one half of the rhombus.

Next, hold up an orange square. Look through the pattern blocks. Can you find one that's half the size of the square? How did you decide?

Students might say:

"We tried two of each piece to see if they would fit on top of the square, and nothing worked."

On your piece of paper, trace around the square. Even though you don't have a pattern block that's half of the square, can you still draw a line that splits the square in half? Show one way to do it.

Distribute copies of Halves or Not? (R59).

ELL English Language Learners

Provide a Word List Have students color half of each diagram they drew during the activity. Then have the student write *half* under each one. Also, discuss the term *halves*. You might want to review the names of the geometric shapes shown on their papers and have students write those names also.

Additional Resource

Student Math Handbook page 86

Extension

15 MIN PAIRS

Sharing the Cost of Toys

Use anytime after Session 1.2.

Math Focus Points

- Solving problems about finding halves of quantities in different contexts

Materials: pennies (50 per pair), R60

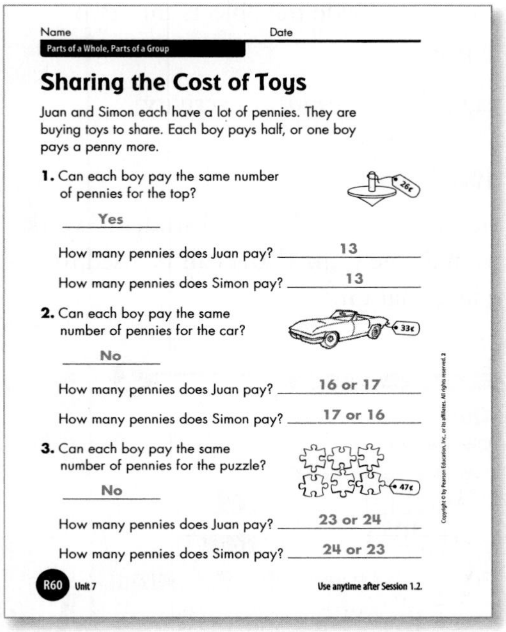
Name Date

Parts of a Whole, Parts of a Group

Sharing the Cost of Toys

Juan and Simon each have a lot of pennies. They are buying toys to share. Each boy pays half, or one boy pays a penny more.

1. Can each boy pay the same number of pennies for the top? Yes

   How many pennies does Juan pay? 13

   How many pennies does Simon pay? 13

2. Can each boy pay the same number of pennies for the car? No

   How many pennies does Juan pay? 16 or 17

   How many pennies does Simon pay? 17 or 16

3. Can each boy pay the same number of pennies for the puzzle? No

   How many pennies does Juan pay? 23 or 24

   How many pennies does Simon pay? 24 or 23

R60 Unit 7 Use anytime after Session 1.2.

On the board, sketch a toy airplane and write its price, 29¢.

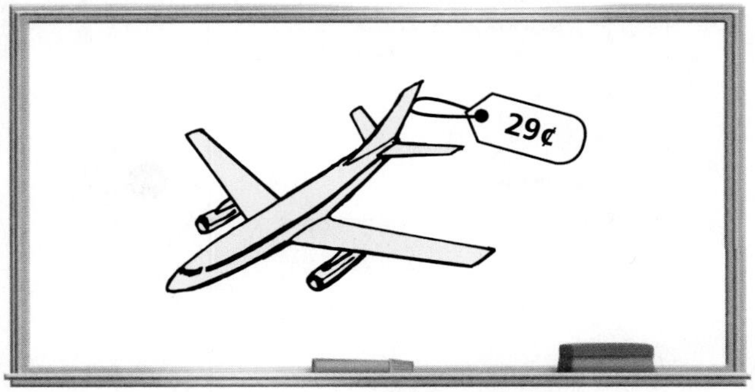

Suppose you and your partner have lots of pennies—enough to buy a small toy. How can you share the cost of the toy airplane evenly or almost evenly? Work with your partner to find the answer. After students have worked on this for a few minutes, ask volunteers to explain their reasoning.

Students might say:

"We made a group of 29 pennies. Then we shared the pennies and found that each person would pay 14¢. We had 1 penny left. One person needs to pay an extra penny."

Pose a similar problem. Discuss ways to make equal groups, such as making two stacks of pennies or making two rows with pennies matched one-to-one. Is there a way to tell ahead of time whether the pennies can be shared evenly? Some students may realize that an even number of pennies can be shared evenly, but an odd number of pennies cannot.

Each of you should think of another toy problem for your partner to solve. Name a different toy and a price less than 50¢.

Distribute copies of Sharing the Cost of Toys (R60).

ELL English Language Learners

Suggest a Sequence A sequence may help students explain the steps in sharing the pennies between two students. For example:

1. Count out pennies.
2. Put the pennies into groups. Groups should be the same size, or one group may have 1 more penny.
3. Find the number of pennies each person gets.

Additional Resource

Student Math Handbook page 86

Unit 7

Differentiation in Investigation 2

Mathematics in This Investigation

The mathematics focuses on understanding fractions as equal parts of a whole or of a group, with emphasis on halves, thirds, and fourths.

Understanding the Mathematics

Students recognize that fractions always involve equal parts. They identify halves, thirds, and fourths of a region and accurately color halves, thirds, and fourths of a rectangle. They identify and name fractional parts with numerators greater than one (e.g., $\frac{2}{3}$, $\frac{3}{4}$), and they recognize and use fraction notation for mixed numbers (e.g., $1\frac{1}{2}$). They can find one half of a set of objects and may use their knowledge of combinations to solve a problem about halves of a group (e.g., $8 + 8 = 16$, so $\frac{1}{2}$ of 16 is 8).

Option: Assign the **Extension** activity.

Partially Understanding the Mathematics

Students identify halves, thirds, and fourths of a region and color halves, thirds, and fourths of a rectangle. Their coloring may not always show equal parts. They can solve a problem about finding one half of a set of objects by using cubes to model the problem or tally marks to record their work, but they may make errors in their counting or recording.

Option: Assign the **Practice** activity.

Not Understanding the Mathematics

Students may associate one half as a whole divided into 2 parts, one third as a whole divided into 3 parts, and one fourth as a whole divided into 4 parts. However, they do not understand that one half is 1 of 2 *equal* parts, one third is 1 of 3 *equal* parts, and one fourth is 1 of 4 *equal* parts. When asked to solve a problem about finding one half of a set of objects, they divide the objects into two unequal groups.

Option: Assign the **Intervention** activity.

Investigation 2 Quiz

In addition to your observations and students' work in Investigation 2, the Quiz (R61) can be used to gather more information.

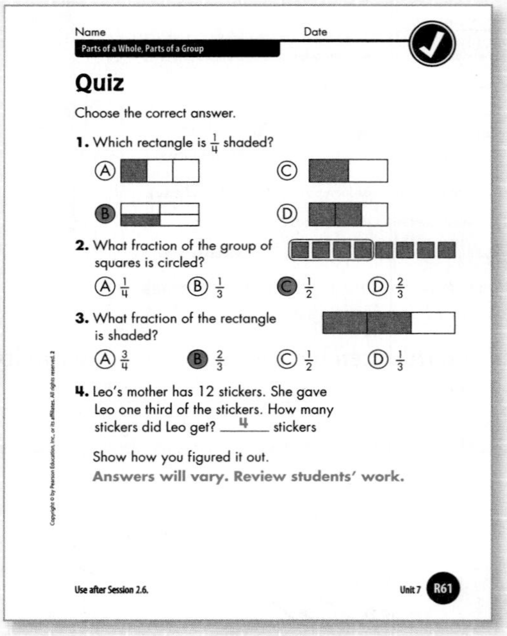
Name Date

Parts of a Whole, Parts of a Group

Quiz

Choose the correct answer.

1. Which rectangle is $\frac{1}{4}$ shaded?

Ⓐ Ⓑ Ⓒ Ⓓ

2. What fraction of the group of squares is circled?

Ⓐ $\frac{1}{4}$ Ⓑ $\frac{1}{3}$ Ⓒ $\frac{1}{2}$ Ⓓ $\frac{2}{3}$

3. What fraction of the rectangle is shaded?

Ⓐ $\frac{3}{4}$ Ⓑ $\frac{2}{3}$ Ⓒ $\frac{1}{2}$ Ⓓ $\frac{1}{3}$

4. Leo's mother has 12 stickers. She gave Leo one third of the stickers. How many stickers did Leo get? 4 stickers

Show how you figured it out.

Answers will vary. Review students' work.

Copyright © by Pearson Education, Inc., or its affiliates. All rights reserved. 2

Use after Session 2.6.

Unit 7 R61

Intervention

20 MIN INDIVIDUALS

Fractions and Flags

Use anytime after Session 2.3.

Math Focus Points

- Learning the terms and notation for fractions that contain more than one part (e.g., $\frac{2}{3}$, $\frac{2}{4}$, $\frac{3}{4}$)
- Identifying halves, thirds, and fourths of regions
- Identifying and naming fractional parts that have numerators greater than 1 (e.g., $\frac{2}{3}$, $\frac{2}{4}$, $\frac{3}{4}$)

Vocabulary: one third, two thirds, one fourth

Materials: blank paper (1 half sheet per student), crayons or markers

Draw a 3-part flag on the board, with shading in the middle part.

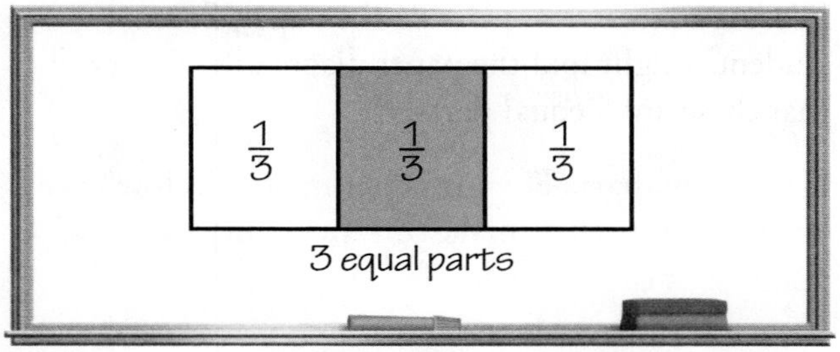

Here is a picture of a flag. How many equal parts does the flag have? Emphasize that the three parts are equal in size. Write 3 equal parts on the board. What are the parts called? How do we write one third using a fraction? Label each section $\frac{1}{3}$. What fraction of the flag is shaded? What fraction of the flag is not shaded?

Students might say:

"There are 3 parts. 1 part is shaded. So $\frac{1}{3}$ is shaded."

"2 parts are white and there are 3 parts. The fraction for white is $\frac{2}{3}$."

Emphasize that a fraction names a part of the *whole* flag. Review that the bottom number in a fraction indicates the number of equal parts in the whole and the top number shows the number of parts out of the total. Also, remind students of the importance of equal parts as you illustrate a flag with unequal parts. Is $\frac{1}{3}$ of this flag shaded? Why or why not?

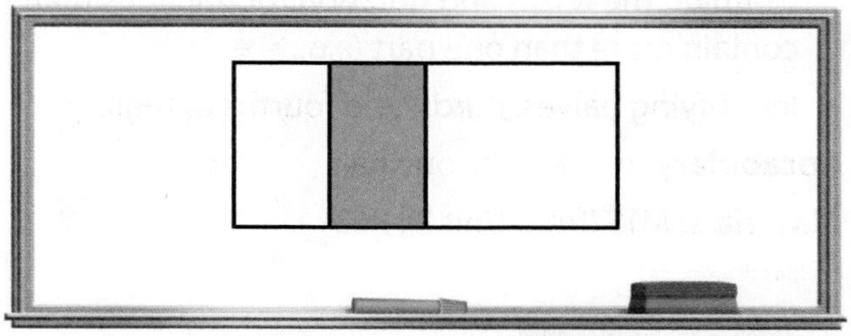

Next, give each student a half sheet of paper and a crayon or marker. Have them fold the sheet in half, then in half again, to make fourths. Ask them to open the sheet and color one of the four parts. Suppose your paper is a flag. What fraction of your flag is shaded? What fraction of your flag is white? Have students label each part using fraction notation and label each part with a fraction.

Write $\frac{1}{4}$ green, $\frac{2}{4}$ yellow, and $\frac{1}{4}$ orange on the board. Have students turn their flags over, color them accordingly, and label each part with a fraction.

ELL English Language Learners

Model Thinking Aloud Show students a flag that is divided into fourths, with one fourth green. Help students relate the number of parts to the numbers in a fraction. 1 out of 4 equal parts is green. One fourth of the flag is green. Have students practice describing other flags in the same way.

Additional Resource

Student Math Handbook pages 86–91

Practice

15 MIN PAIRS

Making Fractions

Use anytime after Session 2.4.

Math Focus Points

- Identifying and naming fractional parts that have numerators greater than 1 (e.g., $\frac{2}{3}, \frac{2}{4}, \frac{3}{4}$)
- Learning the terms and notation for fractions that contain more than one part (e.g., $\frac{2}{3}, \frac{2}{4}, \frac{3}{4}$)
- Identifying halves, thirds, and fourths of regions

Vocabulary: one fourth, one half

Materials: M15 (from Unit 2), R62

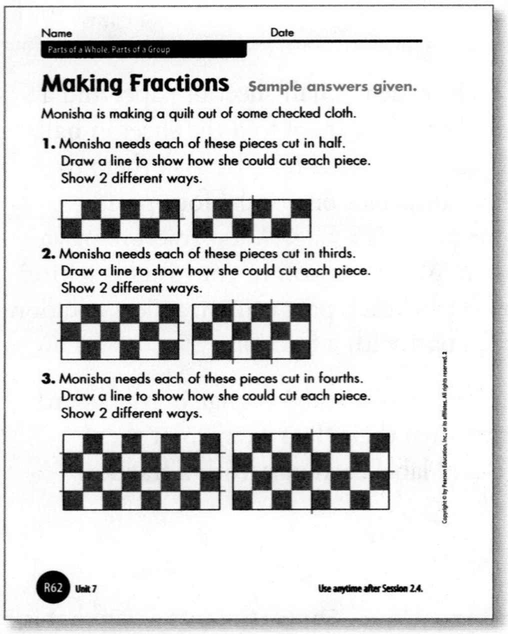

Name Date

Parts of a Whole, Parts of a Group

Making Fractions Sample answers given.

Monisha is making a quilt out of some checked cloth.

1. Monisha needs each of these pieces cut in half. Draw a line to show how she could cut each piece. Show 2 different ways.
2. Monisha needs each of these pieces cut in thirds. Draw a line to show how she could cut each piece. Show 2 different ways.
3. Monisha needs each of these pieces cut in fourths. Draw a line to show how she could cut each piece. Show 2 different ways.

Copyright © by Pearson Education, Inc., or its affiliates. All rights reserved. 2

R62 Unit 7 Use anytime after Session 2.4.

Materials to Prepare: Cut 4-inch squares from Inch Grid Paper (M15). Distribute one 4 × 4 square to each student.

How can you divide your paper into fourths? Is there more than one way? Give students a few minutes to work on making fourths. Ask a volunteer to share his or her work.

Students might say:

"I folded the paper in half and then did it again the other way."

"There are 4 squares going down. So I drew a line under each row of squares."

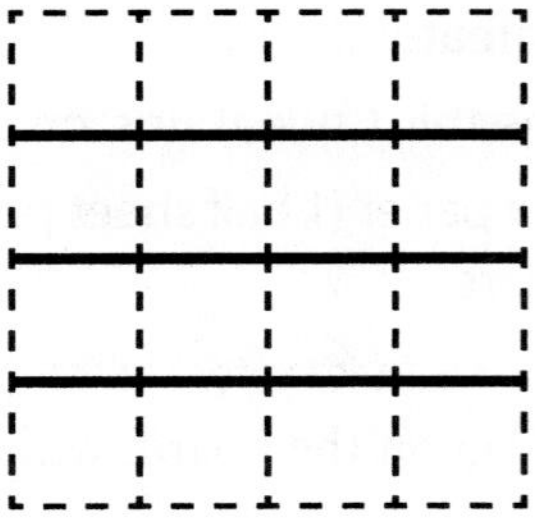

Discuss other ways to divide the paper. Some students might fold the paper diagonally. Point out that these are 4 equal parts.

How many parts of your paper make $\frac{1}{4}$? How many parts of your paper make $\frac{2}{4}$? How many parts make $\frac{3}{4}$? Is there another fraction that names the same amount as $\frac{2}{4}$?

Have each student use fractions to tell his or her partner how to color the paper. For example: *Color $\frac{1}{2}$ of your paper red. Color $\frac{1}{4}$ of your paper blue. Color $\frac{1}{4}$ of your paper green.* Students should label each part using fraction notation. Partners should check that their instructions were carried out correctly.

Distribute copies of Making Fractions (R62).

ELL English Language Learners

Provide a Word List Write the words *halves, thirds,* and *fourths* on the board. Review how to say and write the fractions. Have students copy each word and make a simple diagram to illustrate each fraction.

Additional Resource

Student Math Handbook pages 86–91

Extension

20 MIN PAIRS

Sharing Snacks

Use anytime after Session 2.5.

Math Focus Points

- Finding thirds and fourths of sets
- Identifying halves, thirds, and fourths of regions

Vocabulary: mixed number

Materials: color tiles, R63

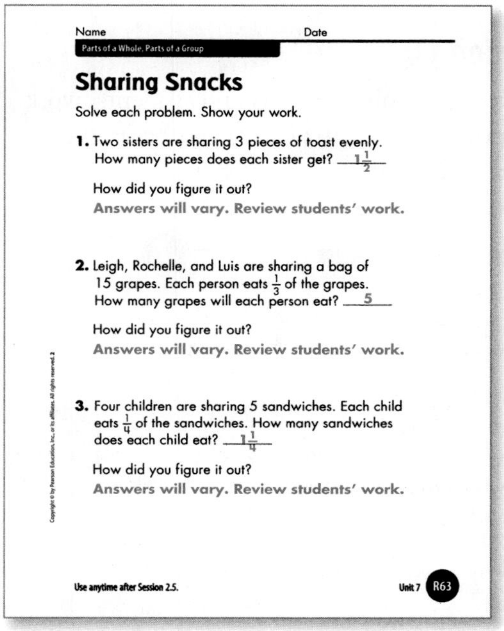

Name Date

Parts of a Whole, Parts of a Group

Sharing Snacks

Solve each problem. Show your work.

1. Two sisters are sharing 3 pieces of toast evenly. How many pieces does each sister get? $1\frac{1}{2}$

   How did you figure it out?

   Answers will vary. Review students' work.

2. Leigh, Rochelle, and Luis are sharing a bag of 15 grapes. Each person eats $\frac{1}{3}$ of the grapes. How many grapes will each person eat? 5

   How did you figure it out?

   Answers will vary. Review students' work.

3. Four children are sharing 5 sandwiches. Each child eats $\frac{1}{4}$ of the sandwiches. How many sandwiches does each child eat? $1\frac{1}{4}$

   How did you figure it out?

   Answers will vary. Review students' work.

Copyright © by Pearson Education, Inc., or its affiliates. All rights reserved. 2

Use anytime after Session 2.5. Unit 7 R63

In this activity, students decide how to share snacks. The answers are either whole numbers or mixed numbers.

Work with your partner. How can the two of you share 7 crackers evenly? Use color tiles or drawings to find the answer. Ask students to share their solutions and strategies.

Students might say:

"We used 7 tiles to stand for the crackers. We each took 3 tiles. There was 1 tile left. If it's a cracker, we could cut it in half. Each of us gets $3\frac{1}{2}$ crackers."

On the board, write the following two problems for partners to solve. Encourage students to use drawings or tiles to solve each problem.

1. How can 3 children share 10 crackers equally?
2. Travis had 18 crackers. He ate one fourth of them. How many crackers did he eat?

After completing both problems, discuss and record students' solutions and strategies. For Problem 1, students may suggest to circle and label each group of 3 crackers and label the remaining crackers with $\frac{1}{3}$.

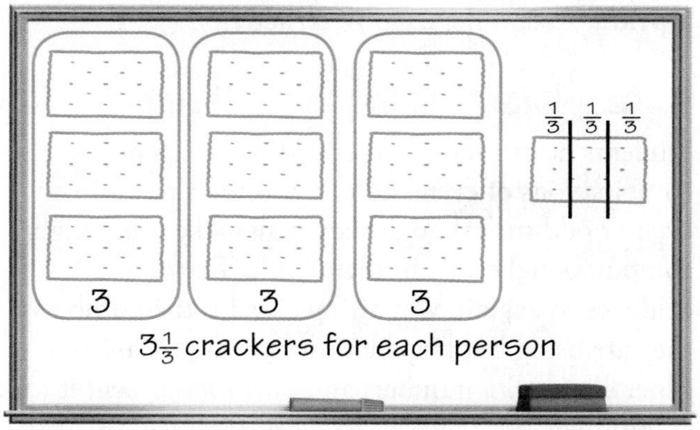

3
3
3
1/3 1/3 1/3
3 1/3 crackers for each person

Distribute copies of Sharing Snacks (R63).

ELL English Language Learners

Rephrase Many English Language Learners have difficulty with story problems like those on R63. Before students begin their work on this page, read through each problem with them. Rephrase and clarify difficult words, as necessary. Ask students to tell you in their own words what each problem says.

Additional Resource

Student Math Handbook page 92

Differentiation in Investigation 1

Mathematics in This Investigation

The mathematics focuses on adding even and odd numbers and making and justifying generalizations about what happens when even and odd numbers are added.

Additional Resource: *What Does Proof Look Like in Second Grade?*, pages 154–155 (See Curriculum Unit 8)

Understanding the Mathematics

Students accurately determine whether adding different combinations of even and odd numbers result in an even or odd sum. They make and justify generalizations about even and odd numbers by reasoning about problems involving partners and teams. They may make models or drawings to represent their generalizations.

Option: Assign the **Extension** activity.

Partially Understanding the Mathematics

Students determine whether adding different combinations of even and odd numbers result in an even or odd sum though they may make some slight computational errors in their work. They provide evidence to explain why this works for the numbers they are using but may be unsure if their reasoning generalizes to *all* numbers and how to represent it for all numbers.

Option: Assign the **Practice** activity.

Not Understanding the Mathematics

Students may or may not accurately add even and odd numbers. They may make lists of problems with correct answers but they do not reason about their work to determine whether different combinations always result in an even or odd number. They may recognize patterns in their answers but are unsure how to interpret these patterns.

Option: Assign the **Intervention** activity.

Investigation 1 Quiz

In addition to your observations and students' work in Investigation 1, the Quiz (R64) can be used to gather more information.

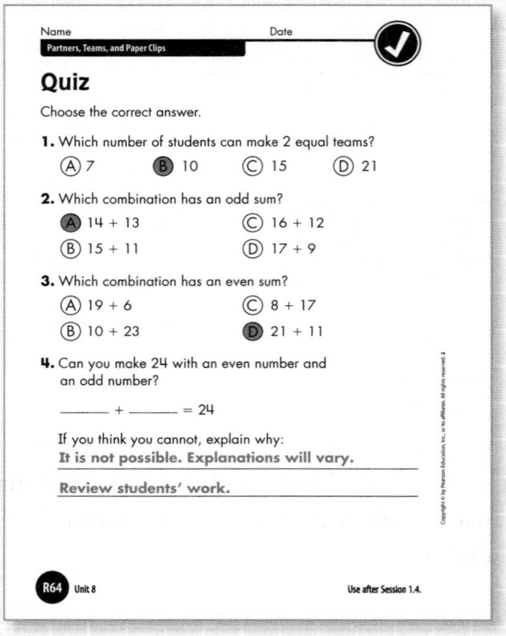

Name Date

Partners, Teams, and Paper Clips

Quiz

Choose the correct answer.

1. Which number of students can make 2 equal teams?
   Ⓐ 7   Ⓑ 10   Ⓒ 15   Ⓓ 21
2. Which combination has an odd sum?
   Ⓐ 14 + 13   Ⓒ 16 + 12
   Ⓑ 15 + 11   Ⓓ 17 + 9
3. Which combination has an even sum?
   Ⓐ 19 + 6   Ⓒ 8 + 17
   Ⓑ 10 + 23   Ⓓ 21 + 11
4. Can you make 24 with an even number and an odd number?
   ____ + ____ = 24
   If you think you cannot, explain why:
   It is not possible. Explanations will vary.
   Review students' work.

R64 Unit 8 Use after Session 1.4.

Intervention

30 MIN INDIVIDUALS

Combinations of Odd and Even Numbers

Use anytime after Session 1.3.

Math Focus Points

- Finding combinations of odd and even numbers that make given numbers or determining that these combinations are not possible

Materials: connecting cubes (23 per pair), blank paper

Begin by reviewing what students know about even and odd numbers. Refer to the charts generated in Session 1.1. Focus specifically on even numbers making equal teams and odd numbers always having one left over when making groups of two.

We have been exploring what happens when we add 2 even numbers or 2 odd numbers or an even number plus an odd number. In our discussion [yesterday], some of you said that 2 even numbers *cannot* have a sum of 23. Do you still think this is true? Why or why not?

Discuss students' reasoning but do not make any generalizations. Explain to students that today they will investigate this in more detail. Ask students for the set of even numbers and odd numbers from 1–24. Record each set on the board in two lists.

Display a cube train with 23 cubes. Have students verify that there are 23 cubes. Is 23 even or odd? How do you know? Could you make 2 equal teams? If there were 23 students could everyone have a partner? Ask a volunteer to break 12 cubes off the train. Write ____ + ____ = 23.

Have students count the cubes in each part. Write the numbers on the blanks in the equation: [12] + [11] = 23. There are [12] cubes in the first part. Is [12] even or odd? There are [11] cubes in the other part. Is that even or odd? Label each number as even or odd. Remember, we are looking for 2 even numbers that make 23. Do these 2 numbers work?

Distribute blank paper to each student. Have them write 23 at the top and then record 12 + 11 = 23 on their papers, noting even + odd under 12 + 11. Put the tower of 23 cubes back together and repeat the process. Ask another volunteer to break an even number of cubes off the train and then write an equation. There are [8] cubes in the first part and [15] cubes in the other part. [8] is an even number, but [15] is an odd number. Record this equation on the board, and label each number as even or odd. Have students do the same.

Repeat the process a few more times. Do you think it is possible to make 23 with 2 even numbers?

Students might say:

"It is possible. So far, it has always been an even plus an odd, but we haven't tried all the numbers yet."

"It is not possible. One of the numbers you add has to have 1 left over. That means one number has to be odd."

Distribute connecting cubes to each pair. Have students generate addition equations with 2 addends for 23 and record them on paper.

After pairs have worked for 10–15 minutes, bring them together for discussion. As each pair gives an equation, record it on the board and ask students whether or not they agree and why. You have tried many examples. Do you think it is possible to make 23 by adding 2 even numbers? Why not?

ELL English Language Learners

Suggest a Sequence Some students might benefit from the following sequence of steps. *First,* break the cube train into two parts. *Next,* count the cubes in each part. *Then,* write an equation.

Additional Resource

Student Math Handbook pages 41–42

Practice

25 MIN PAIRS

Even and Odd Sums

Use anytime after Session 1.3.

Math Focus Points

- Making and testing conjectures about adding even and odd numbers

Materials: index cards (10 per pair), connecting cubes, blank paper, R65

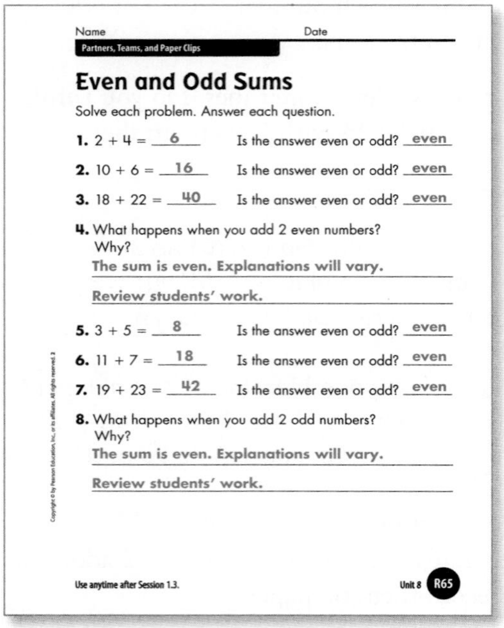

Name Date

Partners, Teams, and Paper Clips

Even and Odd Sums

Solve each problem. Answer each question.

1. 2 + 4 = 6 Is the answer even or odd? even
2. 10 + 6 = 16 Is the answer even or odd? even
3. 18 + 22 = 40 Is the answer even or odd? even
4. What happens when you add 2 even numbers? Why?
   The sum is even. Explanations will vary.
   Review students' work.
5. 3 + 5 = 8 Is the answer even or odd? even
6. 11 + 7 = 18 Is the answer even or odd? even
7. 19 + 23 = 42 Is the answer even or odd? even
8. What happens when you add 2 odd numbers? Why?
   The sum is even. Explanations will vary.
   Review students' work.

Use anytime after Session 1.3. Unit 8 R65

Materials to Prepare: Cut index cards in half. Write the numbers 1–20 on the cards, one number per card. Make one set for each pair.

Briefly review what students know about odd and even numbers. Then have each student fold a sheet of blank paper into three columns. Label each column: even + even, even + odd, odd + odd. Explain that today they will practice adding odd and even numbers. Model the following activity, using one set of numbered cards, with a volunteer.

- Arrange cards facedown in a 4-by-5 array.
- Players take turns turning over 2 cards and identifying the numbers as even or odd.
- Both students record and solve the addition equation using the 2 numbers in the appropriate column.
- They decide whether the sum is even or odd and record that information.
- The cards are returned to their original facedown position and 2 new cards are selected.

7 + 13 = 20
even

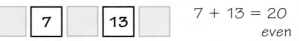

Distribute the numbered index cards. Allow pairs to work for 10–15 minutes. Bring students together for discussion. Using students' equations write 5–6 examples in each column of the chart. Compare the equations in the first column. What do you notice about the sums of these even + even equations? Do you think this is true for *all* even + even equations? Why or why not? Ask students if they can use cubes to explain their thinking. Repeat the questions for the other columns. Then distribute copies of Even and Odd Sums (R65).

ELL English Language Learners

Suggest a Sequence Refer to a visual list of steps while the activity is modeled. Write the steps on the board.

1. Make 4 rows of 5 cards.
2. Pick 2 cards. Say if they are odd or even.
3. Record the equation.
4. Add. Say if the sum is even or odd.
5. Replace cards. Choose 2 new cards.

Additional Resource

Student Math Handbook pages 41–42

Extension

35 MIN INDIVIDUALS

Subtracting Even and Odd Numbers

Use anytime after Session 1.4.

Math Focus Points

- Making and testing conjectures about subtracting even and odd numbers

Materials: connecting cubes, blank paper, R66

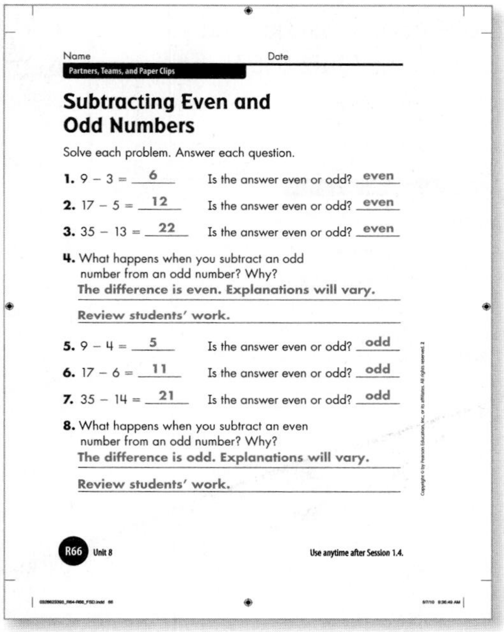

Name Date

Partners, Teams, and Paper Clips

Subtracting Even and Odd Numbers

Solve each problem. Answer each question.

1. 9 − 3 = 6   Is the answer even or odd? even
2. 17 − 5 = 12   Is the answer even or odd? even
3. 35 − 13 = 22   Is the answer even or odd? even
4. What happens when you subtract an odd number from an odd number? Why?
   The difference is even. Explanations will vary.
   Review students' work.
5. 9 − 4 = 5   Is the answer even or odd? odd
6. 17 − 6 = 11   Is the answer even or odd? odd
7. 35 − 14 = 21   Is the answer even or odd? odd
8. What happens when you subtract an even number from an odd number? Why?
   The difference is odd. Explanations will vary.
   Review students' work.

R66 Unit 8   Use anytime after Session 1.4.

We have been investigating what happens when we add even and odd numbers. Today we will explore *subtracting* even and odd numbers.

Make 4 columns on the board and label each column as follows: even − even, odd − odd, even − odd, and odd − even.

Point to the first column. What happens when you subtract an even number from an even number? Is the answer even or odd?

Record 10 − 4 = 6 on the board. Is the difference even or odd? Ask students to suggest a few more equations to test even − even. Discuss whether the answers are even or odd. Do you think this is true for *all* even − even equations? Why or why not?

Students might say:

"If you subtract even − even, you won't break up any pairs, so the answer will be even, too."

Have students fold a sheet of blank paper into 4 sections so they have 4 columns. They should copy the subtraction situations listed on the board at the top of each column. Students generate 4–5 equations for each situation to see if the differences are even or odd. Once students have done this, explain that they should select one situation to investigate further. Your work will be to decide if this is true for all numbers of this type. You should build a model, draw pictures, or use numbers to explain your thinking.

When students have finished developing their proofs, bring them together to discuss their work. Select one situation and have the students who investigated share their work.

Distribute copies of Subtracting Even and Odd Numbers (R66).

ELL English Language Learners

Provide Sentence Stems If students need support verbalizing responses, provide sentence stems to help structure their answers. When you subtract an ______ from an ______, the difference is ______. I think this is true for all ______ − ______ equations because ______.

Additional Resource

Student Math Handbook pages 41–42

Differentiation in Investigation 2

Mathematics in This Investigation

The mathematics focuses on reasoning about known addition combinations to solve unknown combinations and developing fluency with the addition combinations: Plus 9 and the Remaining Combinations.

Additional Resource: *Plus 9 and Remaining Combinations,* pages 188–189 (See Curriculum Unit 8)

Understanding the Mathematics

Students are fluent with all the addition combinations.

Option: Assign the **Extension** activity.

Partially Understanding the Mathematics

Students are fluent with almost all the combinations but may pause to figure out one or two they are unsure of. They use combinations they know to help them figure out other combinations.

Option: Assign the **Practice** activity.

Not Understanding the Mathematics

Students are not yet fluent with the addition combinations. They may not see or use combinations they know to figure out unknown combinations. They use fingers to count on to find the solution to unknown combinations.

Option: Assign the **Intervention** activity.

Investigation 2 Quiz

In addition to your observations and students' work in Investigation 2, the Quiz (R67) can be used to gather more information.

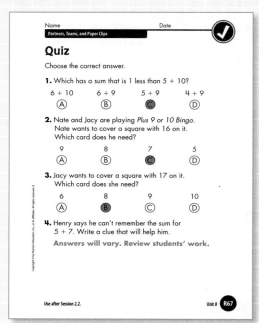

Name Date

Partners, Teams, and Paper Clips

Quiz

Choose the correct answer.

1. Which has a sum that is 1 less than 5 + 10?

Ⓐ	Ⓑ	Ⓒ	Ⓓ
6 + 10	6 + 9	5 + 9 (filled)	4 + 9

2. Nate and Jacy are playing *Plus 9 or 10 Bingo.* Nate wants to cover a square with 16 on it. Which card does he need?

Ⓐ	Ⓑ	Ⓒ	Ⓓ
9	8	7 (filled)	5

3. Jacy wants to cover a square with 17 on it. Which card does she need?

Ⓐ	Ⓑ	Ⓒ	Ⓓ
6	8 (filled)	9	10

4. Henry says he can't remember the sum for 5 + 7. Write a clue that will help him.

Answers will vary. Review students' work.

Copyright © by Pearson Education, Inc., or its affiliates. All rights reserved. 2

Use after Session 2.2. Unit 8 R67

Intervention

25 MIN PAIRS

Using Plus 10 to Solve Plus 9 Combinations

Use anytime after Session 2.1.

Math Focus Points

- Relating unknown combinations to known combinations

Vocabulary: sum

Materials: connecting cubes (20 per pair)

In this activity, students model the relationship between plus 9 and plus 10 combinations. Today we are going to work on how you can use what you know about one combination of numbers to help you solve a related combination. Suppose I am working on 5 + 9. Record 5 + 9 = _____ on the board.

Show students a tower of 5 cubes and a tower of 9 cubes. Move 1 cube from the tower of 5 to the tower of 9, making towers of 4 and 10.

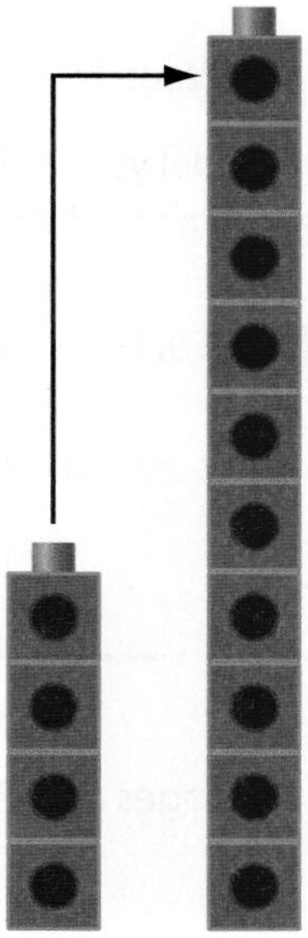

I am going to take 1 cube from the 5, so the 5 becomes a 4. Then I am going to add that cube to 9, so the 9 becomes a 10. How many cubes are in each tower now? On the board, record 4 + 10 under 5 + 9.

What is the sum of 5 + 9? What is the sum of 4 + 10? Record each sum on the board. Why are these two answers the same? If students do not mention it, point out that nothing was added or taken away from the total set of cubes; the towers were just rearranged, thus the total remains the same.

Now, how can you use what you know about 8 + 10 to solve 8 + 9? Direct pairs of students to use cubes to solve the problem on their own and then record their work. When students have solved the problem, gather them together and discuss their solutions and strategies. How can you use what you know about Plus 10 combinations to help you solve Plus 9 combinations?

ELL English Language Learners

Model Thinking Aloud Some students may confuse the meaning of the word *sum* with the meaning of *some.* Write 5 + 9 = 14 and 4 + 10 = 14 on the board. 14 is the total or the *sum* of 5 + 9 and 4 + 10. The total or sum of 5 + 9 and 4 + 10 is the same. They both equal 14. Circulate as students work on 8 + 9. Have them verbalize their thoughts and explain their reasoning. Listen for correct usage of the term *sum* in their explanations.

Additional Resource

Student Math Handbook

Game: *Plus 9 or 10 Bingo* SMH G11

Materials: Primary Number Cards, two kinds of counters, M11

Variation: Play on teams of two. Team members can work together to complete turns.

Practice

30 MIN PAIRS

Sorting and Solving Addition Combinations

Use anytime after Session 2.2.

Math Focus Points

- Developing fluency with the plus 9 and remaining combinations

Materials: students' sets of Addition Combination Cards (1 set per pair), blank paper, R68

Name Date

Partners, Teams, and Paper Clips

Sorting and Solving Addition Combinations

Choose 3 pairs of problems that might be hard for you to remember.

Answers will vary for Problems 1–3. Review students' work.

4 + 7 7 + 4	4 + 8 8 + 4	5 + 7 7 + 5
5 + 8 8 + 5	7 + 9 9 + 7	6 + 8 8 + 6

1. ________ is hard for me to remember.
Here is a clue that can help me:

2. ________ is hard for me to remember.
Here is a clue that can help me:

3. ________ is hard for me to remember.
Here is a clue that can help me:

R68 Unit 8 Use anytime after Session 2.2.

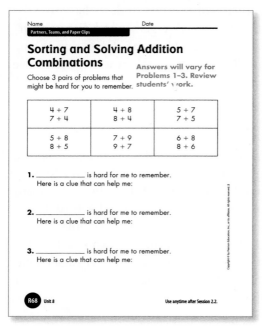

Explain that students will practice addition combinations with emphasis on the Plus 9 and remaining combinations. Have each student fold a sheet of paper in half vertically, twice, and then in half horizontally, once, to make 8 boxes. Ask them to label each box with 1 of the addition combination categories:

Plus 1 Plus 2 Doubles

Doubles plus or minus 1

Make 10 Plus 10 Plus 9

Remaining Combinations

Each pair of students will only need one set of their Addition Combination Cards.

Students shuffle the cards and turn them facedown in a pile. Partners take turns turning one card over at a time. Both partners write the combination and sum in the appropriate box on their papers. They compare to see if they both placed them in the same category and got the same sum.

Give students about 15 minutes to work. Then gather students to discuss their progress. Draw 8 columns on the board and label them with the addition combination categories. Who has an equation for [plus 1 combinations]? Write students' equations in the appropriate columns.

Ask students to explain their reasoning and talk about how they remember the sums, especially for the 7 remaining combinations. They can continue sorting and solving the combinations as time allows.

Distribute copies of Sorting and Solving Addition Combinations (R68).

ELL English Language Learners

Model Thinking Aloud Model your thinking for how to determine which category an addition combination belongs to. I chose the combination 2 + 3. I know that 2 + 2 is a doubles fact. So, I can use the doubles fact, 2 + 2, and add to get 2 + 3. The combination 2 + 3 belongs in the doubles plus or minus 1 category.

Additional Resource

Student Math Handbook pages 51–53

Extension

30 MIN PAIRS

More *Plus 9 or 10 Bingo*

Use anytime after Session 2.1.

Math Focus Points

- Relating unknown combinations to known combinations
- Developing fluency with the plus 9 and remaining combinations

Vocabulary: sum, vertical, horizontal, diagonal

Materials: counters (72 per pair), Primary Number Cards (1 deck per group), M11 (1 per group), R69

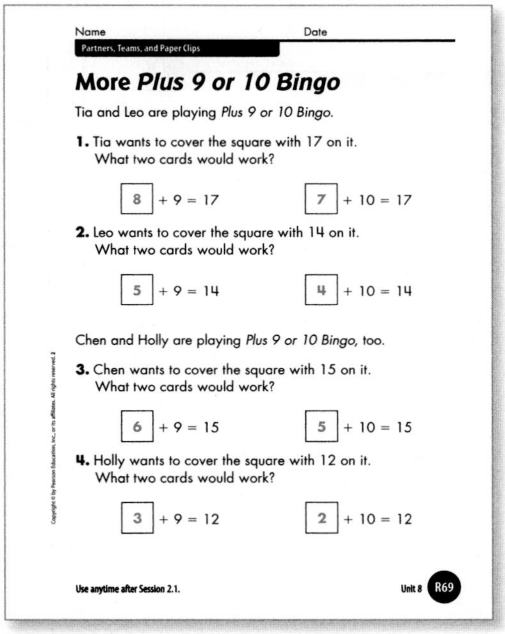

Name Date

Partners, Teams, and Paper Clips

More *Plus 9 or 10 Bingo*

Tia and Leo are playing *Plus 9 or 10 Bingo.*

1. Tia wants to cover the square with 17 on it. What two cards would work?

   8 + 9 = 17 7 + 10 = 17

2. Leo wants to cover the square with 14 on it. What two cards would work?

   5 + 9 = 14 4 + 10 = 14

Chen and Holly are playing *Plus 9 or 10 Bingo,* too.

3. Chen wants to cover the square with 15 on it. What two cards would work?

   6 + 9 = 15 5 + 10 = 15

4. Holly wants to cover the square with 12 on it. What two cards would work?

   3 + 9 = 12 2 + 10 = 12

Use anytime after Session 2.1. Unit 8 R69

Students play a variation of *Plus 9 or 10 Bingo* in which students must cover the entire gameboard with counters. Briefly review the original rules to *Plus 9 or 10 Bingo* and explain the new rules. Just like the old version of *Plus 9 or 10 Bingo,* players turn over number cards, add 9 or 10, and cover the sums with counters. In this version, players must cover the entire gameboard with counters instead of just 1 vertical, horizontal, or diagonal row.

Distribute a deck of Primary Number Cards, a copy of the *Plus 9 or 10 Bingo* Gameboard (M11), and counters to pairs. Have partners play the new version of the game for 15–20 minutes, saving at least 5 minutes at the end of class for discussion.

How did you decide which square to cover? What card did you need to pick to cover the 9 square? Why was there only 1 possible card you could pick to cover the 9? What card did you need to pick to cover the 20 square? Why was there only 1 possible card you could pick to cover the 20?

Students might say:

"If you want to cover a 9 square, you have to pick a 0 card because only 0 + 9 = 9."

"To cover the 20 square, you have to pick a 10 card and add 10 to it. You can't pick a 9 card because that's too little."

Distribute copies of More *Plus 9 or 10 Bingo* (R69).

ELL English Language Learners

Provide a Word List Students may need support using math vocabulary. Post a word list on the wall to which they can refer during discussion. Include the words *vertical, horizontal, diagonal,* and *sum* on the list. Check students' understanding of these words. Be sure that students are not confusing the meaning of *sum* with that of *some.*

Additional Resource

Student Math Handbook pages 51–52

Differentiation in Investigation 3

Mathematics in This Investigation

The mathematics focuses on making sense of and developing strategies to solve subtraction problems with totals to 100.

Understanding the Mathematics

Students understand what is being asked in a subtraction problem. They accurately and efficiently solve the problem choosing from a variety of strategies including subtracting one number in parts, adding up, or subtracting back to find the difference. They show flexibility in their strategy use, depending on the numbers they are working with. They use a variety of tools (e.g., stickers, a number line), to show their work.

Option: Assign the **Extension** activity.

Partially Understanding the Mathematics

Students recognize subtraction situations and are able to articulate what a problem is asking. They tend to rely on the same strategy to solve any problem. They may also make minor computational errors.

Option: Assign the **Practice** activity.

Not Understanding the Mathematics

Students use inefficient and error-prone strategies to solve problems. They may directly model the problems with ones and then count back by ones to solve it. They may lose track and make computational errors.

Option: Assign the **Intervention** activity.

Investigation 3 Quiz

In addition to your observations and students' work in Investigation 3, the Quiz (R70) can be used to gather more information.

Name Date

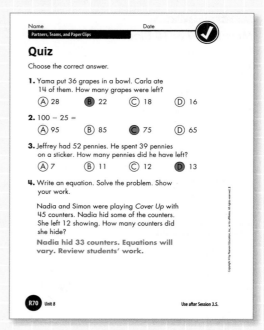

Partners, Teams, and Paper Clips

Quiz

Choose the correct answer.

1. Yama put 36 grapes in a bowl. Carla ate 14 of them. How many grapes were left?
   Ⓐ 28 Ⓑ 22 Ⓒ 18 Ⓓ 16
2. 100 − 25 =
   Ⓐ 95 Ⓑ 85 Ⓒ 75 Ⓓ 65
3. Jeffrey had 52 pennies. He spent 39 pennies on a sticker. How many pennies did he have left?
   Ⓐ 7 Ⓑ 11 Ⓒ 12 Ⓓ 13
4. Write an equation. Solve the problem. Show your work.

   Nadia and Simon were playing *Cover Up* with 45 counters. Nadia hid some of the counters. She left 12 showing. How many counters did she hide?

   Nadia hid 33 counters. Equations will vary. Review students' work.

Copyright © by Pearson Education, Inc., or its affiliates. All rights reserved. 2

R70 Unit 8 Use after Session 3.5.

Intervention

35 MIN PAIRS

Modeling Paper Clip Problems

Use anytime after Session 3.1.

Math Focus Points

- Subtracting amounts from 100

Materials: paper clips (100 per pair), connecting cubes organized into single color towers of 10 (10 towers per pair), M14–M16

Briefly review Pinching Paper Clips from Session 3.1. Show students a box of 100 paper clips. Do you remember what we did in Pinching Paper Clips? We started with a box of 100 paper clips, pinched some out of the box, and then found out how many paper clips were left in the box. We will solve another problem like that now.

Distribute cubes. Let's use these cubes to show the paper clip problem. Each cube represents 1 paper clip. Take 100 cubes and organize them into a 10 × 10 array. Display a box of 100 paper clips. Ask a student to pinch some of them and count them aloud. [Darren] pinched [22] paper clips. With the cubes, show how many paper clips [Darren] pinched. Verify that students removed [2] towers of 10 and [2] singles.

How can you use the cubes to figure out how many paper clips are left in the box? On the board, write 100 − [22] = ______.

Have partners count the remaining cubes. Then together as a group, count one set of cubes to verify that there are [78] cubes. So if [Darren] pinched [22] paper clips, how many are left in the box? Write the difference in the equation on the board.

Display one grid from Pages in a Sticker Book (M16). We can think of this as a picture of our 100 cubes. This grid has 10 rows of 10 squares. How many squares should I shade to show the [22] that [Darren] pinched? Demonstrate shading the grid. Label the section [22].

How can we use this grid to find how many paper clips are left in the box? Ask a student to demonstrate how to count the remaining squares and label this section [78]. Write 100 − [22] = [78] below the grid.

Distribute a box of paper clips to each pair and a copy of Pinching Paper Clips (M14–M15) and M16 to each student. For 15–20 minutes, have partners work together to generate, model, and solve Pinching Paper Clips problems.

- Partner A pinches some paper clips out of a box of 100.
- Both partners enter the number on M14–M15.
- Partner B uses cubes to show the problem.
- Both partners shade a grid on M16 to show the problem. They label each part of the grid then write the equation beneath it.
- Partners solve the problem together and record their work on M14–M15.
- Partners switch roles and solve a new problem.

Bring students together in the last 5–10 minutes of the activity to discuss how they figured out the number of paper clips left in the box.

ELL English Language Learners

Rephrase Explain the steps in this activity a second time using terminology that is more familiar to the student. The first partner pinches or *takes* some paper clips. *Write* the number of paper clips [he] *took* on this line. *Color* in the *squares* to show the cubes. Now it is your turn. Model each step as you explain it.

Additional Resource

Student Math Handbook pages 67–68

Practice

25 MIN INDIVIDUALS

Subtraction Problems: Starting with 100

Use anytime after Session 3.2.

Math Focus Points

- Visualizing, retelling, and modeling the action of subtraction situations

Materials: connecting cubes organized into single color towers of 10, M16, M17, R71

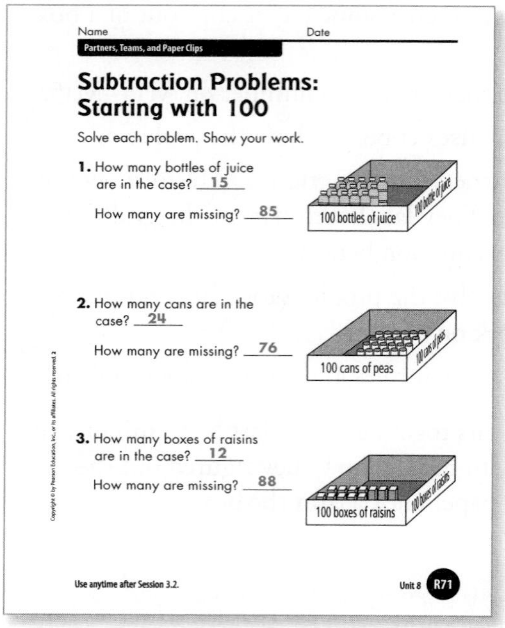
Name Date

Partners, Teams, and Paper Clips

Subtraction Problems: Starting with 100

Solve each problem. Show your work.

1. How many bottles of juice are in the case? 15
   How many are missing? 85
2. How many cans are in the case? 24
   How many are missing? 76
3. How many boxes of raisins are in the case? 12
   How many are missing? 88

100 bottles of juice
100 cans of peas
100 boxes of raisins

Use anytime after Session 3.2. Unit 8 R71

Write the following problem on the board and read it aloud. A store had a case of 100 bottles of juice. Many people bought them. After a few days, there were only 19 bottles of juice left. How many bottles of juice did the store sell?

Ask a volunteer to retell the story. What information do we know? What do we need to find out? Post a list of the information given in the problem. Draw a diagram of the case of juice showing 19 left. Some people might write this equation to think about the problem, 100 − ______ = 19. Can someone explain how this equation represents the problem? Other people might write 19 + ______ = 100. How are they thinking about the problem?

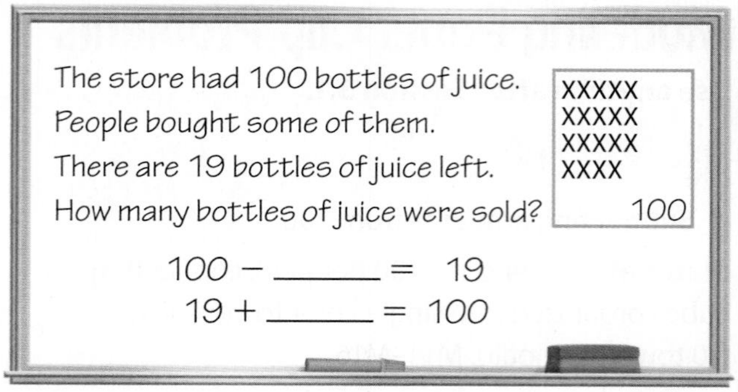
The store had 100 bottles of juice.
People bought some of them.
There are 19 bottles of juice left.
How many bottles of juice were sold?
XXXXX
XXXXX
XXXXX
XXXX
100
100 − ______ = 19
19 + ______ = 100

Students solve the problem. Provide cubes, 100 Grids (M16), and 100 Charts (M17). They record their work and write an equation. When finished, discuss strategies. How did you solve the problem?

Students might say:

"I shaded in 19 squares on a 100 chart. Those were for the juice boxes left. Then I counted the other squares and got 81."

"I counted up to 100. 19 + 1 is 20 then 20 plus 80 is 100. So that's 81 bottles of juice."

As students share, draw diagrams and write equations to illustrate their strategies. Present a new problem for them to solve by changing the number of juice bottles left. Then distribute copies of Subtraction Problems: Starting with 100 (R71).

ELL English Language Learners

Rephrase Some English Language Learners may be intimidated by the length of the story problem. Rephrase the problem giving only the necessary information. A store had 100 bottles of juice. Some bottles of juice were sold. Now there are only 19 bottles left. How many bottles of juice were sold?

Additional Resource

Student Math Handbook pages 67–68, 70

Extension

25 MIN GROUPS

Visualizing Problems, Writing Equations

Use anytime after Session 3.2.

Math Focus Points

- Visualizing, retelling, and modeling the action of subtraction situations
- Representing the action of subtraction situations using notation (−, +, =)

Materials: connecting cubes, M17 (as needed), R72

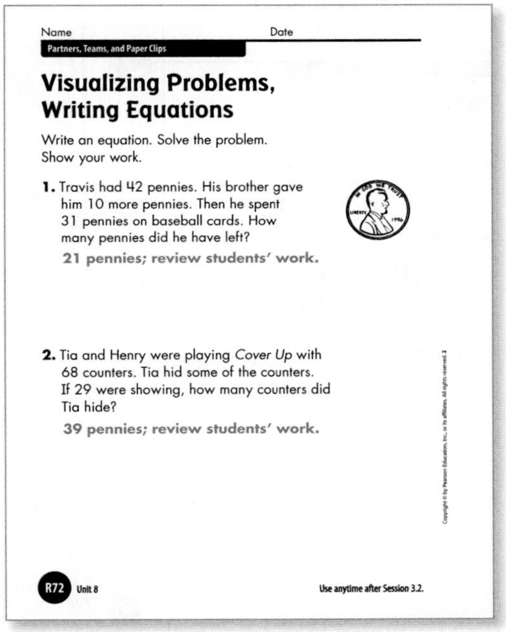
Name Date

Partners, Teams, and Paper Clips

Visualizing Problems, Writing Equations

Write an equation. Solve the problem. Show your work.

1. Travis had 42 pennies. His brother gave him 10 more pennies. Then he spent 31 pennies on baseball cards. How many pennies did he have left?
   21 pennies; review students' work.

2. Tia and Henry were playing *Cover Up* with 68 counters. Tia hid some of the counters. If 29 were showing, how many counters did Tia hide?
   39 pennies; review students' work.

R72 Unit 8 Use anytime after Session 3.2.

Read the following problem to students. Juanita had 87 pennies. She spent 22 pennies on a pencil and 54 pennies on a pen. How many pennies did she have left?

Follow the established story problem routine. Visualize the actions taking place in the story. What information is the problem giving us? What do we need to find out?

Ask students to solve the problem. Give them about 5 minutes to work and then call them back together. How did you solve the problem?

Students might say:

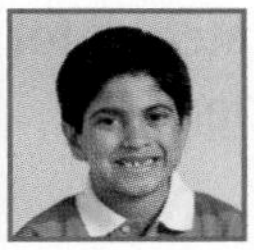

"First I subtracted 87 − 22. That equals 65. Then I subtracted 65 − 54. That equals 11, so Juanita had 11 pennies left."

"I added 22 + 54 and got 76. That's what Juanita spent. Then I subtracted 87 − 76 and got 11."

Record the equations that match each strategy.

$87 - 22 = 65$	$22 + 54 = 76$
$65 - 54 = 11$	$87 - 76 = 11$

Have students solve another problem and write an equation. Leigh and Alberto were playing *Cover Up* with 92 counters. Leigh hid some of the counters. If 16 were showing, how many counters did Leigh hide? After students finish, have them share their strategies. Then distribute copies of Visualizing Problems, Writing Equations (R72).

ELL English Language Learners

Provide Sentence Stems Some students may benefit from having a model to help record the known information and determine which value they are trying to find. For these students, provide sentence stems. For example:

- Juanita had ______ pennies. She spent ______ pennies. Now she has ______ pennies.
- Leigh and Alberto had ______ counters. They hid ______ counters. Now they have ______ counters.

Additional Resource

Student Math Handbook pages 71–75

Differentiation in Investigation 4

Mathematics in This Investigation

The mathematics focuses on developing strategies for adding 2-digit numbers accurately and efficiently.

Understanding the Mathematics

Students interpret an addition story problem, write an equation, and choose from a variety of strategies to accurately and efficiently solve it. They may add by place, keep one number whole, or change the numbers often selecting a strategy based on the numbers and the problem situation. They use a variety of tools (e.g., stickers, a number line) to show their work.

Option: Assign the **Extension** activity.

Partially Understanding the Mathematics

Students interpret and solve addition problems but may make minor computational errors in their work. They may not have a variety of strategies to choose from to solve any problem.

Option: Assign the **Practice** activity.

Not Understanding the Mathematics

Students do not have efficient strategies for solving addition problems. They may count on by ones to solve a problem and make computational errors because they lose track of their count.

Option: Assign the **Intervention** activity.

Investigation 4 Quiz

In addition to your observations and students' work in Investigation 4, the Quiz (R73) can be used to gather more information.

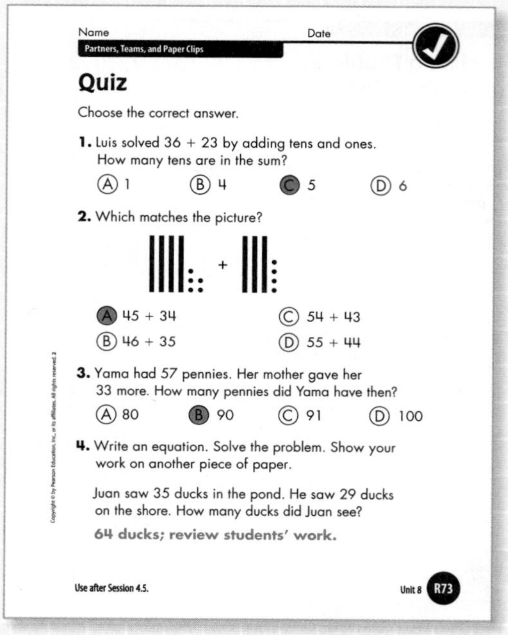

Name Date

Partners, Teams, and Paper Clips

Quiz

Choose the correct answer.

1. Luis solved 36 + 23 by adding tens and ones. How many tens are in the sum?

   (A) 1 (B) 4 (C) 5 (D) 6

2. Which matches the picture?

   (A) 45 + 34 (C) 54 + 43
   (B) 46 + 35 (D) 55 + 44

3. Yama had 57 pennies. Her mother gave her 33 more. How many pennies did Yama have then?

   (A) 80 (B) 90 (C) 91 (D) 100

4. Write an equation. Solve the problem. Show your work on another piece of paper.

   Juan saw 35 ducks in the pond. He saw 29 ducks on the shore. How many ducks did Juan see?

   64 ducks; review students' work.

Use after Session 4.5. Unit 8 R73

Intervention

30 MIN PAIRS

Using Different Addition Strategies

Use anytime after Session 4.1.

Math Focus Points

- Visualizing, retelling, and modeling the action of addition situations
- Representing the action of addition situations using notation (+, =)

Materials: connecting cubes organized into single color towers of 10 (7 per student)

Read the following problem aloud. Carolina had 37 rocks in her collection. Her brother gave her 25 more rocks. How many rocks did Carolina have in all? Ask students to visualize the action and retell the story. Identify and record the known and unknown information

Distribute cubes and have students model the addends. Show the number of rocks Carolina had. How many towers of 10 is that? How many single cubes? Now show the number of rocks her brother gave her. Verify this number in tens and ones. Record these two amounts on the board using sticker notation.

We can add numbers by grouping the tens and the ones. How many tens in 37? In 25? How many tens in all? What equation shows this? Record $30 + 20 = 50$. Repeat these questions for grouping the ones.

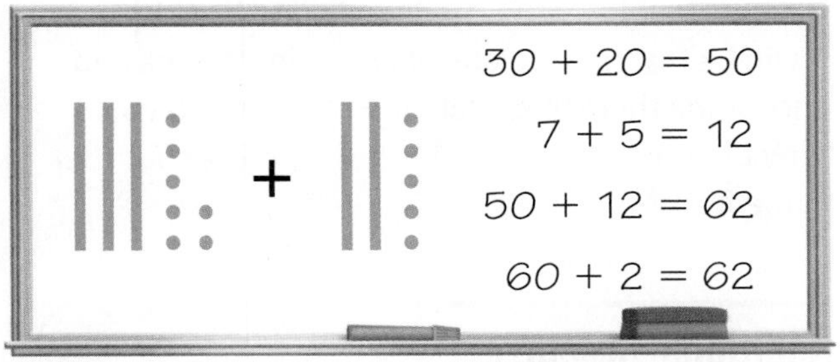

Now we have 5 tens and 12 ones. Do you have enough ones to make a tower of 10? If so, snap them together. How many towers of 10 do you have? How many singles? How many rocks does Carolina have? Record $60 + 2 = 62$. Ask students to explain how they know there are 62 cubes. Depending on your students, either practice combining tens and ones with a new problem or practice keeping one number whole and adding on the other, using the same problem.

We can also add two numbers by keeping one number whole and adding the other on in parts. With cubes, show me how many rocks Carolina started with. Now add on the rocks her brother gave her. How many was that? Let's add on 10 at a time.

Record $37 + 10 = 47$ and $47 + 10 = 57$ asking students to verify each total. We have added on 20 so far. How many rocks are left? Record $57 + 5 =$ ____ and ask students how they would figure this out before filling in the total.

Let's look at the equations. Where is the number of rocks Carolina started with? Where are the 25 her brother gave her? Record $10 + 10 + 5 = 25$ as you point out these amounts in each equation. Where is the answer to the problem?

Compare the different strategies. Which strategy seems easiest and most efficient for you? Point out that no matter which strategy is used, the answer remains the same. Provide similar problems for pairs to solve. Remind students to show their work using equations. Discuss strategies for each problem.

ELL English Language Learners

Provide a Word List Post a chart showing the different strategies students used in this activity. Use sticker notation and equations to match the steps. Encourage students to refer to this chart if they need support explaining their methods.

Additional Resource

Student Math Handbook pages 63–66

Practice

25 MIN INDIVIDUALS

Adding on Tens and Ones

Use anytime after Session 4.2.

Math Focus Points

- Adding 2-digit numbers by keeping one number whole

Materials: connecting cubes organized into single color towers of 10, pocket 100 chart, M17, R74

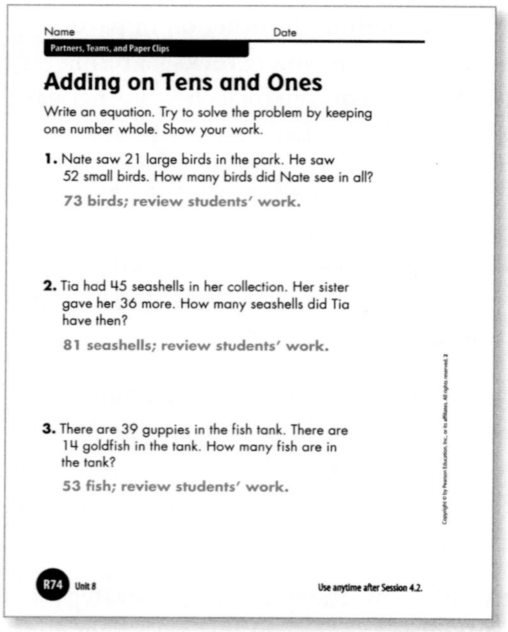
Name Date
Partners, Teams, and Paper Clips

Adding on Tens and Ones

Write an equation. Try to solve the problem by keeping one number whole. Show your work.

1. Nate saw 21 large birds in the park. He saw 52 small birds. How many birds did Nate see in all?
   73 birds; review students' work.

2. Tia had 45 seashells in her collection. Her sister gave her 36 more. How many seashells did Tia have then?
   81 seashells; review students' work.

3. There are 39 guppies in the fish tank. There are 14 goldfish in the tank. How many fish are in the tank?
   53 fish; review students' work.

R74 Unit 8 Use anytime after Session 4.2.

In this activity, students practice solving addition problems by keeping one addend whole and adding the other number in parts. Read the following problem aloud to students. Alberto saw 46 butterflies in the butterfly house. Chen saw 37 butterflies. How many butterflies did Alberto and Chen see in all?

Ask students to visualize the action. Are groups being combined or separated? Review the important information and write an equation on the board: $46 + 37 =$ ______. Ask a student to represent each addend with cubes.

Today we are going to practice the addition strategy of keeping one number whole and adding the other one in parts. Does it matter if we keep 46 whole and add on 37 or if we keep 37 whole and add on 46? Demonstrate adding by keeping one number whole. We'll keep 46 whole and add 37 in parts. What part of 37 should we add first? Some students might suggest adding on 4 from the 37 to get to 50 and then add on the remaining 33 either in parts or whole ($50 + 33$). Other students are likely to suggest adding the 37 on by breaking it into 10s (30) and 1s (7). Use cubes to demonstrate both of these ways of adding on the 37. Record each using equations.

How can you use a 100 chart to add 46 and 37 using this strategy?

Students might say:

"Move 3 rows down from 46. Now you're at 76. Then move 7 squares forward. That's $76 + 7$. That's 83 in all."

Demonstrate methods students suggest on the class 100 chart.

Give students similar problems to solve on their own using the strategy of keeping one number whole. Remind them to record their work using equations. Supply cubes and copies of the 100 Chart (M17), as needed. Then distribute copies of Adding on Tens and Ones (R74).

ELL English Language Learners

Model Thinking Aloud While modeling strategies, explain your thinking to students. I could count on by ones, but if I count on by tens and then by ones, it will be faster. Circulate while students work and encourage them to explain their thinking to you. Why did you add [3] tens? Where did that number come from?

Additional Resource

Student Math Handbook pages 63–66

Extension

25 MIN GROUPS

Two-Digit Addition Challenges

Use anytime after Session 4.2.

Math Focus Points

- Developing efficient methods for adding and notating strategies

Materials: connecting cubes, M17, R75

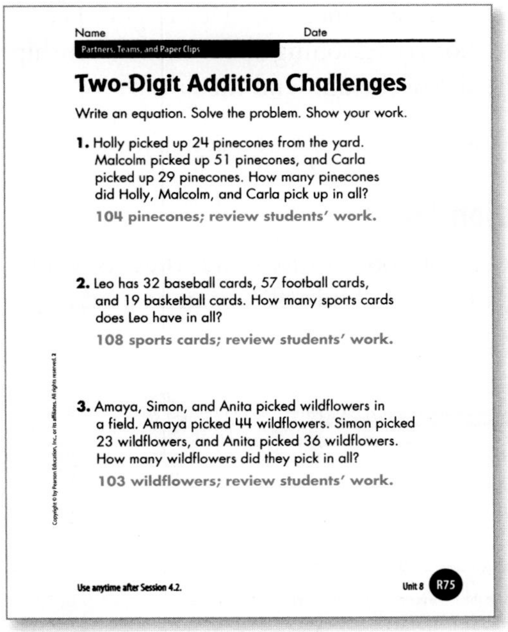

Name Date

Partners, Teams, and Paper Clips

Two-Digit Addition Challenges

Write an equation. Solve the problem. Show your work.

1. Holly picked up 24 pinecones from the yard. Malcolm picked up 51 pinecones, and Carla picked up 29 pinecones. How many pinecones did Holly, Malcolm, and Carla pick up in all?
104 pinecones; review students' work.

2. Leo has 32 baseball cards, 57 football cards, and 19 basketball cards. How many sports cards does Leo have in all?
108 sports cards; review students' work.

3. Amaya, Simon, and Anita picked wildflowers in a field. Amaya picked 44 wildflowers. Simon picked 23 wildflowers, and Anita picked 36 wildflowers. How many wildflowers did they pick in all?
103 wildflowers; review students' work.

Copyright © by Pearson Education, Inc., or its affiliates. All rights reserved. 2

Use anytime after Session 4.2. Unit 8 R75

This activity gives students an opportunity to solve more challenging problems. Students will be working with 3 addends and sums to 110.

Read the following problem aloud. A second-grade class collected 28 cans for recycling. A third-grade class collected 41 cans, and a fourth-grade class collected 40 cans. How many cans did all 3 classes collect?

Ask a student to retell the problem while you write the important information on the board.

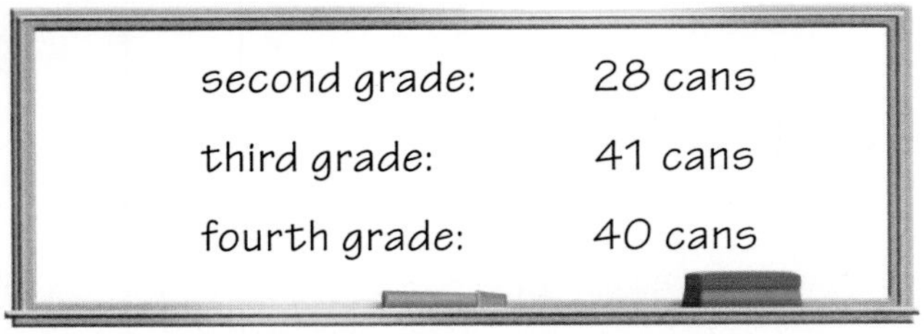

Point out that this problem has 3 addends. Have a volunteer write an equation for the problem. Ask students whether or not they think the order of the addends matters when solving the problem.

Students solve the problem individually and record their work. When they have finished, bring them together for discussion. How did you solve the problem?

Students might say:

"I added all the tens together first. 20 + 40 + 40. That's 100. Then I added the ones. 8 + 1 = 9. The answer is 109."

"I started with 28 and counted on 4 tens and then 4 more tens. That was 108. Then I added on 1 more because of the 1 in 41. That made 109."

Have students demonstrate their strategies using a 100 Chart (M17) or connecting cubes. You can provide more problems for students by changing the numbers in the original story, keeping sums to 110 or less. Supply cubes and additional 100 charts, as needed.

Distribute copies of Two-Digit Addition Challenges (R75).

ELL English Language Learners

Use Repetition Students may need support solving a multistep problem like this one. Ask questions that help them focus on the information needed to solve the problem. How many cans did the second-grade class collect? How many cans did the third-grade class collect? How many cans did the fourth-grade class collect? What operation do you use to find the total number of cans collected?

Additional Resource

Student Math Handbook pages 63–66

Differentiation in Investigation 1

Mathematics in This Investigation

The mathematics focuses on understanding and measuring length accurately using nonstandard units.

Understanding the Mathematics

Students accurately use nonstandard units to measure the length of objects by counting how many unit lengths match the length of the object. They choose an appropriate unit to use and iterate it along the length to measure. They recognize that measuring the same length with larger units yields smaller counts and reason about sources of measurement errors.

Option: Assign the **Extension** activity.

Partially Understanding the Mathematics

Students measure length using nonstandard units by iterating a single unit or by joining several units along the length. They may make some errors because of the choice of measuring unit. They may also line up the units incorrectly or they lose track of the number of units counted.

Option: Assign the **Practice** activity.

Not Understanding the Mathematics

Students do not consistently identify the length of an object. When asked to measure length, they may be unsure which side of the object they should measure. They may or may not use a single unit to iterate and may often struggle with keeping track of the beginning and end of the unit. They have difficulty understanding why it is important not to leave gaps or overlap the unit and measure in a straight line. Students are not yet reasoning about the relationship between the size of the unit and the number of units.

Option: Assign the **Intervention** activity.

Investigation 1 Quiz

In addition to your observations and students' work in Investigation 1, the Quiz (R76) can be used to gather more information.

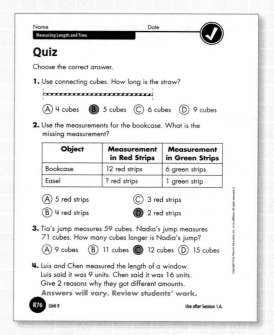

Name Date

Measuring Length and Time

Quiz

Choose the correct answer.

1. Use connecting cubes. How long is the straw?

Ⓐ 4 cubes Ⓑ 5 cubes Ⓒ 6 cubes Ⓓ 9 cubes

2. Use the measurements for the bookcase. What is the missing measurement?

Object	Measurement in Red Strips	Measurement in Green Strips
Bookcase	12 red strips	6 green strips
Easel	? red strips	1 green strip

Ⓐ 5 red strips Ⓒ 3 red strips
Ⓑ 4 red strips Ⓓ 2 red strips

3. Tia's jump measures 59 cubes. Nadia's jump measures 71 cubes. How many cubes longer is Nadia's jump?

Ⓐ 9 cubes Ⓑ 11 cubes Ⓒ 12 cubes Ⓓ 15 cubes

4. Luis and Chen measured the length of a window. Luis said it was 9 units. Chen said it was 16 units. Give 2 reasons why they got different amounts.

Answers will vary. Review students' work.

R76 Unit 9 Use after Session 1.6.

Copyright © by Pearson Education, Inc., or its affiliates. All rights reserved. 2

Intervention

20 MIN INDIVIDUALS

Blue and Yellow Strips

Use anytime after Session 1.2.

Math Focus Points

- Iterating units to measure length
- Estimating and calculating length using units that are related by a 2:1 ratio
- Identifying strategies for accurate measurement

Vocabulary: measure, width, length, estimate

Materials: 6-inch blue strips and 3-inch yellow strips (from Session 1.2)

On the board, list three things to measure. Some suggestions are given below.

Objects to Measure:

width of your student desk

width of door

length (from top to bottom) of your math book

Today we will measure objects using your blue and yellow strips. Begin by using the blue strips to measure the width of your desk. How you will start to measure?

Students might say:

"I will start along this side. I need to line up the end of the blue strip with the edge of the desk."

"I will place the first strip. Then I need to put the second strip next to the first one without any space or overlap."

Have students measure the width of a desk with their blue strips. Make sure they know how to continue measuring if they run out of strips. Then ask a volunteer to share his or her measurement. Write the measurement on the board next to the name of the object.

How many yellow strips long do you think your desk will measure? How can you estimate? After students brainstorm ideas, have students place 2 or 3 yellow strips and then predict the total number that will fit across. Now measure the width of your desk with yellow strips. Where will you start measuring? After students have found the measurement, have a volunteer write the measurement on the board. Have students look at how the two measurements for the desk are related. So the desk measured about 6 blue strips and 12 yellow strips. What do you notice about these two numbers?

Students measure the other objects listed on the board with blue strips and record their measurements.

Without using any strips, can you predict the results if you measured with only the yellow strips? Suppose a box is close to 3 blue strips long. What would be its length in yellow strips?

Now measure the other objects with the yellow strips. How good were your predictions? Because the objects might be a little longer or shorter than an exact number of blue strips, the answers using yellow strips might vary from double the number of blue strips. Discuss students' estimates and measurements. Make sure to emphasize the 2:1 ratio and that the smaller the unit the bigger the number.

ELL English Language Learners

Rephrase You may need to rephrase questions using words or phrases that are more familiar to students. For example, instead of *estimate* you might say *predict* or *make a smart guess.*

Additional Resource

Student Math Handbook pages 146–148

Practice

25 MIN PAIRS

Find the Object

Use anytime after Session 1.2.

Math Focus Points

- Iterating units to measure length
- Estimating and calculating length using units that are related by a 2:1 ratio
- Identifying strategies for accurate measurement

Vocabulary: measure, length, estimate

Materials: blank paper (1 sheet per pair), 6-inch blue strips and 3-inch yellow strips (from Session 1.2), R77

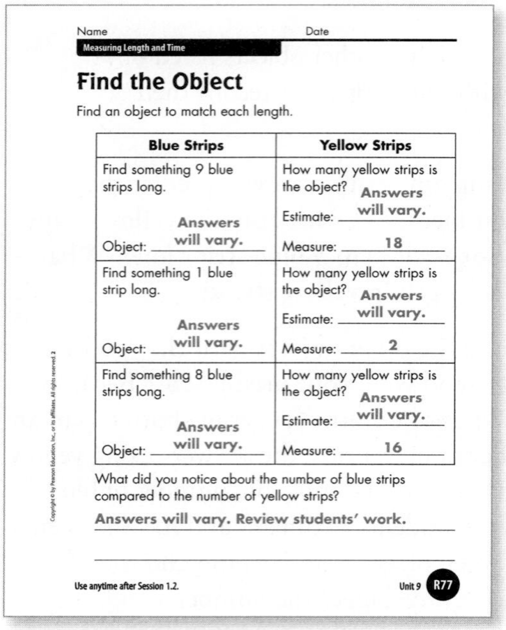
Name Date

Measuring Length and Time

Find the Object

Find an object to match each length.

Blue Strips	Yellow Strips
Find something 9 blue strips long. Object: **Answers will vary.**	How many yellow strips is the object? Estimate: **Answers will vary.** Measure: **18**
Find something 1 blue strip long. Object: **Answers will vary.**	How many yellow strips is the object? Estimate: **Answers will vary.** Measure: **2**
Find something 8 blue strips long. Object: **Answers will vary.**	How many yellow strips is the object? Estimate: **Answers will vary.** Measure: **16**

What did you notice about the number of blue strips compared to the number of yellow strips?

Answers will vary. Review students' work.

Use anytime after Session 1.2. Unit 9 R77

Length of whiteboard ______ blue strips	______ yellow strips
Length of window ______ blue strips	______ yellow strips
Find something 11 blue strips long. Object: ______	

On the board, draw a table similar to the one shown. You may wish to change the objects being measured based on your classroom.

Have pairs copy the table onto their pieces of paper. Work with your partner to fill in the missing measurements in the table. What do you need to be careful of when you measure a long object with your blue or yellow strips?

Students might say:

"I need to be sure that I put the strips end to end without space between."

"I need to make sure the strips are in a straight line."

Most students will have already recognized the 2-to-1 relationship that exists between the blue and yellow strips. Encourage groups to estimate the number of yellow strips before measuring.

After groups have completed the table, have volunteers share their measurements.

Distribute copies of Find the Object (R77).

ELL English Language Learners

Provide a Word List Write the following words on the board: *measure, length, estimate*. Review the meaning of each word and have students write a definition for each in their own words. As pairs work together, encourage students to use these words as much as possible.

Additional Resource

Student Math Handbook pages 146–148

Extension

15 MIN GROUPS

More Blue and Yellow Strips

Use anytime after Session 1.2.

Math Focus Points

- Using direct and indirect comparisons to identify equal lengths
- Iterating units to measure length
- Estimating and calculating length using units that are related by a 2:1 ratio
- Identifying strategies for accurate measurement

Vocabulary: measure

Materials: 6-inch blue strips and 3-inch yellow strips (from Session 1.2), R78

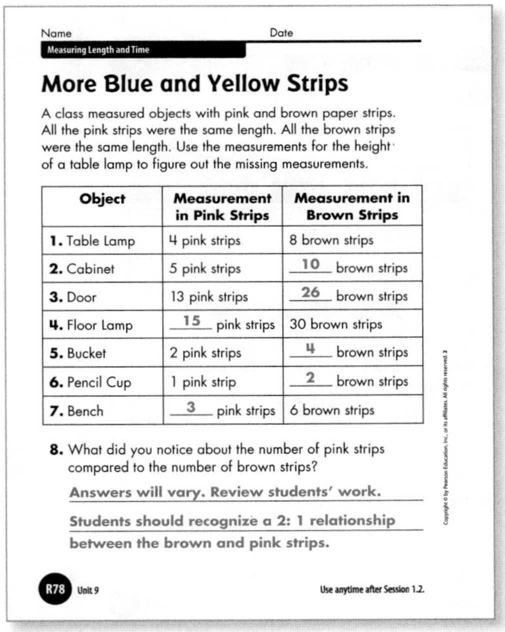

Name Date

Measuring Length and Time

More Blue and Yellow Strips

A class measured objects with pink and brown paper strips. All the pink strips were the same length. All the brown strips were the same length. Use the measurements for the height of a table lamp to figure out the missing measurements.

Object	Measurement in Pink Strips	Measurement in Brown Strips
1. Table Lamp	4 pink strips	8 brown strips
2. Cabinet	5 pink strips	10 brown strips
3. Door	13 pink strips	26 brown strips
4. Floor Lamp	15 pink strips	30 brown strips
5. Bucket	2 pink strips	4 brown strips
6. Pencil Cup	1 pink strip	2 brown strips
7. Bench	3 pink strips	6 brown strips

8. What did you notice about the number of pink strips compared to the number of brown strips?

Answers will vary. Review students' work.

Students should recognize a 2: 1 relationship between the brown and pink strips.

Copyright © by Pearson Education, Inc., or its affiliates. All rights reserved. 2

R78 Unit 9 Use anytime after Session 1.2.

Materials to Prepare: On the board, draw a 3-column table similar to the one shown below.

Things to Measure	Yellow Strips	Blue Strips
width of chalkboard		
height of door		
length of bookcase		

Today you will measure several things using the yellow and blue strips. Copy the table from the board. Choose two more things to measure and write them in the first column.

Some of the items are large. What can you do if you don't have enough strips?

Students might say:

"After we place the first 2 strips, we can move the first strip to the end of the second strip. We need to count each strip until we get to the end of what we're measuring."

"We can put a chalk mark or piece of tape after each strip and use the same strip over and over."

With your group, measure the items in the table with yellow strips. Then predict each length in blue strips. Finally, measure the object with blue strips. Discuss student predictions and compare measurements. For each object, the number of yellow strips should be about double the number of blue strips.

Distribute copies of More Blue and Yellow Strips (R78).

ELL English Language Learners

Suggest a Sequence Provide a format for sequencing the steps to compare the yellow strip measurements to the blue strip measurements.

1. Measure each object with the yellow strips.
2. Estimate the lengths of each item using the blue strips.
3. Measure each object with blue strips and compare.

Additional Resource

Student Math Handbook pages 146–149

Differentiation in Investigation 2

Mathematics in This Investigation

The mathematics focuses on understanding length and measuring accurately using standard units.

Understanding the Mathematics

Students recognize that the same count of different–sized units yields different lengths. They reason about measuring errors and articulate the need for using a common unit to measure accurately. They measure length accurately using standard units.

Option: Assign the **Extension** activity.

Partially Understanding the Mathematics

Students reason about measuring errors. They make slight errors when measuring using standard units either because they lose track iterating their unit or in their calculations.

Option: Assign the **Practice** activity.

Not Understanding the Mathematics

Students do not measure accurately because they do not measure in a straight line or because they do not iterate their measuring unit correctly and leave gaps or overlaps as they measure. Some students understand the basics of using a measuring tool but have difficulty measuring lengths longer than 12 inches.

Option: Assign the **Intervention** activity.

Investigation 2 Quiz

In addition to your observations and students' work in Investigation 2, the Quiz (R79) can be used to gather more information.

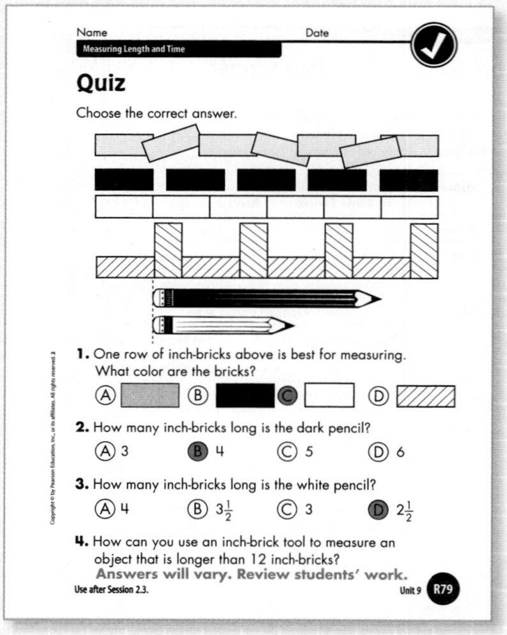

Name Date

Measuring Length and Time

Quiz

Choose the correct answer.

1. One row of inch-bricks above is best for measuring. What color are the bricks?

Ⓐ Ⓑ Ⓒ Ⓓ

2. How many inch-bricks long is the dark pencil?

Ⓐ 3 Ⓑ 4 Ⓒ 5 Ⓓ 6

3. How many inch-bricks long is the white pencil?

Ⓐ 4 Ⓑ $3\frac{1}{2}$ Ⓒ 3 Ⓓ $2\frac{1}{2}$

4. How can you use an inch-brick tool to measure an object that is longer than 12 inch-bricks?

Answers will vary. Review students' work.

Copyright © by Pearson Education, Inc., or its affiliates. All rights reserved. 2

Use after Session 2.3. Unit 9 R79

Intervention

20 MIN INDIVIDUALS

Using Inch-Bricks

Use anytime after Session 2.2.

Math Focus Points

- Identifying strategies for accurate measurement

Vocabulary: accurately

Materials: inch-brick tools (from Session 2.1)

Students having difficulty measuring with the inch-brick tool may benefit from measuring more objects that are less than 12 inches long. On the board, list three objects to measure.

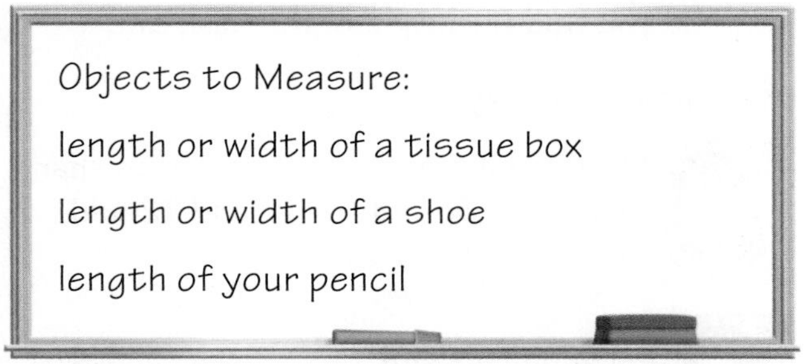

Today you will measure several more objects using the inch-brick tool. How can you measure more *accurately*? Accuracy is related to how well something is measured. If you measure with separate inch-bricks, rather than the inch-brick tool, do you think you will get the same answer?

Students might say:

"It is harder to keep the little bricks lined up, so the answer might be different than when I use the strip of inch-bricks."

"The tool is more accurate because the bricks are connected."

If students numbered their inch-brick tool from Session 2.1, they may be looking at the middle of each brick instead of the end. Check students' understanding by showing an object that is a little longer than a whole number of bricks, such as this crayon.

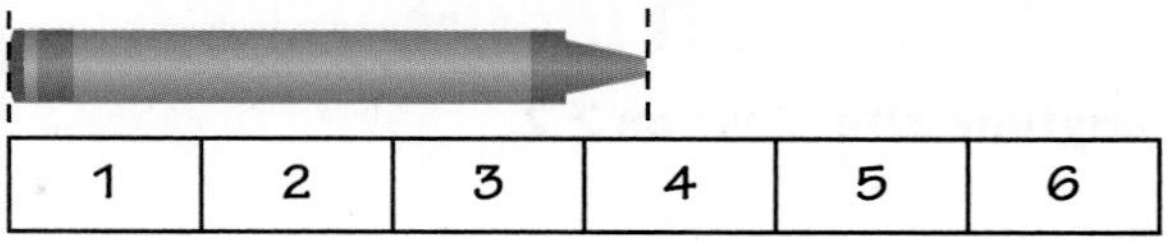

Remind students that the number in the middle tells how many whole units between the start of the first brick and the end of an inch-brick. So this crayon is closer to 3 inch-bricks long.

Measure the objects listed on the board. Measure carefully to the nearest inch-brick and record the lengths on the board.

When students have finished, ask comparison questions, such as the following. Which object is the shortest? How much longer is [the shoe] than [the tissue box]? How do you find the difference between the length of [the pencil] and the length of [the shoe]?

ELL English Language Learners

Suggest a Sequence Suggesting steps for the students to follow may help them measure an object using the inch-brick tool more accurately.

1. Line up the end of the tool with the end of the object.
2. Find the number of bricks that is closest to the end of the object.
3. Read the number on the inch-brick tool or count the number of bricks.

Additional Resource

Student Math Handbook page 152

Practice

20 MIN PAIRS

Measuring with Inch-Bricks

Use anytime after Session 2.2.

Math Focus Points

- Identifying strategies for accurate measurement
- Iterating a 12-inch measuring tool

Vocabulary: accurately

Materials: inch-brick tools (from Session 2.1), R80

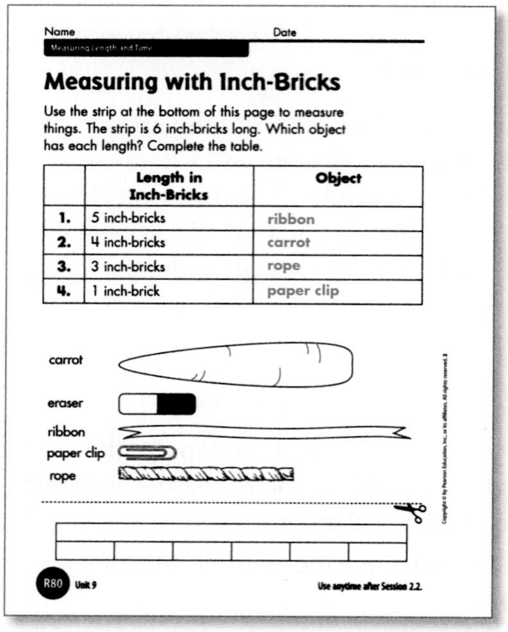

Name Date

Measuring Length and Time

Measuring with Inch-Bricks

Use the strip at the bottom of this page to measure things. The strip is 6 inch-bricks long. Which object has each length? Complete the table.

	Length in Inch-Bricks	Object
1.	5 inch-bricks	ribbon
2.	4 inch-bricks	carrot
3.	3 inch-bricks	rope
4.	1 inch-brick	paper clip

carrot

eraser

ribbon

paper clip

rope

R80 Unit 9 Use anytime after Session 2.2.

On the board, list several large objects that students can measure within the classroom.

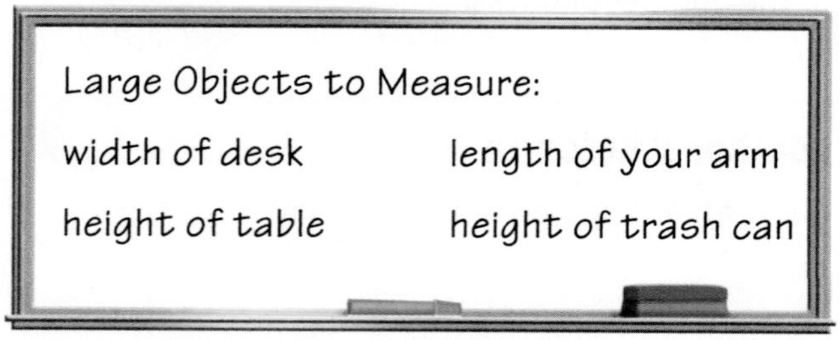

Today you will measure several large objects with your inch-brick tool. How can you measure more *accurately*? Accuracy is related to how well something is measured.

Work with your partner. Take turns measuring the objects listed on the board. Measure carefully to the nearest inch-brick.

When students have finished, write several of the measurements on the board and talk about the process. How did you measure when the inch-brick tool was not long enough? Discuss the process of marking the position of the end of the tool with a fingertip or a pencil mark and then picking up the tool and moving the zero point to the previous mark. Count how many times the tool is moved. If the last part to measure is less than the size of the tool, see how many more inch-bricks will fit in that part.

How did you find the height of the trash can?

Students might say:

"The height was just an inch less than two 12s. So I added 12 and 12 and then subtracted 1."

"I added 12 and 11 to get an answer of 23 inch-bricks."

Ask several comparison questions and discuss the answers. Which object is the longest? How much longer is [the desk] than [your arm]? How do you find the difference between two lengths?

Distribute copies of Measuring with Inch-Bricks (R80).

ELL English Language Learners

Provide a Word List Discuss the words *width, length,* and *height.* Write the words on chart paper and draw several examples of each. Post this list in the classroom for reference.

Additional Resource

Student Math Handbook pages 153, 155–156

Extension

20 MIN PAIRS

Fractions of Inch-Bricks

Use anytime after Session 2.2.

Math Focus Points

- Identifying strategies for accurate measurement

Vocabulary: accurately

Materials: inch-brick tools (from Session 2.1), R81

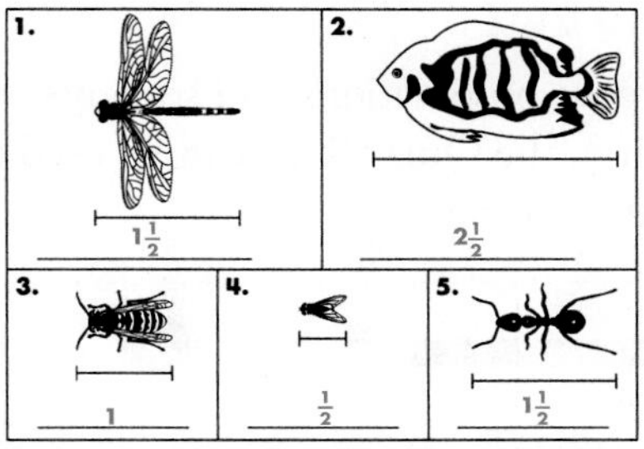

Name Date

Measuring Length and Time

Fractions of Inch-Bricks

Measure using the inch-brick tool.

1. $1\frac{1}{2}$
2. $2\frac{1}{2}$
3. 1
4. $\frac{1}{2}$
5. $1\frac{1}{2}$
6. Draw or trace around an object that is $3\frac{1}{2}$ inch-bricks long.
Review students' work.

Object: Answers will vary.

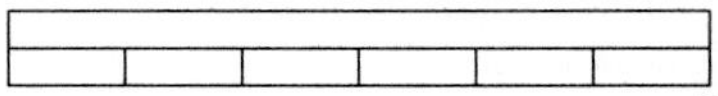

Use anytime after Session 2.2. Unit 9 R81

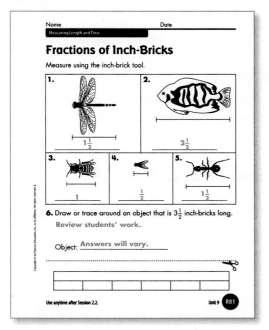

On the board, list several small objects that students can measure within the classroom.

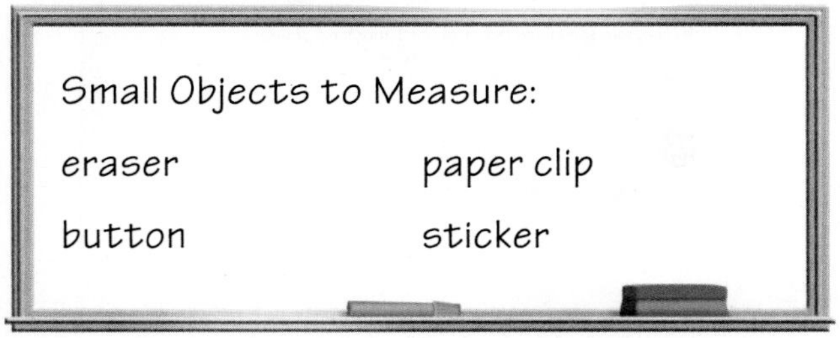

Today you will measure several small objects using your inch-brick tool. Hold up a small object that is about an inch long and another that is a little more than a half-inch long.

If you measure these objects to the nearest inch-brick, you find the same measurement for both. Are they the same length? Is there a better way to describe the lengths?

Students might say:

"I can use fractions because one object looks like it is only half as long as an inch-brick."

"I can say that an object is *more than* or *less than* an inch-brick."

Why is it helpful to use fractions when comparing some lengths? Discuss how fractions make the measurements more specific so that you can compare more easily. Remind students how to write the fraction one-half as $\frac{1}{2}$ and to write a mixed number such as one and one half as $1\frac{1}{2}$.

How can you measure more *accurately*? Accuracy is related to how well something is measured. Students may mention that you should line up the inch-bricks without leaving gaps and put them in a straight line. The measurement is also more accurate if you measure carefully to the nearest half-inch instead of the nearest inch.

Work with your partner. Take turns measuring the objects listed on the board. Measure carefully to the nearest half of an inch-brick. When students have finished, write several of the measurements on the board and compare them. Then distribute copies of Fractions of Inch-Bricks (R81).

ELL English Language Learners

Provide a Word List Encourage students to explain their thinking to each other as they are measuring. Suggest using words such as *closest to*, *more than*, *less than*, or *in the middle*. Review the meanings of each with students, as needed.

Additional Resource

Student Math Handbook pages 152–153

Differentiation in Investigation 3

Mathematics in This Investigation

The mathematics focuses on establishing the need for a common unit of measurement and measuring with, and comparing, U.S. and Metric units.

Understanding the Mathematics

Students make mathematical arguments to illustrate their reasoning about a measuring discrepancy and the need for a common unit of measurement. They measure accurately using both inches and centimeters and can easily measure longer lengths. They compare a variety of measuring tools and can articulate why different-sized units yield different counts.

Option: Assign the **Extension** activity.

Partially Understanding the Mathematics

Students measure accurately in inches and centimeters but may have difficulty keeping track of their work when measuring objects over 12 inches in length. They articulate that different-sized units yield different counts but may not be certain that this is always true.

Option: Assign the **Practice** activity.

Not Understanding the Mathematics

Students find lengths of objects in inches and in centimeters but their measurements are not accurate. They do not have a reliable strategy for measuring objects over 12 inches. They may say that measuring with centimeters gives a greater number but are not sure why. They have difficulty understanding that different-sized units yield different measurements (e.g., the smaller the unit, the higher the count).

Option: Assign the **Intervention** activity.

Investigation 3 Quiz

In addition to your observations and students' work in Investigation 3, the Quiz (R82) can be used to gather more information.

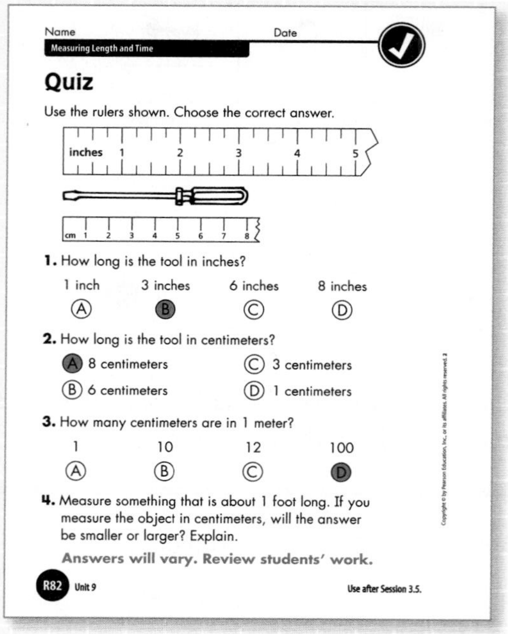
Name Date

Measuring Length and Time

Quiz

Use the rulers shown. Choose the correct answer.

1. How long is the tool in inches?

1 inch (A) 3 inches (B) 6 inches (C) 8 inches (D)

2. How long is the tool in centimeters?

(A) 8 centimeters (C) 3 centimeters
(B) 6 centimeters (D) 1 centimeters

3. How many centimeters are in 1 meter?

1 (A) 10 (B) 12 (C) 100 (D)

4. Measure something that is about 1 foot long. If you measure the object in centimeters, will the answer be smaller or larger? Explain.

Answers will vary. Review students' work.

Copyright © by Pearson Education, Inc., or its affiliates. All rights reserved. 2

R82 Unit 9 Use after Session 3.5.

Intervention

20 MIN INDIVIDUALS

Hand Measurements

Use anytime after Session 3.2.

Math Focus Points

- Solving comparison problems by finding the difference between two measurements
- Becoming familiar with the terms *inches*, *feet*, and *yards* as standard units of measure
- Using a ruler as a standard measuring tool

Vocabulary: inch

Materials: blank paper, crayons or markers (optional), 12-inch rulers, yardstick

Materials to Prepare: On the board, label two tracings of your hand as shown below.

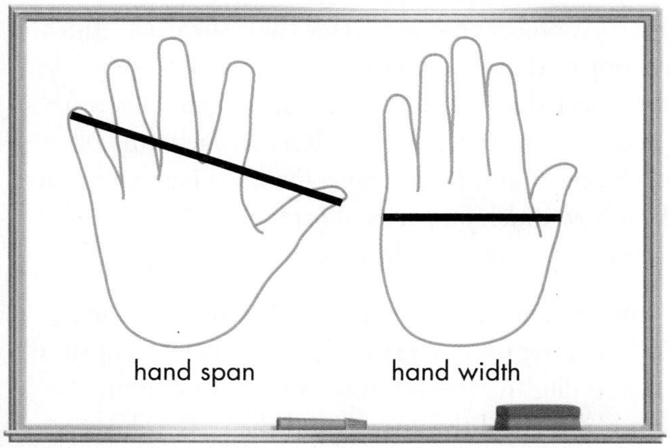

Distribute paper to each student and direct students' attention to the board. Trace around your hand two times. First, trace your hand with your fingers spread out as much as possible. Then trace your hand with your fingers close together. Suggest to students that they work with a partner to trace each other's hands. Students should use a pencil for the first tracings, although you may suggest that they later darken the line with a crayon or marker.

When your fingers are stretched apart, the distance from your thumb tip to the tip of your little (pinkie) finger is called your *hand span*. When your fingers are together, the distance from one side of your hand to the other is called your *hand width*.

Demonstrate how to use a ruler to draw a line showing your hand span and hand width. Label your drawing and have students do the same. Draw a line, and then measure your hand span and hand width in inches with your ruler. Review with students how to accurately measure with a ruler. Watch students to make sure they have measured starting with the correct end of the ruler. Students familiar with half-inch measurements may use fractions in their answers. How much wider is your hand span than your hand width? How can you find the answer?

Students might say:

"My hand span is 6 inches. My hand width is $3\frac{1}{2}$ inches. On the ruler, I see that the difference is $2\frac{1}{2}$ inches."

"I measured 5 inches and 3 inches. I can subtract $5 - 3$. My hand span is 2 inches wider than my hand width."

If students have difficulty finding the difference when one or both lengths involve a partial inch, suggest that they round the measurements to the nearest whole inch.

ELL English Language Learners

Model Thinking Aloud For students having difficulty finding the difference between their hand span and hand width, model your thinking aloud. First, I measured my hand span. My hand span is 7 inches. Then, I measured my hand width. It is $3\frac{1}{2}$ inches. $3\frac{1}{2}$ inches is close to 4 inches so I will use 4 inches. I can find how much wider my hand span is by subtracting. $7 - 4 = 3$, so my hand span is 3 inches wider than my hand width.

Additional Resource

Student Math Handbook pages 153–154

Practice

20 MIN PAIRS

Cat Comparisons

Use anytime after Session 3.4.

Math Focus Points

- Becoming familiar with the terms *centimeters* and *meters* as standard units of measure
- Using centimeters and meters to describe length

Materials: metersticks or meter strips (from Session 3.4), string or yarn, scissors, blank paper (1 sheet per pair), R83

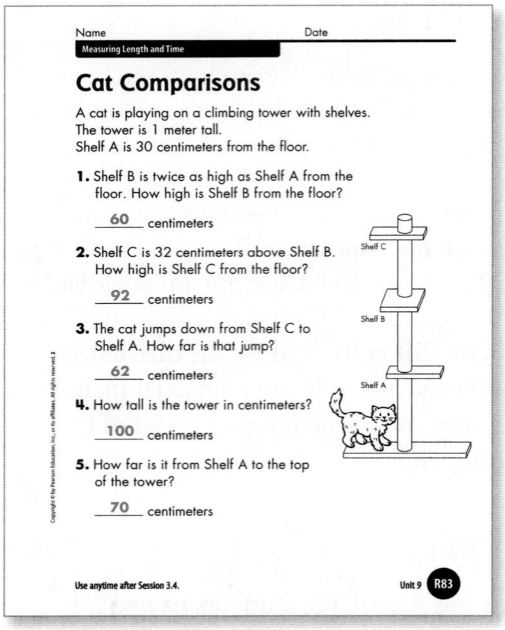
Name Date

Measuring Length and Time

Cat Comparisons

A cat is playing on a climbing tower with shelves.
The tower is 1 meter tall.
Shelf A is 30 centimeters from the floor.

1. Shelf B is twice as high as Shelf A from the floor. How high is Shelf B from the floor?
   60 centimeters
2. Shelf C is 32 centimeters above Shelf B. How high is Shelf C from the floor?
   92 centimeters
3. The cat jumps down from Shelf C to Shelf A. How far is that jump?
   62 centimeters
4. How tall is the tower in centimeters?
   100 centimeters
5. How far is it from Shelf A to the top of the tower?
   70 centimeters

Use anytime after Session 3.4. Unit 9 R83

Show students a meterstick. Remind them that it is like their inch measuring tool, however, instead of being made up of inches, it is made up of centimeters which are about the size of a thumbnail. 100 centimeters equals 1 meter. What are some objects that have a length or width of about 1 meter?

Students might say:

"A door is about 1 meter wide."

Do any of you have a pet cat? Not including the tail, about how long is your cat? Show me the length with your hands. Choose a student who seems to be making a good estimate with his or her hands and have another student measure the distance with a meterstick or meter strip. Write the measurement on the board.

Length of a cat (without tail):
45 centimeters

Have pairs measure and cut a piece of string or yarn that is the same length as the measurement on the board.

You and your partner will go on a scavenger hunt. Find an object that is shorter than the cat's length, an object that is longer than the cat's length, and an object that is about the same length. Use your piece of [yarn] to help you. Record the name of each object and the measurements. Then have pairs find how much longer or shorter each object is compared to the cat's length.

Now, pretend the cat's tail is 30 centimeters long. What is the total length of the cat? Is the length of a cat including the tail more or less than a meter? Have pairs find the answer and then ask volunteers to share their findings.

Distribute copies of Cat Comparisons (R83).

ELL English Language Learners

Provide Sentence Stems For comparison questions, it may help to provide sentence stems, such as the following. The longer measurement is ______. The shorter measurement is ______. The difference is ______.

Additional Resource

Student Math Handbook pages 153–154

Extension

30 MIN PAIRS

Room Comparisons

Use anytime after Session 3.3.

Math Focus Points

- Using inches, feet, and yards to describe lengths
- Measuring lengths that are longer than 12 inches

Materials: yardsticks (1 per pair), R84

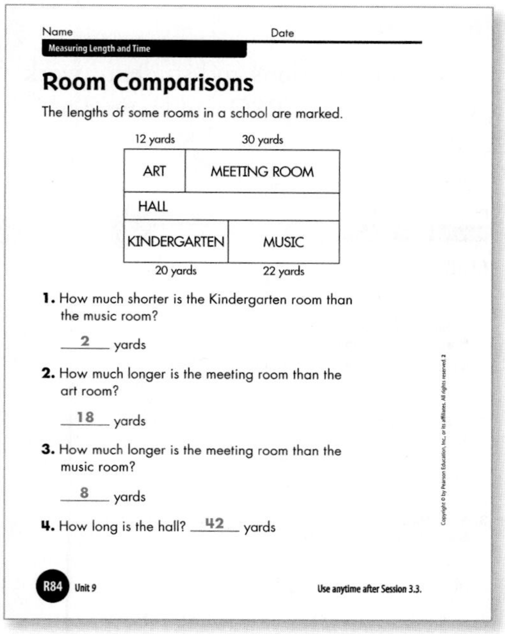

Name Date

Measuring Length and Time

Room Comparisons

The lengths of some rooms in a school are marked.

12 yards	30 yards
ART	MEETING ROOM
HALL	
KINDERGARTEN	MUSIC
20 yards	22 yards

1. How much shorter is the Kindergarten room than the music room?

   2 yards

2. How much longer is the meeting room than the art room?

   18 yards

3. How much longer is the meeting room than the music room?

   8 yards

4. How long is the hall? 42 yards

R84 Unit 9 Use anytime after Session 3.3.

Students work in pairs to measure and compare different classrooms or halls in the school. Make arrangements ahead of time with other teachers whose rooms will be measured.

Today you will be measuring large spaces with a yardstick. Assign each pair of students a length to measure, such as a specific classroom, the cafeteria, or a hallway. Have them measure the longest dimension of the room. How will you keep track of how many yards you have measured?

Students might say:

"We can start with 1 yard. Each time we move the yardstick, we can count the next number out loud."

"We can put a tally mark on paper each time we shift the yardstick to the end of where it was before."

Have students make the measurements. After you find the measurements, write them on the board.

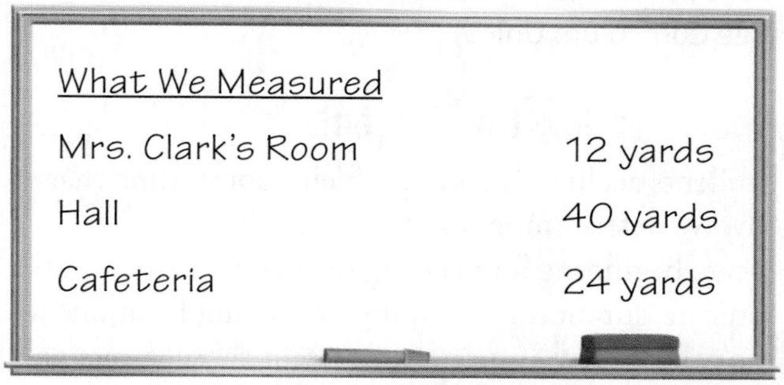

Did you find any shortcuts for measuring long distances? Students may have noticed that there were a certain number of floor tiles or carpet squares in 1 yard. Discuss any patterns on the floor or wall that could help with measurement. For example, if floor tiles are 1 foot by 1 foot, students can count every third tile to find the number of yards.

Discuss questions such as the following:

- Which room was the longest/shortest?
- How much longer is the [hall] than the [cafeteria]?

Students write two comparison statements using numbers, such as stating how much longer one room is than another room. Then distribute copies of Room Comparisons (R84).

ELL English Language Learners

Suggest a Sequence Suggesting a sequence may help students compare measurements. *First,* write the longer measurement. *Then,* write the shorter measurement. *Last,* subtract the shorter distance from the longer distance. This is the difference.

Additional Resource

Student Math Handbook page 157

Differentiation in Investigation 4

Mathematics in This Investigation

The mathematics focuses on representing time on a timeline and using a timeline to determine and calculate the duration of an event.

Additional Resource: *Not Even a Second Has Gone By: Calculating Duration,* pages 170–171 (See Curriculum Unit 9)

Understanding the Mathematics

Students accurately solve problems about time that involve determining durations and times. They locate beginning and ending times on a timeline and indicate duration by jumping or moving from one to the other. They accurately represent those events on a timeline. Students also are able to connect time, its digital notation, and its representation on an analog clock to a timeline using 15-minute intervals.

Option: Assign the **Extension** activity.

Partially Understanding the Mathematics

Students solve problems about duration using a timeline. They locate beginning and ending times and articulate that the space between those points show duration. They may make minor errors in representing events on a timeline and minor computational errors when calculating duration. Overall, they are familiar with digital and analog notation of time and can represent this on a timeline.

Option: Assign the **Practice** activity.

Not Understanding the Mathematics

Students may or may not be able to tell time on a digital and/or analog clock. When representing time as a horizontal sequence, they may place events in a chronological order but have difficulty determining the duration of time between events on a timeline.

Option: Assign the **Intervention** activity.

Investigation 4 Quiz

In addition to your observations and students' work in Investigation 4, the Quiz (R85) can be used to gather more information.

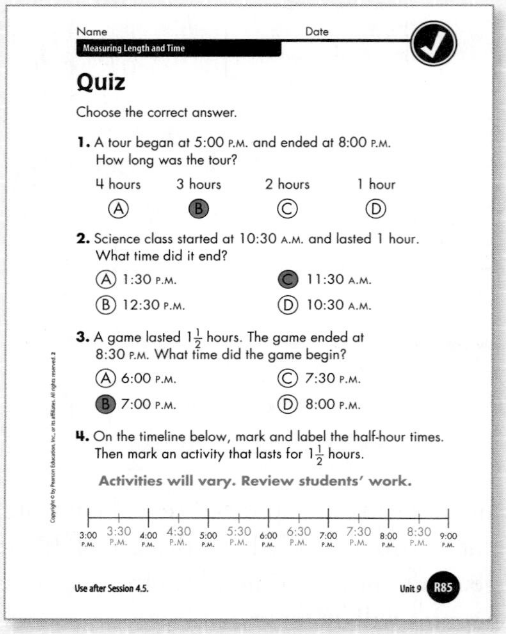

Name Date

Measuring Length and Time

Quiz

Choose the correct answer.

1. A tour began at 5:00 P.M. and ended at 8:00 P.M. How long was the tour?

4 hours	3 hours	2 hours	1 hour
(A)	(B)	(C)	(D)

2. Science class started at 10:30 A.M. and lasted 1 hour. What time did it end?

(A) 1:30 P.M. (C) 11:30 A.M.

(B) 12:30 P.M. (D) 10:30 A.M.

3. A game lasted $1\frac{1}{2}$ hours. The game ended at 8:30 P.M. What time did the game begin?

(A) 6:00 P.M. (C) 7:30 P.M.

(B) 7:00 P.M. (D) 8:00 P.M.

4. On the timeline below, mark and label the half-hour times. Then mark an activity that lasts for $1\frac{1}{2}$ hours.

Activities will vary. Review students' work.

Copyright © by Pearson Education, Inc., or its affiliates. All rights reserved. 2

Use after Session 4.5. Unit 9 R85

Intervention

20 MIN INDIVIDUALS

Using Timelines

Use anytime after Session 4.3.

Math Focus Points

- Moving forward and backward along a timeline in multiples of hours and half hours
- Using a timeline to determine duration

Vocabulary: timeline, half hour

Materials: student clocks

Materials to Prepare: Write the following information about a field trip and draw the corresponding timeline on the board.

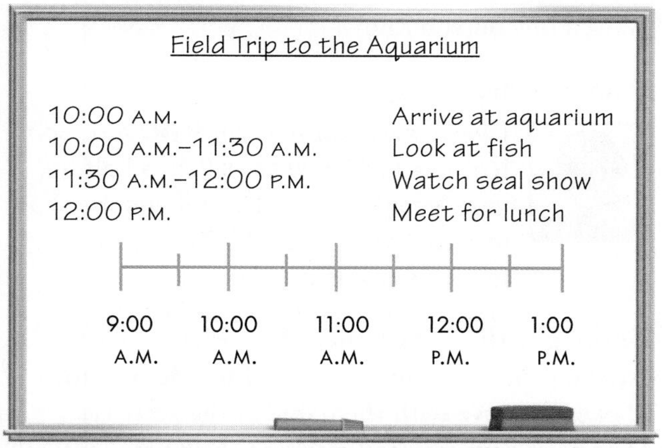

Distribute a clock to each student. Today we will talk about a class that went on a field trip to an aquarium. Look at the board. What time did the class arrive at the aquarium? How can you show this on your clock?

How can we mark 10:00 A.M. on this timeline? Have a volunteer draw an arrow above the timeline, pointing down to the 10:00 mark and label it. Point out that 10:00 A.M. is represented by a long slash line. Point to 10:30 on the timeline. 10:30 A.M. is between 10:00 A.M. and 11:00 A.M. and has a small slash mark. Remind students that the longer slash lines show the hours and the shorter slash lines show the half-hour marks.

What happens next? What time do they start looking at fish? Have a volunteer mark 10:00 A.M. with a dot. What time do they stop looking at fish? Have a volunteer mark 11:30 A.M. with a dot. To show that they were looking at fish from 10:00 A.M. until 11:30 A.M., we can connect the dots to make a curve. Show this on the board. Write "Look at fish" above the curve. How long did they look at fish? How do you know?

Students might say:

"10:00 to 11:00 is 1 hour. Then it's another half hour, so $1\frac{1}{2}$ hours."

"On the timeline, 10:00 to 11:00 is an hour. The curve goes halfway from 11:00 to 12:00, which is a half hour. So they looked at fish for an hour and a half."

Repeat the process to have students find the duration of the seal show. Then have students label when the class met for lunch.

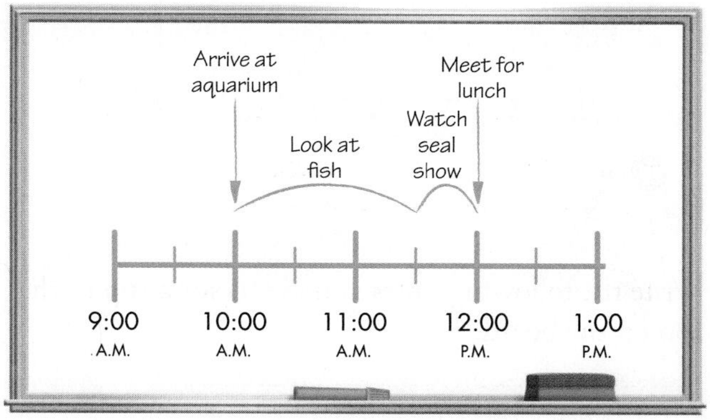

ELL English Language Learners

Suggest a Sequence To help English Language Learners, suggest a sequence to find the duration of an event. *First*, mark the start time. *Next*, mark the end time. *Then*, connect the start and end times with a curve. *Last*, find the amount of time under the curve.

Additional Resource

Student Math Handbook pages 143–145

Practice

20 MIN PAIRS

Trip to the Zoo

Use anytime after Session 4.3.

Math Focus Points

- Moving forward and backward along a timeline in multiples of hours and half hours
- Using a timeline to determine duration

Materials: scissors, tape, M17 (1 per pair), R86

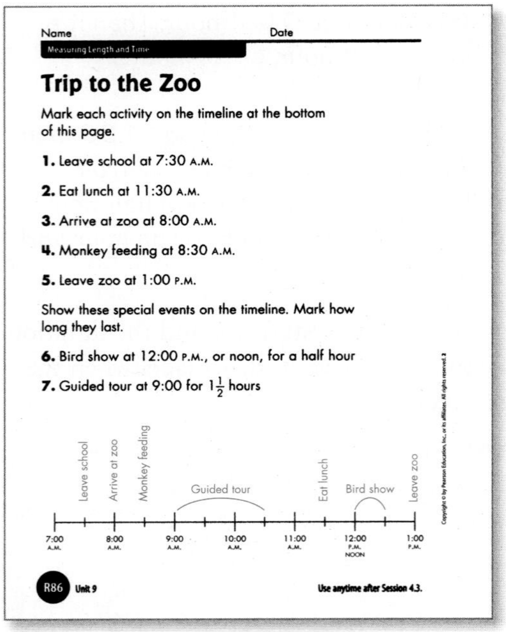
Name Date

Measuring Length and Time

Trip to the Zoo

Mark each activity on the timeline at the bottom of this page.

1. Leave school at 7:30 A.M.
2. Eat lunch at 11:30 A.M.
3. Arrive at zoo at 8:00 A.M.
4. Monkey feeding at 8:30 A.M.
5. Leave zoo at 1:00 P.M.

Show these special events on the timeline. Mark how long they last.

6. Bird show at 12:00 P.M., or noon, for a half hour
7. Guided tour at 9:00 for $1\frac{1}{2}$ hours

R86 Unit 9 Use anytime after Session 4.3.

Write the following times and events for a trip to the zoo on the board.

Trip to the Zoo

9:30 A.M.	Arrive at zoo
9:30 A.M.–10:30 A.M.	Dolphin show
10:30 A.M.–11:00 A.M.	Zoo babies show
11:00 A.M.–12:30 P.M.	African animals movie
12:30 P.M.	Lunch

Today we will talk about a class that took a trip to a zoo. Distribute a copy of the School Day Timeline (M17), scissors, and tape to each pair. Have them cut out and assemble their timelines. What time did the class arrive at the zoo? How can you show this on your timeline?

Students might say:

"I can draw an arrow pointing to 9:30 A.M. It is halfway between 9:00 A.M. and 10:00 A.M. I will label it 'Arrive at zoo.'"

What happens next? What time does the dolphin show start? When does it end? How will you mark this on your timeline? How long is the dolphin show? How do you know?

Students might say:

"I will draw a curve from 9:30 A.M. to 10:30 A.M. I know that it is a half an hour from 9:30 to 10 and another half an hour from 10 to 10:30. So, the dolphin show is an hour long."

Working with your partner, show each activity listed on the board on your timeline. Be sure to label each curve with the name of the activity. After pairs have finished marking their timelines, ask questions about the length of each activity and have them explain how they found the duration. Then distribute copies of Trip to the Zoo (R86).

ELL English Language Learners

Provide a Word List Write the following words and phrases on the board: *timeline, half hour,* A.M., P.M., *start time, end time*. Review the meaning of each, then have students illustrate each word. As partners work together, encourage them to use as many of these words as possible.

Additional Resource

Student Math Handbook pages 142–145

Extension

30 MIN PAIRS

Garden Timeline

Use anytime after Session 4.3.

Math Focus Points

- Moving forward and backward along a timeline in multiples of hours and half hours
- Using a timeline to determine duration

Materials: scissors, tape, M29 (1 per pair), R87

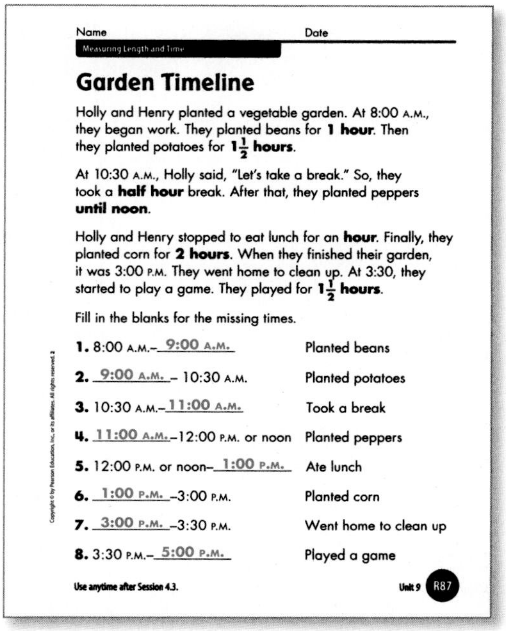

Name Date

Measuring Length and Time

Garden Timeline

Holly and Henry planted a vegetable garden. At 8:00 A.M., they began work. They planted beans for **1 hour**. Then they planted potatoes for **$1\frac{1}{2}$ hours**.

At 10:30 A.M., Holly said, "Let's take a break." So, they took a **half hour** break. After that, they planted peppers **until noon**.

Holly and Henry stopped to eat lunch for an **hour**. Finally, they planted corn for **2 hours**. When they finished their garden, it was 3:00 P.M. They went home to clean up. At 3:30, they started to play a game. They played for **$1\frac{1}{2}$ hours**.

Fill in the blanks for the missing times.

1. 8:00 A.M.–9:00 A.M. Planted beans
2. 9:00 A.M. – 10:30 A.M. Planted potatoes
3. 10:30 A.M.–11:00 A.M. Took a break
4. 11:00 A.M.–12:00 P.M. or noon Planted peppers
5. 12:00 P.M. or noon–1:00 P.M. Ate lunch
6. 1:00 P.M.–3:00 P.M. Planted corn
7. 3:00 P.M.–3:30 P.M. Went home to clean up
8. 3:30 P.M.–5:00 P.M. Played a game

Use anytime after Session 4.3. Unit 9 R87

Students work in pairs to create a schedule and timeline for planting a garden.

Today you will think about a schedule for planting a garden. What types of plants grow in a garden? What vegetables would you like to grow? What flowers do you enjoy? Discuss possible vegetables, such as beans, tomatoes, lettuce, or squash, or other plants, such as flowers or herbs. You may want to focus on plants that are common in your area.

What type of activities will be part of the workday? How long might something take in hours or half hours?

Students might say:

"We might need to pull weeds first. This might take an hour."

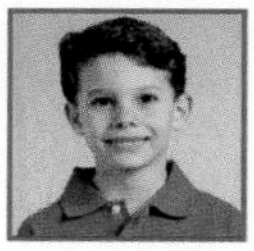

"If we put in tomato plants, it takes time to put up stakes to hold up the plants. I like lots of tomatoes, so I'll work $1\frac{1}{2}$ hours."

Distribute a copy of Special Day Timeline (M29), scissors, and tape to each pair. Give them a few minutes to cut out and assemble their timelines. Work with your partner to list 4 types of plants you want to have in your garden and write a length of time for planting. It's not important to know if the planting will really take as long as you say. Each plant will take at least a half hour to plant. After making your list, write a schedule and draw a timeline that matches the schedule. The schedule can start at 6:00 A.M. or later but must end by 5:00 P.M.

After pairs finish, have them share their schedules and timelines with other pairs of students. Then distribute copies of Garden Timeline (R87).

ELL English Language Learners

Provide Sentence Stems As pairs are listing what to plant, it may help to provide sentence stems to use for each type of plant.

We want to plant ________.

The planting begins at ________.

The planting ends at ________.

The length of the planting is ________ hours.

Additional Resource

Student Math Handbook pages 142–145

Resource Masters

Name Date

Counting, Coins, and Combinations

Quiz

Choose the correct answer.

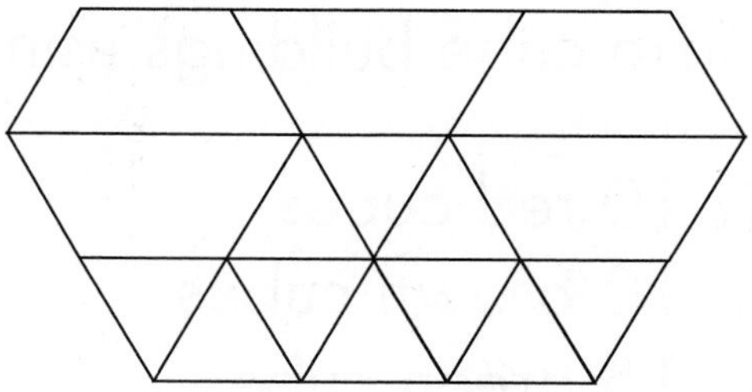

1. How many pattern block shapes are used in the design?

(A) 10 (B) 12 (C) 14 (D) 15

2. Which number matches these clues?
My number is greater than 27.
My number is 10 less than 45.

(A) 25 (B) 35 (C) 43 (D) 55

3. A Cube Thing is made with the following:

10 red cubes 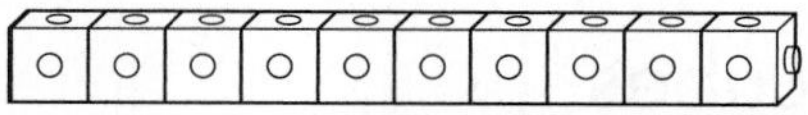

15 blue cubes 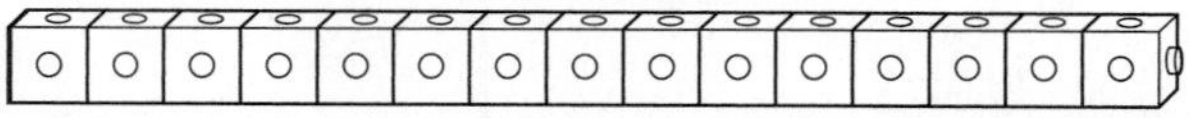

21 green cubes 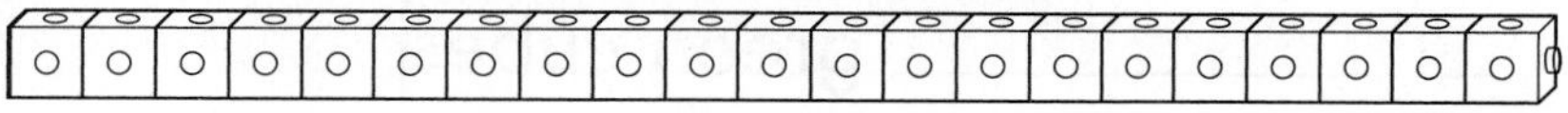

How many cubes are in the Cube Thing?

(A) 46 (B) 45 (C) 36 (D) 25

4. How did you find the answer to Problem 3? Explain your strategy.

Copyright © by Pearson Education, Inc., or its affiliates. All rights reserved. 2

Name Date

Cube Buildings

Make cube buildings using the following number of cubes.

1. 10 red cubes
10 brown cubes
15 green cubes
20 yellow cubes

How many cubes will you use in all? ________

2. 20 white cubes
30 orange cubes
15 black cubes
5 blue cubes

How many cubes will you use in all? ________

3. Decide how many cubes you will use for your cube building.

________ red cubes

________ blue cubes

________ green cubes

________ yellow cubes

How many cubes will you use in all? ________

Copyright © by Pearson Education, Inc., or its affiliates. All rights reserved. 2

Use anytime after Session 1.3.

Name Date

Cube Building Riddles

1. Use the clues to figure out how many cubes to use in the Cube Building. Then make the Cube Building.

Clue 1: The number of black cubes is 20.

Clue 2: The number of orange cubes is 1 less than 11.

______________ orange cubes

Clue 3: The number of yellow cubes is 10 more than 25.

______________ yellow cubes

Clue 4: The number of green cubes is 5 more than 15.

______________ green cubes

Total number of cubes in Cube Building: ______________

2. Write your own clues for the number of cubes in a Cube Building. Write at least 3 clues, and then trade with a partner to solve.

____

____

____

Total number of cubes in Cube Building: ______________

Copyright © by Pearson Education, Inc., or its affiliates. All rights reserved. 2

Name Date

Quiz

Choose the correct answer.

1. How many pockets are there on all the students?

Pockets	Students
0	1
1	5
2	3

(A) 3 (B) 5 (C) 9 (D) 11

2. Which number is just after 39 on the number line?

(A) 50 (B) 49 (C) 40 (D) 38

3. How many pennies is this set worth?

(A) 37 (B) 27 (C) 15 (D) 6

4. 24 people want to go horseback riding. There are 13 white horses and 14 brown horses. Are there enough horses for everyone to ride one? How do you know?

Copyright © by Pearson Education, Inc., or its affiliates. All rights reserved. 2

Name Date

Enough or Not Enough?

Seth has 23 apples. There are 17 students in his class.

1. Are there enough for the class? YES NO

2. Are there any extra apples? YES NO

If so, how many? ________

3. Does Seth need more apples? YES NO

If so, how many? ________

4. How did you figure it out? Show your work.

Copyright © by Pearson Education, Inc., or its affiliates. All rights reserved. 2

Name Date

Two or More Bones

Fill in the information that your teacher gives you.
At the dog shelter there are:

☐
small dogs

☐
medium dogs

☐
large dogs

1. How many dogs are there in all? ____________________

2. There are ☐ dog bones.

3. Do you have enough bones for the dogs to get ☐ bones each? YES NO

4. Were there any extra bones? YES NO

If so, how many? ____________

5. Do you need more bones? YES NO

If so, how many? ____________

6. How did you figure it out? Show your work.

Copyright © by Pearson Education, Inc., or its affiliates. All rights reserved. 2

Quiz

Choose the correct answer.

1. Which Plus 2 addition combination has a sum of 8?

Ⓐ 4 + 2 Ⓒ 6 + 2

Ⓑ 5 + 2 Ⓓ 7 + 2

2. Luis is playing a game of *Make 10.* Which two number cards make 10?

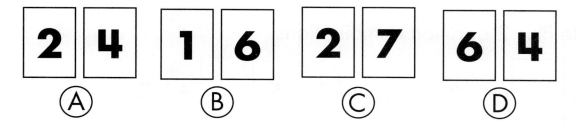

2	4		1	6		2	7		6	4
Ⓐ			Ⓑ			Ⓒ			Ⓓ	

3. Holly is playing a game of *Tens Go Fish.* She has the number *7* card. What number should she ask for to make 10?

Ⓐ 2 Ⓑ 3 Ⓒ 4 Ⓓ 5

4. Show 3 ways to make 10.
Write the numbers on the cards.

☐ + ☐ = 10 ☐ + ☐ = 10 ☐ + ☐ = 10

Copyright © by Pearson Education, Inc., or its affiliates. All rights reserved. 2

Name Date

Plus 1, Plus 2, or Make 10?

Write Plus 1 addition combinations.

1. ☐ + 1 = ____ 2. ☐ + 1 = ____

3. ☐ + 1 = ____ 4. ☐ + 1 = ____

Write Plus 2 addition combinations.

5. ☐ + 2 = ____ 6. ☐ + 2 = ____

7. ☐ + 2 = ____ 8. ☐ + 2 = ____

Write Make 10 addition combinations.

9. 5 + ____ = ____ 10. 9 + ____ = ____

11. 6 + ____ = ____ 12. 7 + ____ = ____

Copyright © by Pearson Education, Inc., or its affiliates. All rights reserved. 2

Use anytime after Session 3.5.

Name Date

More Than Two to Make 10

Choose 3 or more cards to make 10. Record the equations.

1.	2	1	5	7	4
2.	8	5	1	3	1
3.	1	2	4	4	5
4.	3	5	2	1	2
5.	3	2	3	4	2

6. Draw a set of 5 cards. Write equations that equal 10 using 3 or more cards.

Copyright © by Pearson Education, Inc., or its affiliates. All rights reserved. 2

Name Date

Quiz

Choose the correct answer.

1. If you put 13 socks into the magic doubling pot, how many socks will you get back?

(A) 13 (B) 24 (C) 26 (D) 36

2. Which shows a way to make 15?

(A) 9 + 1 + 4

(B) 7 + 3 + 1 + 5

(C) 6 + 3 + 4 + 1

(D) 8 + 2 + 5

3. Leo has 22 pencils. He gives 10 to Tia. How many pencils does Leo have left?

(A) 32 (B) 23 (C) 12 (D) 11

4. Solve the problem. Show your work. Write an equation.

There are 15 boys and 14 girls in the park. How many children are there in all?

Copyright © by Pearson Education, Inc., or its affiliates. All rights reserved. 2

Modeling Story Problems

Solve each problem. Show your work.
Write an equation.

1. A pet store has 14 goldfish in a tank and 13 goldfish in another tank. How many goldfish are there in all?

2. There are 25 turtles at the pet store. Children buy 6 of the turtles. How many turtles are left at the pet store?

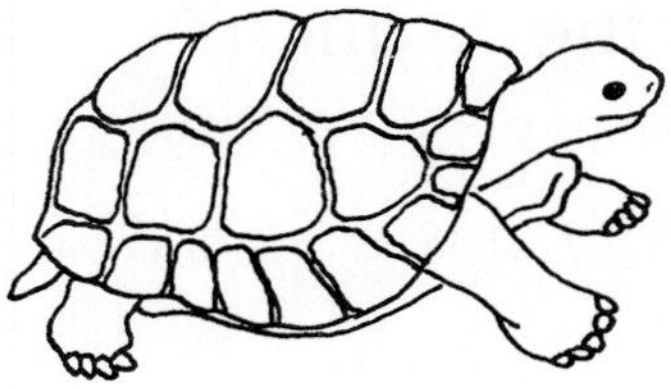

Copyright © by Pearson Education, Inc., or its affiliates. All rights reserved. 2

Name Date

Story Problems with Multiple Parts

Solve each problem. Show your work.
Write an equation.

1. Yama counted 28 ants on a log.
Juan counted 13 ants on a leaf.
Jake counted 17 ants.
How many ants did they count in all?

2. A tree had 34 birds on its branches.
16 of the birds flew away,
then 6 more flew away.
How many birds were left
on the branch?

3. Rochelle had 52 pennies. She spent
24 pennies to buy an eraser, and
10 pennies to buy a pencil. She
also gave 4 pennies to Jake.
How much money does Rochelle
have left?

Copyright © by Pearson Education, Inc., or its affiliates. All rights reserved. 2

Quiz

Choose the correct answer.

1. Which shape has 4 sides?

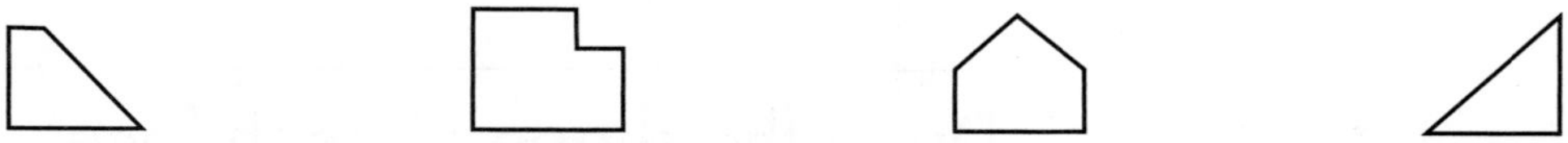

(A) (B) (C) (D)

2. These shapes were made by a tracing a Geoblock.

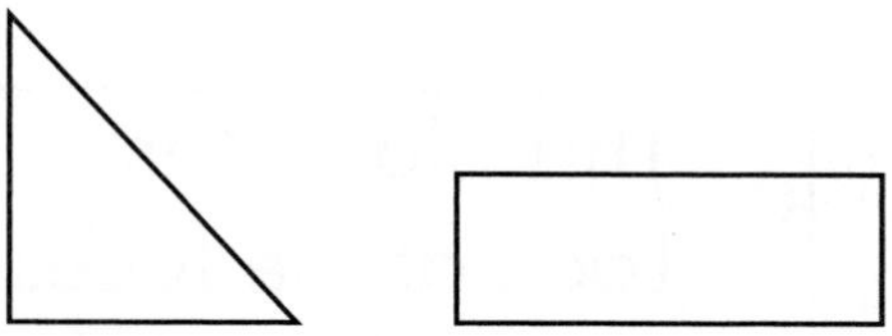

Which block matches the shapes?

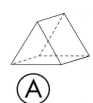

(A) (B) (C) (D)

3. Which shape has 6 faces?

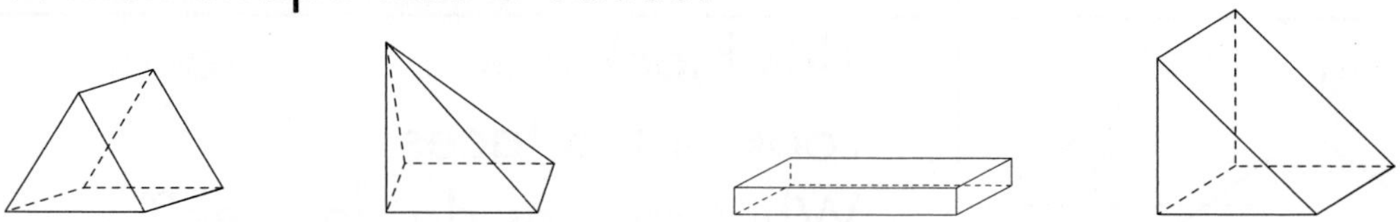

(A) (B) (C) (D)

4. Draw lines to show which pattern block shapes can cover the figures. Show 2 different ways.

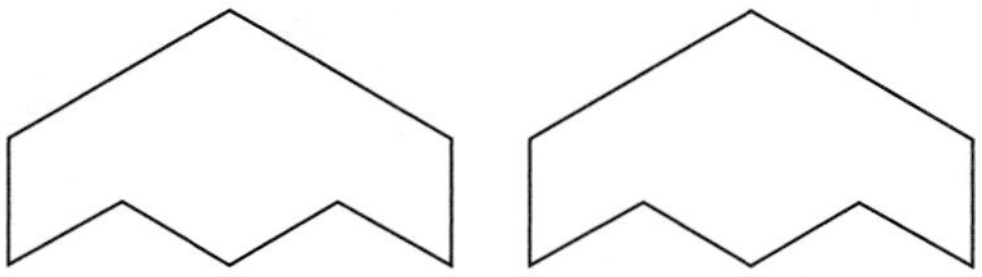

Copyright © by Pearson Education, Inc., or its affiliates. All rights reserved. 2

Name Date

Describing Faces

1. 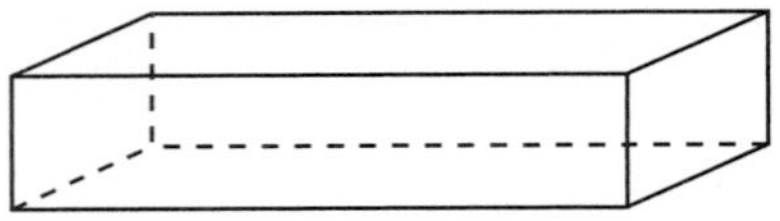

This block has ______ faces.
Look at the faces.
What shapes do you see?

____

Draw the shape of each face.
Write how many of each face.

2. 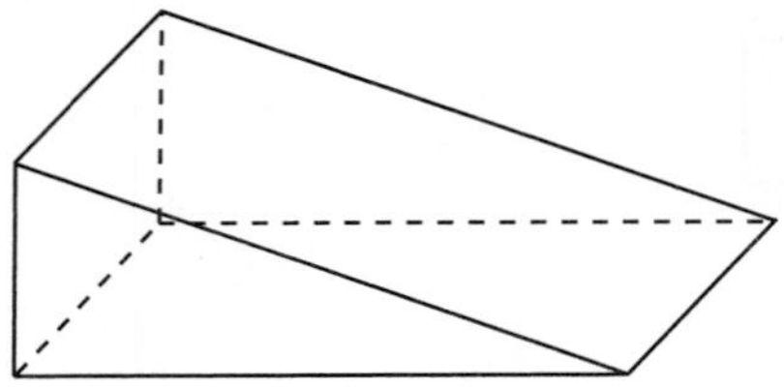

This block has ______ faces.
Look at the faces.
What shapes do you see?

____

Draw the shape of each face.
Write how many of each face.

3. 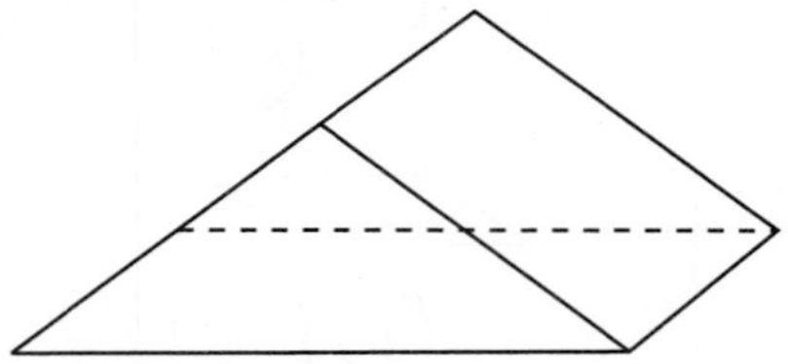

This block has ______ faces.
Look at the faces.
What shapes do you see?

____

Draw the shape of each face.
Write how many of each face.

Copyright © by Pearson Education, Inc., or its affiliates. All rights reserved. 2

Use anytime after Session 1.3.

Name Date

Faces, Vertices, and Edges

Count the faces, vertices, and edges of each 3-D shape.

1.

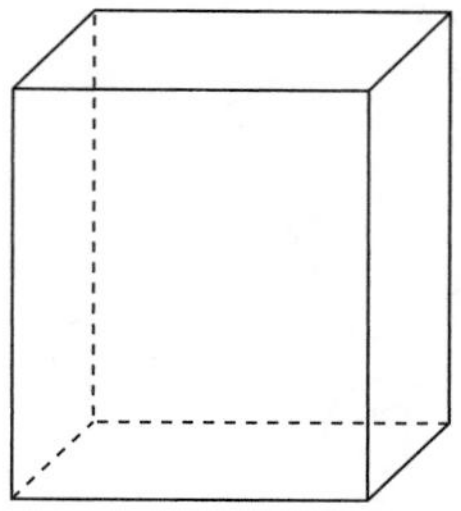

faces ________

edges ________

vertices ________

2.

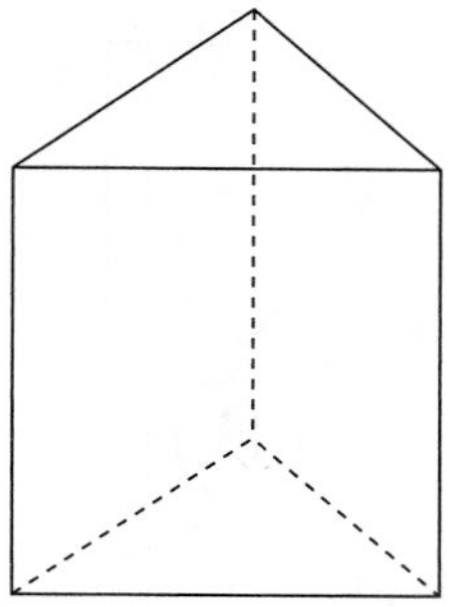

faces ________

edges ________

vertices ________

3.

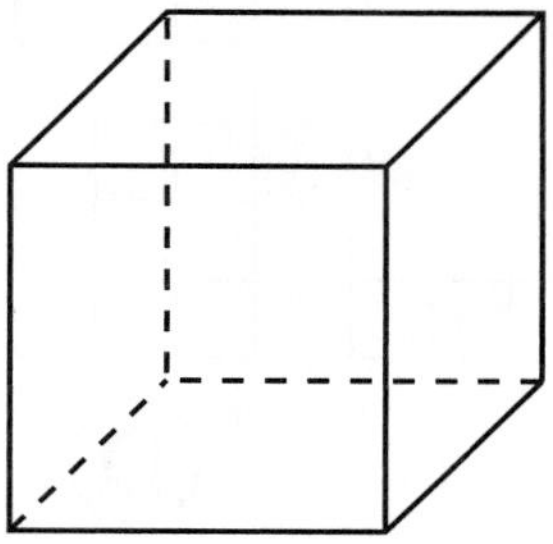

faces ________

edges ________

vertices ________

4.

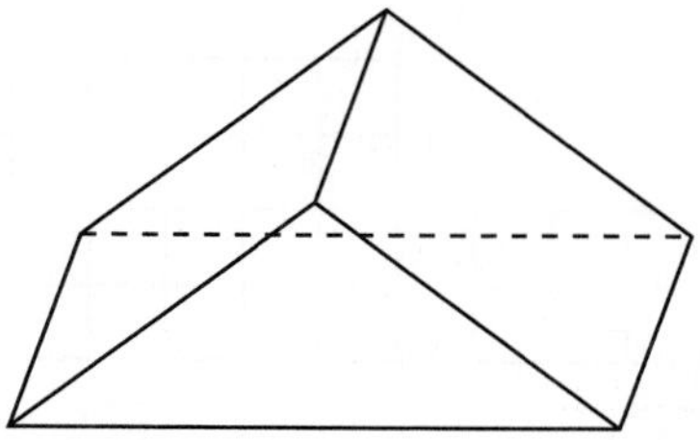

faces ________

edges ________

vertices ________

Copyright © by Pearson Education, Inc., or its affiliates. All rights reserved. 2

Name Date

Shapes, Blocks, and Symmetry

Quiz

Choose the correct answer.

1. Which shape is a rectangle?

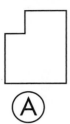

Ⓐ Ⓑ Ⓒ Ⓓ

2. Which corner is a right angle?

Ⓐ Corner A

Ⓑ Corner B

Ⓒ Corner C

Ⓓ Corner D

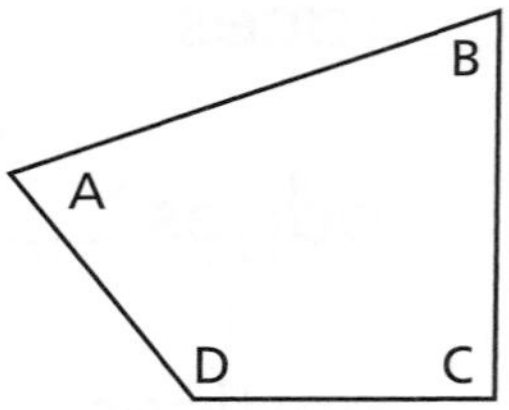

3. Which rectangle is the biggest?

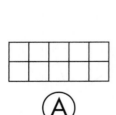

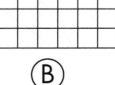

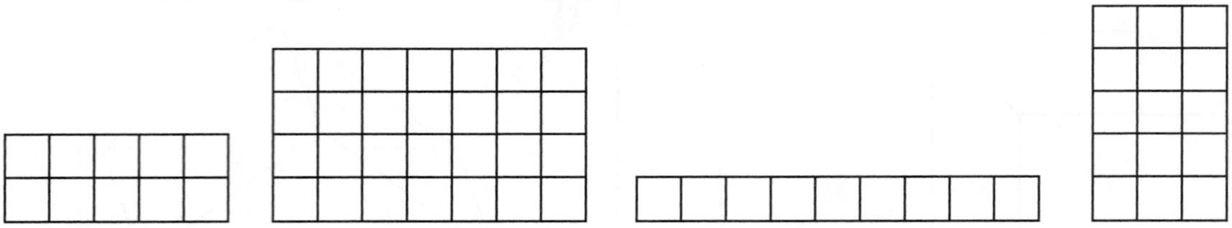

Ⓐ Ⓑ Ⓒ Ⓓ

4. On the grid, draw a rectangle made from 12 squares.

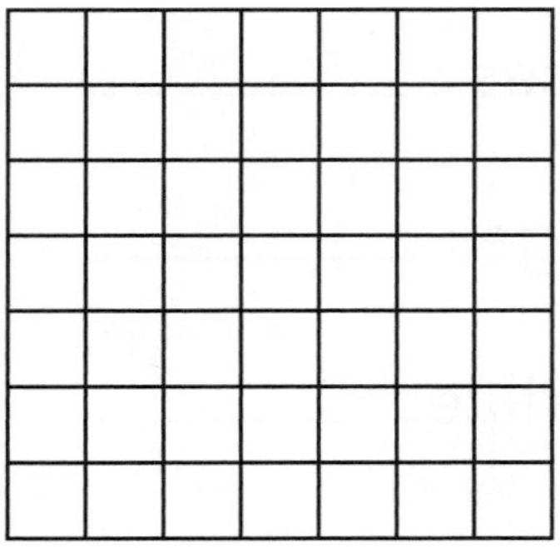

Copyright © by Pearson Education, Inc., or its affiliates. All rights reserved. 2

Name Date

Rectangles and Squares

1. Circle all of the shapes that have 4 sides.
Color all of the squares yellow.
Color all of the rectangles blue.

2. Rectangles have _____ sides.
Squares have _____ sides.
Rectangles have 4 __________ angles.

The sides of a square are all __________.
Squares have _____ right angles.

Copyright © by Pearson Education, Inc., or its affiliates. All rights reserved. 2

Name Date

More Rectangle Riddles

Draw the rectangle that solves the riddle.

1. I have 3 rows and 9 columns.

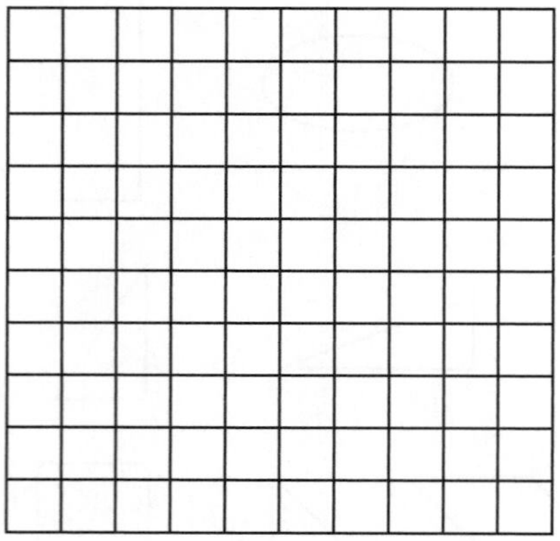

2. I have 20 squares and 4 rows.

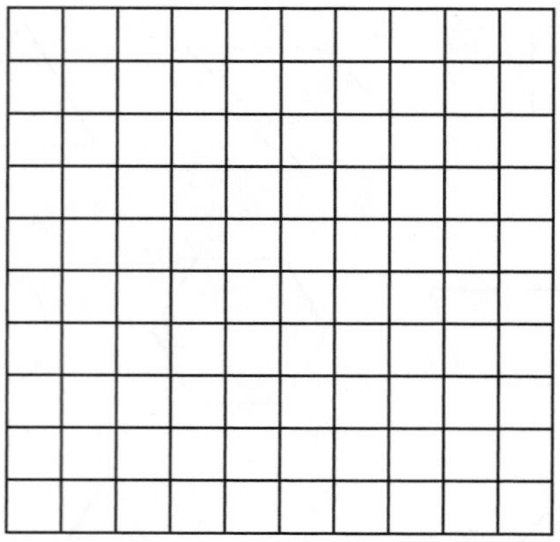

3. I have 4 columns and 8 rows.

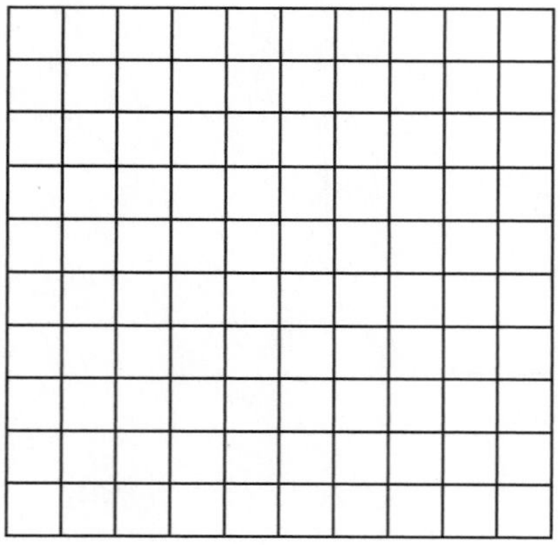

4. I have 35 squares and 5 columns.

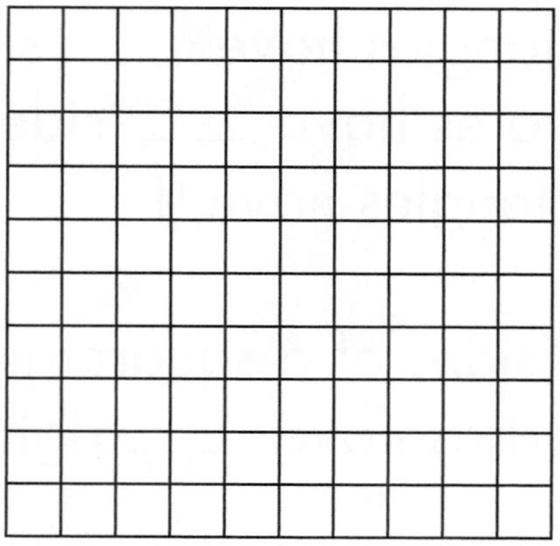

Copyright © by Pearson Education, Inc., or its affiliates. All rights reserved. 2

Use anytime after Session 2.5.

Name Date

Quiz

Choose the correct answer.

1. Which shape is symmetrical?

(A) 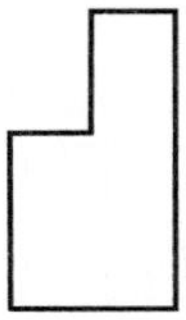
(B) 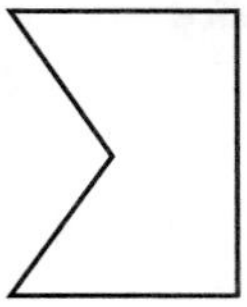
(C) 
(D) 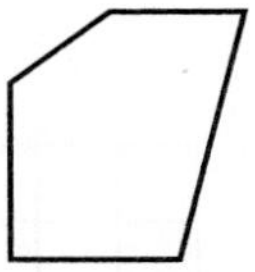

2. Which shows a line of symmetry for the shape?

(A) 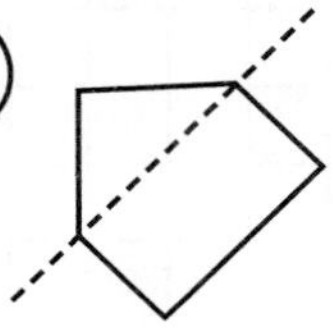
(B) 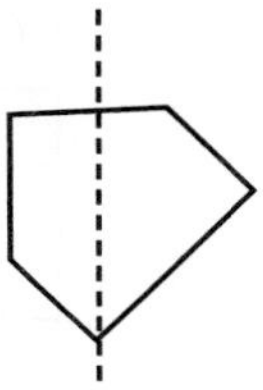
(C) 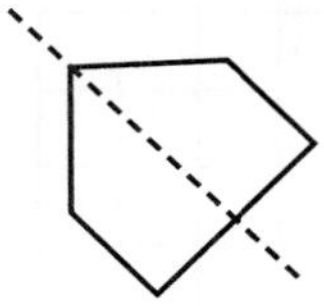
(D) 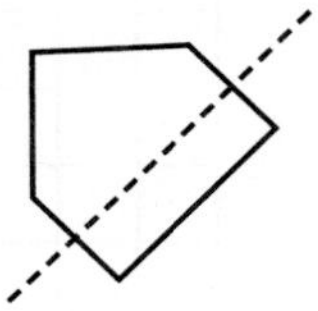

3. Half of a symmetrical design is shown. Which equation shows how many squares will be in the whole design?

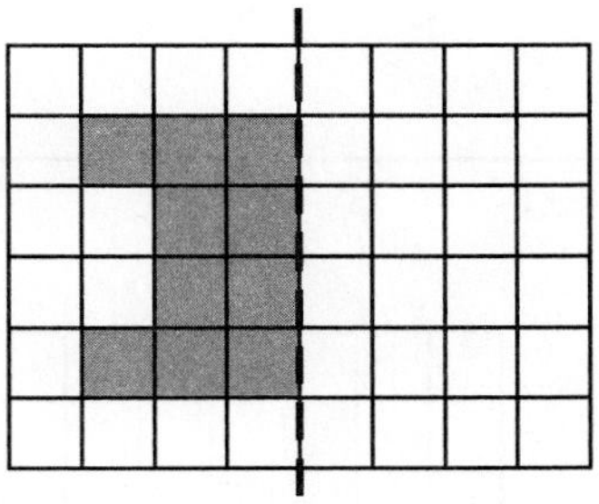

(A) 8 + 8 = 16

(B) 5 + 5 = 10

(C) 12 + 12 = 24

(D) 10 + 10 = 20

4. On the grid, finish a symmetrical design. Then draw the line of symmetry.

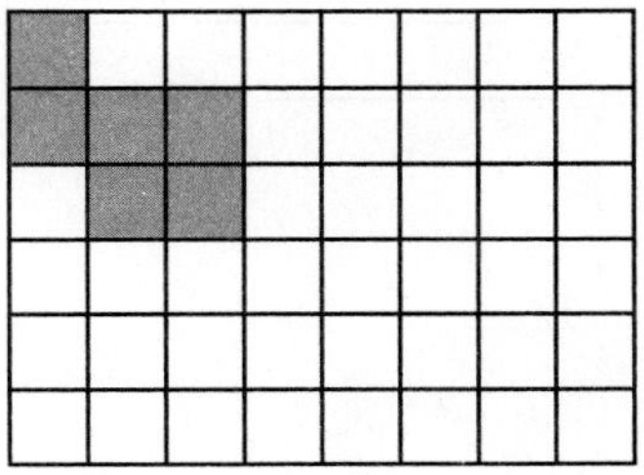

Copyright © by Pearson Education, Inc., or its affiliates. All rights reserved. 2

Grid Pattern Symmetry

Half of each design is shown with a mirror line.
Finish each design to show symmetry.

1.

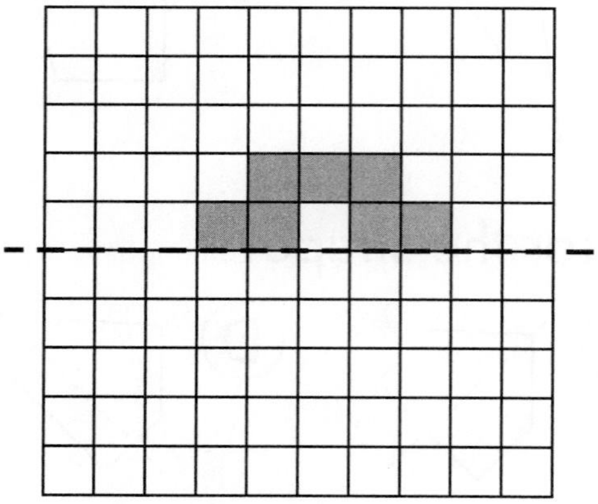

2.

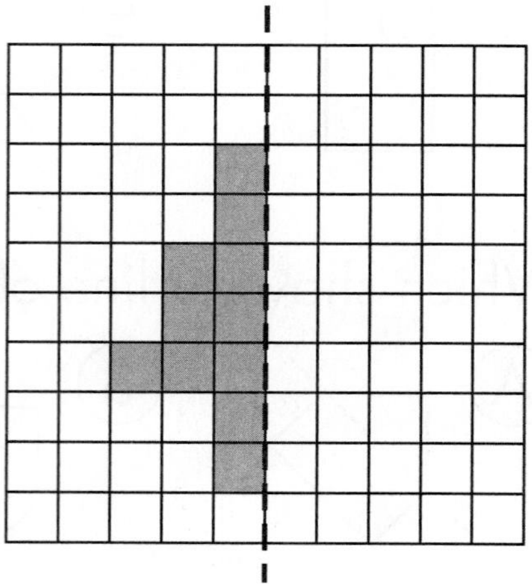

3.

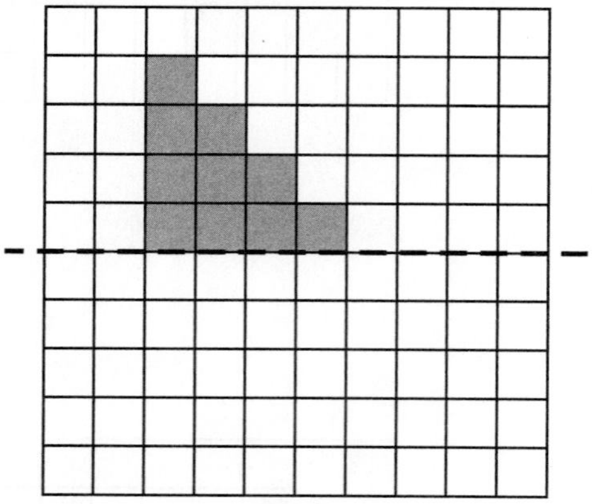

4.

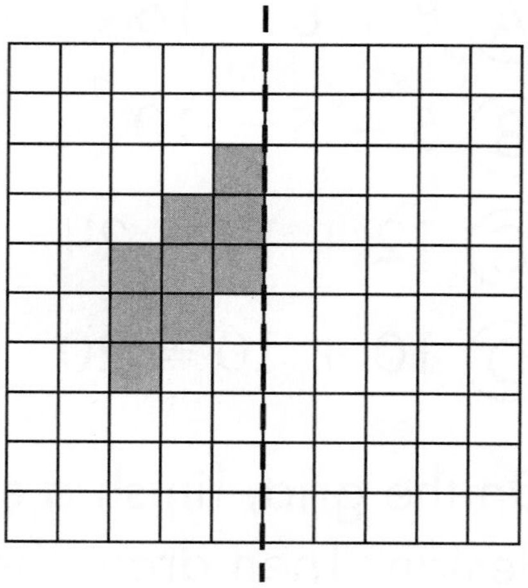

Copyright © by Pearson Education, Inc., or its affiliates. All rights reserved. 2

Use anytime after Session 3.2.

Name Date

More Symmetry

Draw 2 or more lines of symmetry for each shape.

1.

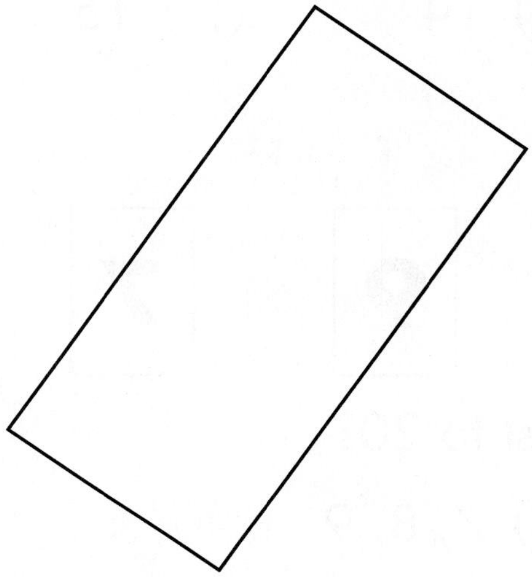

2.

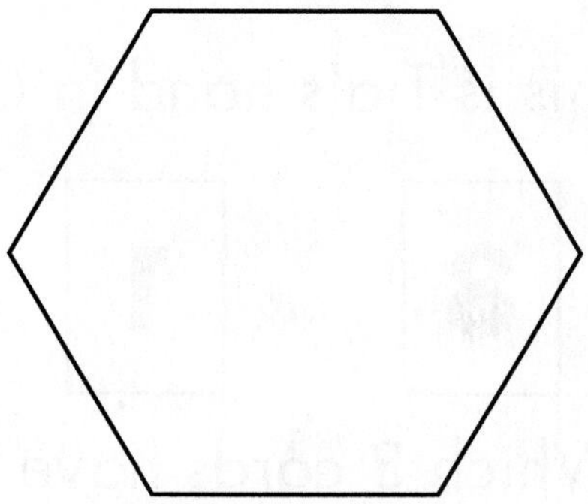

3.

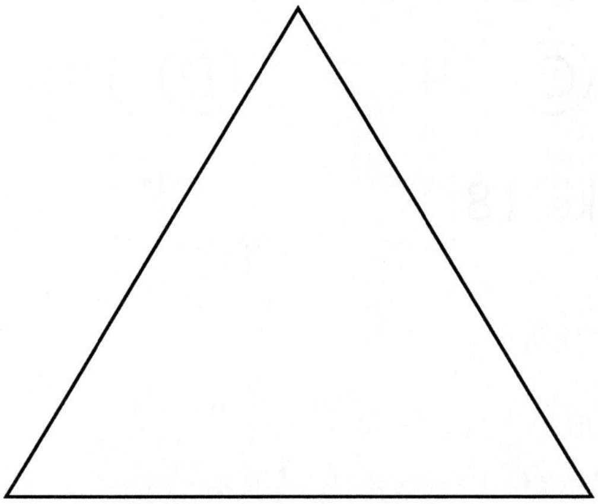

4.

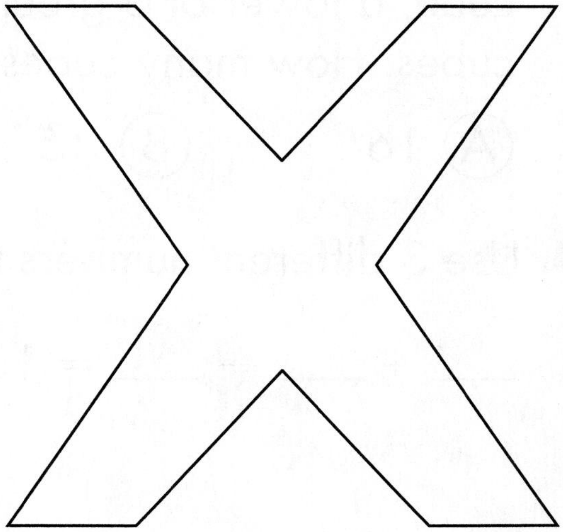

Copyright © by Pearson Education, Inc., or its affiliates. All rights reserved. 2

Use anytime after Session 3.3.

Name Date

Quiz

Choose the correct answer.

1. ☐ = 7 + 3 + 4

Ⓐ 10 Ⓑ 13 Ⓒ 14 Ⓓ 15

2. This is Tia's hand in *Close to 20.*

8	**1**	**2**	**9**	**7**

Which 3 cards have a sum closest to 20?

Ⓐ 8, 2, 9 Ⓒ 7, 8, 9

Ⓑ 8, 1, 9 Ⓓ 7, 2, 9

3. Carla is building with cubes. She has a tower of 1 red cube, a tower of 5 green cubes, and a tower of 9 blue cubes. How many cubes does she have?

Ⓐ 16 Ⓑ 15 Ⓒ 14 Ⓓ 13

4. Use 3 different numbers to make 18.

____ + ____ + ____ = 18

Copyright © by Pearson Education, Inc., or its affiliates. All rights reserved. 2

Name Date

More Than 2 Addends

Solve each number string problem. Remember to look for doubles and for combinations that make 10.

1. 2 + 6 + 2 =	**2.** 3 + 9 + 7 =
3. 5 + 4 + 5 =	**4.** 2 + 6 + 8 =
5. 9 + 8 + 1 =	**6.** 3 + 6 + 3 =

Copyright © by Pearson Education, Inc., or its affiliates. All rights reserved. 2

Use anytime after Session 1.2.

Name Date

More Than 3 Addends and Larger Numbers

Use combinations you know to solve each problem.

More Than 3 Addends	
1. 7 + 1 + 3 + 5 =	**2.** 4 + 9 + 1 + 4 =
3. 5 + 2 + 8 + 5 =	**4.** 6 + 2 + 4 + 2 =
Larger Numbers	
5. 11 + 9 + 10 =	**6.** 10 + 8 + 20 =
7. 6 + 10 + 20 =	**8.** 7 + 10 + 13 + 10 =

Copyright © by Pearson Education, Inc., or its affiliates. All rights reserved. 2

Use anytime after Session 1.1.

Name Date

Stickers, Number Strings, and Story Problems

Quiz

Choose the correct answer.

1. Juan saw 18 birds in a tree. Carla saw 11 birds on the ground. How many birds did they see in all?

Ⓐ 26 Ⓑ 27 Ⓒ 28 Ⓓ 29

2. 9 + ____ = 12

Ⓐ 1 Ⓑ 2 Ⓒ 3 Ⓓ 4

3. Nate and Jacy are playing *Cover Up*. They start with 15 counters. Nate hides 6 under the paper. How many are **not** under the paper?

Ⓐ 10 Ⓑ 9 Ⓒ 8 Ⓓ 5

4. Solve the problem. Show your work. Write an equation.

Holly has 32 peanuts. She gave Leo 11 of them. How many peanuts does Holly have now?

Copyright © by Pearson Education, Inc., or its affiliates. All rights reserved. 2

Name Date

Unknown Change

Solve each problem. Show your work.
Write an equation.

1. Simon has 12 crayons. Holly gave him some more. Now Simon has 20 crayons. How many crayons did Holly give him?

2. Carla has 20 crayons. She gave some of them to Chen. Now Carla has 12 crayons. How many crayons did Carla give to Chen?

3. Can you use what you know from Problem 1 to help you solve Problem 2? How does it help?

Copyright © by Pearson Education, Inc., or its affiliates. All rights reserved. 2

Name Date

Adding Tens and Ones

Solve each problem. Show your work.
Write an equation.

1. Paige is collecting buttons. She has 28 buttons. Her aunt gave her 12 more buttons. How many buttons does Paige have now?

2. Travis is collecting postcards. He has 29 postcards. His brother gave him 16 more postcards. How many postcards does Travis have now?

Copyright © by Pearson Education, Inc., or its affiliates. All rights reserved. 2

Name Date

Stickers, Number Strings, and Story Problems

Quiz

Choose the correct answer.

1. A game in class needs 2 equal teams. Which number will make 2 equal teams?

Ⓐ 13 Ⓑ 15 Ⓒ 16 Ⓓ 17

2. Which number is **not** odd?

Ⓐ 57 Ⓑ 43 Ⓒ 39 Ⓓ 32

3. Which shows numbers you say when you count by 2s?

Ⓐ 5, 10, 15, 20, 25
Ⓑ 22, 24, 26, 28, 30
Ⓒ 1, 10, 20, 30, 40
Ⓓ 1, 2, 3, 4, 5

4. Solve the problem. Show your work.

There are 6 people in the library. How many fingers are in the library?

Copyright © by Pearson Education, Inc., or its affiliates. All rights reserved. 2

Name Date

Counting by 5s and 10s

Each cube train has 5 cubes.

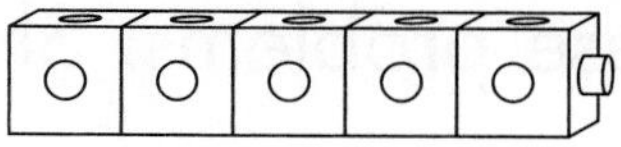

1. If there are 10 cubes, how many cube trains can you make? ______________

2. If there are 20 cubes, how many cube trains can you make? ______________

3. If there are 30 cubes, how many cube trains can you make? ______________

4. If there are 40 cubes, how many cube trains can you make? ______________

5. Count by 5s from 0 to 40. List the numbers you say. What pattern do you see?

Copyright © by Pearson Education, Inc., or its affiliates. All rights reserved. 2

Name Date

More Counting Bags

Solve these problems. Show your work.

1. There are 12 people in the room. How many eyes are in the room?

2. There are 8 people raising their hand to answer a question. How many fingers are on the raised hands?

3. There are 6 people in the gym. How many toes are in the gym?

Copyright © by Pearson Education, Inc., or its affiliates. All rights reserved. 2

Use anytime after Session 3.6.

Name Date

Quiz

Choose the correct answer.

1. 8 + 8 + 1 =

Ⓐ 7 + 8 Ⓑ 8 + 8 Ⓒ 9 + 9 Ⓓ 9 + 8

2. Nate has 43 pennies. If he trades the pennies for as many dimes as he can, how many dimes will he have?

Ⓐ 3 Ⓑ 4 Ⓒ 5 Ⓓ 9

3. Which tells about 27?

Ⓐ 27 tens

Ⓑ 7 tens and 2 ones

Ⓒ 2 tens and 7 ones

Ⓓ 1 ten and 7 ones

4. Draw 58 stickers using strips of 10 and singles.

Copyright © by Pearson Education, Inc., or its affiliates. All rights reserved. 2

Name Date

Strips and Singles

1. 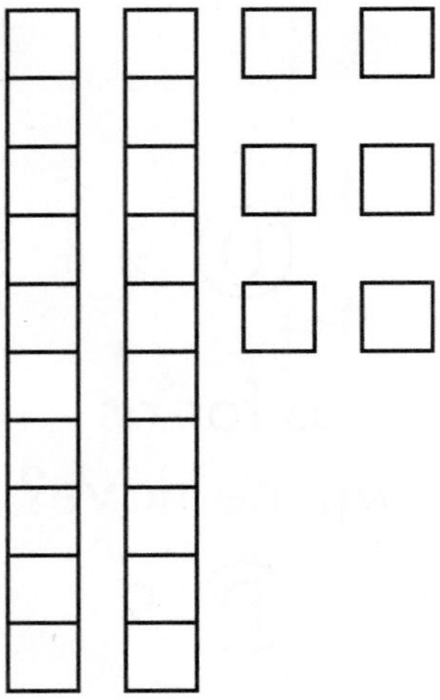

How many stickers? ___

2. 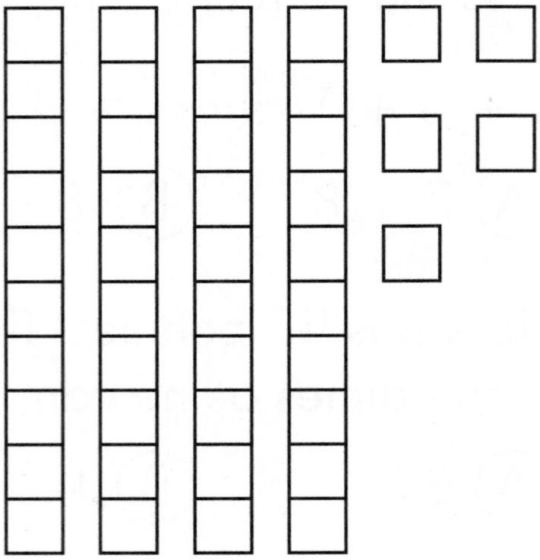

How many stickers? ___

3. Show 54 stickers using strips of 10 and singles.

4. Show all the possible ways to make 31 with stickers (strips of 10 and singles). Use the back of this page.

Copyright © by Pearson Education, Inc., or its affiliates. All rights reserved. 2

Name Date

Combinations of Tens and Ones

Write equations to show all the possible combinations of strips and singles for each number.

1. 32

2. 45

3. 69

Copyright © by Pearson Education, Inc., or its affiliates. All rights reserved. 2

Name Date

Quiz

RULE A: Dark shapes **RULE B:** Shapes with straight sides

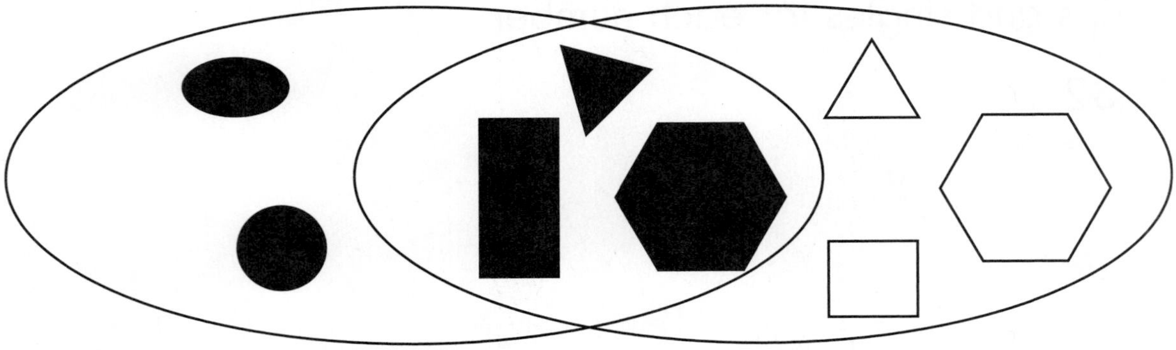

Look at Rule A and Rule B above. Choose the correct answer.

1. Which of these shapes fits Rule A?

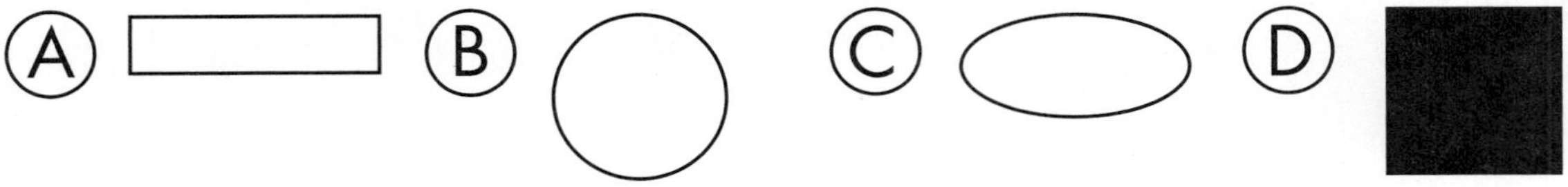

2. Which of these shapes fits Rule B?

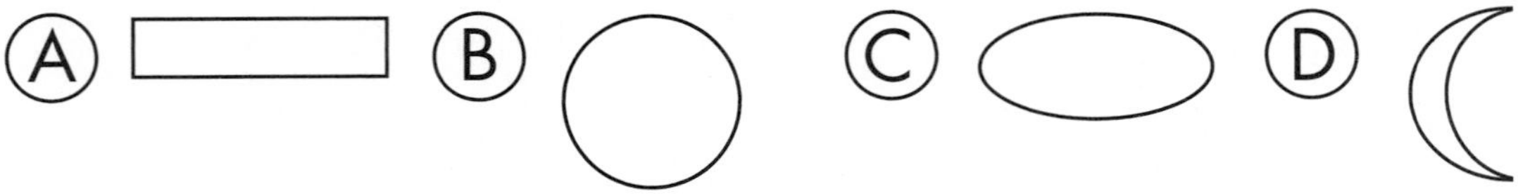

3. Which of these shapes does **not** fit Rule A or Rule B?

4. Draw another shape that fits **both** rules.

Copyright © by Pearson Education, Inc., or its affiliates. All rights reserved. 2

Name Date

Sorting Flower Data

Here are some flowers that one student drew.
Think of a rule for sorting the flowers.

What is your rule?

____

Circle each flower that fits your rule.

How many flowers fit your rule? ______

How many flowers do **not** fit your rule? ______

Copyright © by Pearson Education, Inc., or its affiliates. All rights reserved. 2

Name Date

Two Rules for Data

Here are some buttons. Think of how they are different.

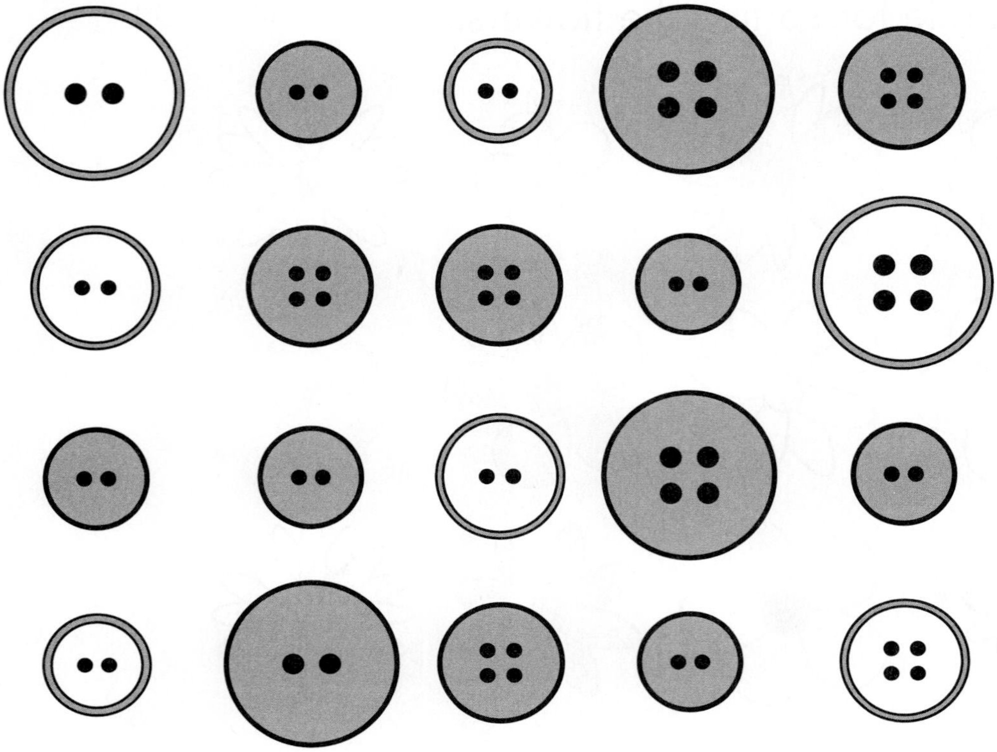

How can you sort the buttons? Write two sorting rules.

Rule A: ______________________________

Rule B: ______________________________

Circle each button that fits Rule A.
Draw an X on each button that fits Rule B.

On a separate piece of paper, draw a Venn diagram.
Represent the button data using your rules.

Copyright © by Pearson Education, Inc., or its affiliates. All rights reserved. 2

Name Date

Quiz

Choose the correct answer.

A group of students went on a field trip to a park. They counted the number of butterflies they saw. The group made this line plot.

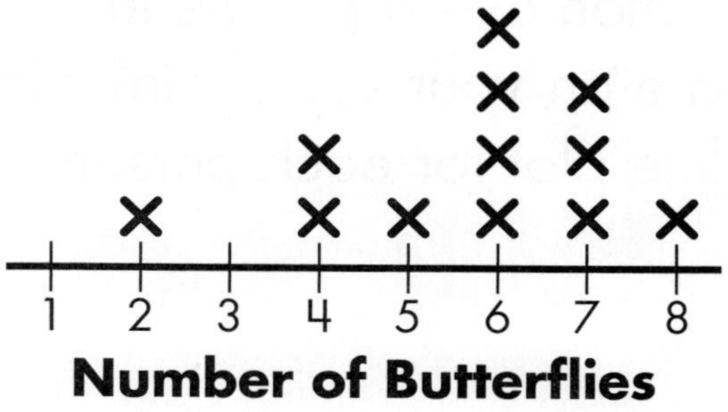

1. What is the most common number of butterflies seen?

Ⓐ 1 Ⓑ 4 Ⓒ 6 Ⓓ 8

2. How many students were in the group?

Ⓐ 6 Ⓑ 8 Ⓒ 10 Ⓓ 12

3. How many students in the group saw more than 6 butterflies?

Ⓐ 1 Ⓑ 4 Ⓒ 6 Ⓓ 8

4. Describe 2 more things you notice about the data.

Copyright © by Pearson Education, Inc., or its affiliates. All rights reserved. 2

Name Date

Line Plots

Simon asked people this question: How many keys are on your key chain? Simon marked an X on the line plot for each person's answer.

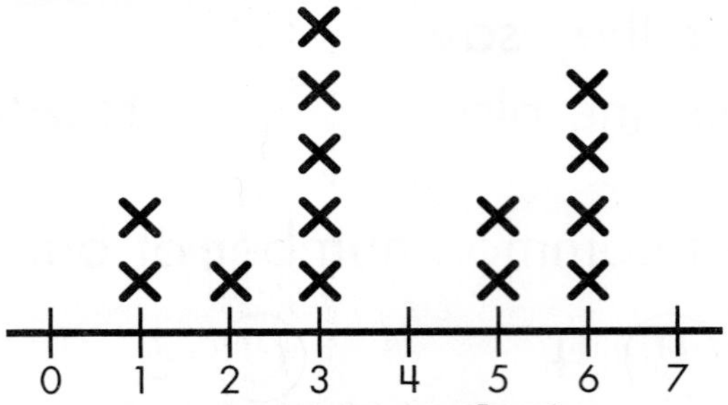

1. How many key chains had 3 keys? ___________

2. How many key chains had 6 keys? ___________

3. Were there more key chains with 5 keys or 2 keys? ___________

4. How many key chains had less than 4 keys? ___________

5. How many people answered Simon's question? ___________

How do you know? ___________

____

____

Copyright © by Pearson Education, Inc., or its affiliates. All rights reserved. 2

Use anytime after Session 2.4.

Name Date

Representing Age Data

Here are the names and ages of students who volunteer at an animal shelter.

Amaya	16	Alberto	13	Chen	17
Darren	18	Holly	17	Juanita	19
Melissa	14	Travis	15	Nadia	17
Jacy	15	Monisha	13	Leo	14
Yama	17	Malcolm	19	Lonzell	19
Jeffrey	13	Carolina	13	Henry	17
Nate	15	Katrina	19		

1. Use a line plot to show the data.

2. What is the mode? ______________________

3. What is the range? ______________________

4. Are there any outliers? ______________________

Copyright © by Pearson Education, Inc., or its affiliates. All rights reserved. 2

Name Date

Quiz

Choose the correct answer.

Alberto is buying cans of tennis balls. The table shows the number of tennis balls in 1, 2, and 3 cans.

Number of Cans	Number of Tennis Balls
1	3
2	6
3	9

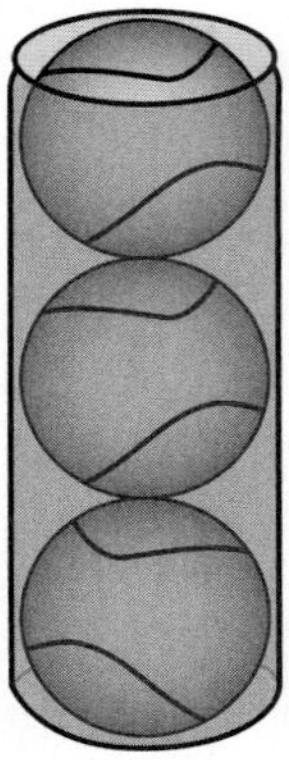

1. How many tennis balls are in 3 cans?

Ⓐ 3 Ⓑ 4 Ⓒ 6 Ⓓ 9

2. How many cans will have a total of 6 tennis balls?

Ⓐ 6 Ⓑ 4 Ⓒ 3 Ⓓ 2

3. How many tennis balls will be in 5 cans?

Ⓐ 3 Ⓑ 10 Ⓒ 15 Ⓓ 18

4. Choose a number greater than 5. ______________

How many tennis balls will be in that number of cans? ______________

Copyright © by Pearson Education, Inc., or its affiliates. All rights reserved. 2

Name Date

Polygons and Stars

Jacy is decorating a wall with pentagons. A pentagon has 5 sides and 5 corners. She will put a star on each corner of each pentagon.

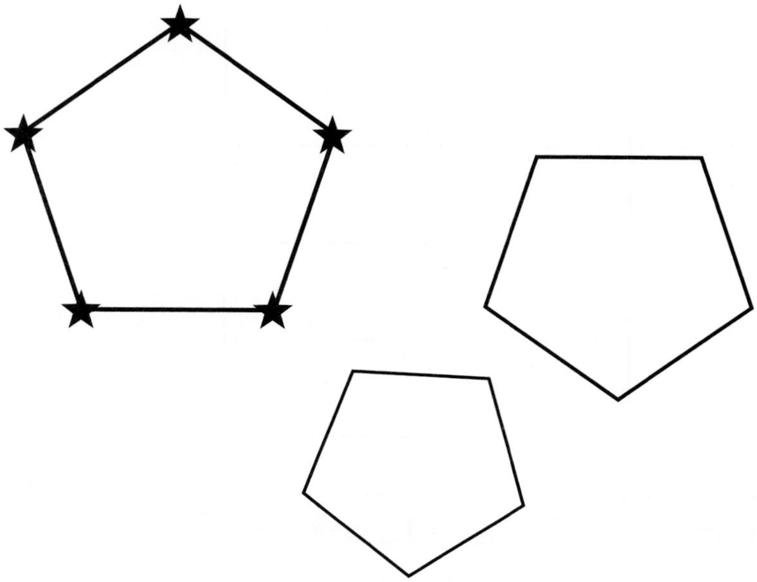

Complete the table.

Number of Pentagons	Total Number of Stars
1	
	10
3	
4	
	25
10	

Copyright © by Pearson Education, Inc., or its affiliates. All rights reserved. 2

Name Date

How Many Floors? How Many Rooms?

Floor Plans and Tables

Draw a floor plan for a cube building with 9 rooms on a floor. Then fill in the table with the missing information.

Total Number of Floors	Total Number of Rooms
1	
2	
	27
4	
	45
10	
20	

As the total number of floors increases, what happens to the total number of rooms? What pattern do you notice in the table?

Copyright © by Pearson Education, Inc., or its affiliates. All rights reserved. 2

Name Date

Quiz

Choose the correct answer.

Use this pattern to answer the questions.

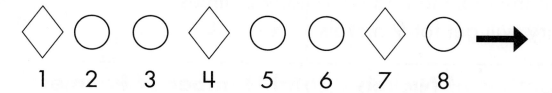

◇	○	○	◇	○	○	◇	○	→
1	2	3	4	5	6	7	8	

1. If the pattern continues, which shapes will be 9th and 10th?

Ⓐ ◇ ◇ Ⓑ ◇ ○ Ⓒ ○ ○ Ⓓ ○ ◇

2. What is the unit that repeats in this pattern?

Ⓐ ◇ ◇ ○

Ⓒ ◇ ○ ○

Ⓑ ○ ○

Ⓓ ○ ◇

3. What number will be under the next ◇?

Ⓐ 9 Ⓑ 10 Ⓒ 11 Ⓓ 12

4. Draw the 15th shape. How do you know?

Copyright © by Pearson Education, Inc., or its affiliates. All rights reserved. 2

Name Date

Working with 5-Element Patterns

Mrs. Mull is giving Henry 5 pennies for every nickel in his piggy bank.

1. Fill in the table to find how many pennies Henry will get for 9 nickels.

Number of Nickels	Total Number of Pennies
1	5
2	10
3	
4	
5	
6	
7	
8	
9	

2. If Henry has 12 nickels, how many pennies would he get? How do you know?

____

Copyright © by Pearson Education, Inc., or its affiliates. All rights reserved. 2

Name Date

More Cube Trains

Color a **blue-blue-green-yellow** pattern on the number strip and answer the questions.

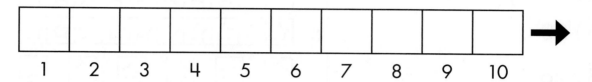

1	2	3	4	5	6	7	8	9	10

→

1. What color is the 5th cube? ______________

2. What color is the 7th cube? ______________

3. If you kept the pattern going, what number would the next **yellow** cube be? ______________

4. Write the numbers matched with **yellow** cubes. Keep going until you get to at least 40.

____

5. Write one thing you notice about the number pattern in Problem 4.

____

____

____

Copyright © by Pearson Education, Inc., or its affiliates. All rights reserved. 2

Name Date

How Many Tens? How Many Ones?

Quiz

Choose the correct answer.

1. How many stickers?

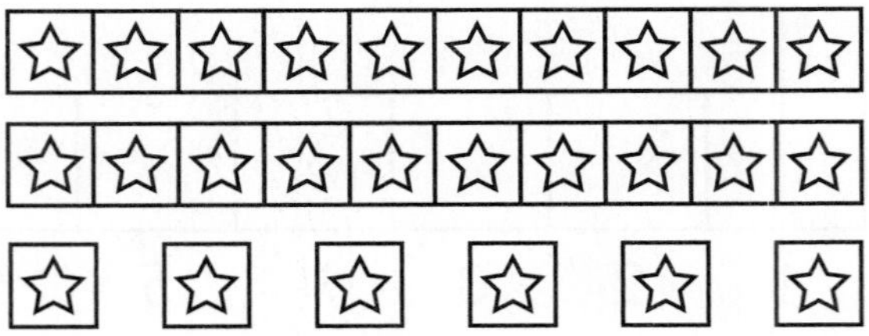

Ⓐ 30

Ⓑ 26

Ⓒ 25

Ⓓ 16

2. 10 + 10 + 3 + 10 + 2 =

Ⓐ 25 Ⓑ 32 Ⓒ 33 Ⓓ 35

3. Tia had 45 sun stickers. She gave 10 to her sister and 10 to her brother. How many stickers did Tia have left?

Ⓐ 65 Ⓑ 35 Ⓒ 25 Ⓓ 15

4. Solve the problem. Show your work and write an equation. Use another sheet of paper.

Darren had 23 car stickers. He went to Sticker Station and bought 1 more strip of ten car stickers and 5 single car stickers. How many car stickers did Darren have then?

Copyright © by Pearson Education, Inc., or its affiliates. All rights reserved. 2

Name Date

Combining Stickers

Simon went to Sticker Station.
He bought 3 strips of ten dog stickers and 4 single dog stickers.
He also bought 2 strips of ten cat stickers and 1 single cat sticker.
How many stickers did Simon buy?

1. Use sticker notation to show how many dog stickers Simon bought. Write an equation using tens and ones to show this amount.

_______ + _______ = _______

2. Use sticker notation to show how many cat stickers Simon bought. Write an equation using tens and ones to show this amount.

_______ + _______ = _______

3. How many total stickers did Simon buy? Use equations to show your work.

Copyright © by Pearson Education, Inc., or its affiliates. All rights reserved. 2

Name Date

Using Strategies to Solve Problems

Write an equation. Then solve the problem and show your work.

1. Chen collected stickers of insects. He bought 4 strips of ten dragonfly stickers and 3 single dragonfly stickers. He also bought 3 strips of ten bee stickers and 6 single bee stickers. How many stickers of insects did Chen buy?

2. Carla collected flower stickers. She bought 2 strips of ten daisy stickers and 7 single daisy stickers. She also bought 4 strips of ten tulip stickers and 1 single tulip sticker. How many flower stickers did Carla buy?

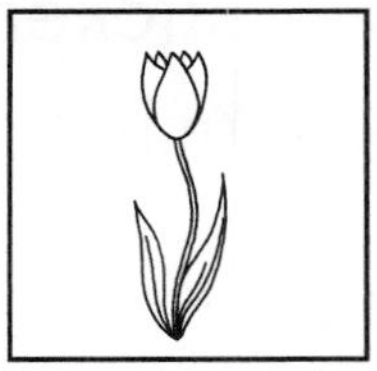

Copyright © by Pearson Education, Inc., or its affiliates. All rights reserved. 2

Use anytime after Session 1.3.

Quiz

Choose the correct answer.

1. 10 + 20 + 10 + 4 =

(A) 24 (B) 34 (C) 35 (D) 44

2. How many more cubes do you need to finish another row of 10?

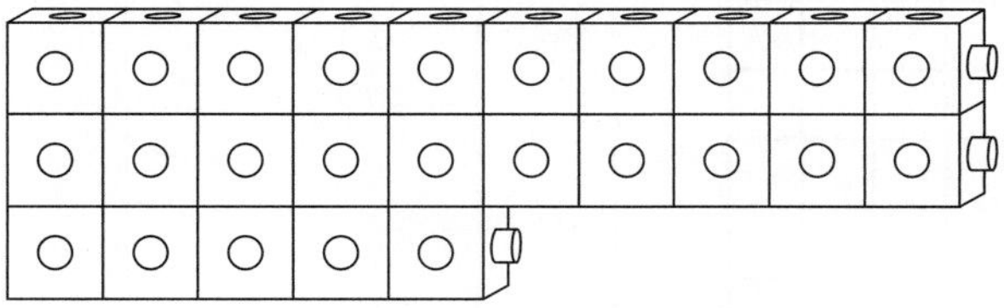

(A) 3 (B) 4 (C) 5 (D) 6

3. Tia and Simon were playing *Roll-a-Square.* They had 48 cubes. They rolled a 7. How many cubes did they have then?

(A) 55 (B) 54 (C) 45 (D) 41

4. Solve the problem. Write an equation. Show your work on another sheet of paper.

Yama has 27 moon stickers. How many more moon stickers does Yama need to have 60 moon stickers?

Copyright © by Pearson Education, Inc., or its affiliates. All rights reserved. 2

Name Date

Problems on a Grid

Use the grid to solve each problem. Write an equation.

1. Nadia has 29 bicycle stickers. How many more does Nadia need to have 50 bicycle stickers? ______

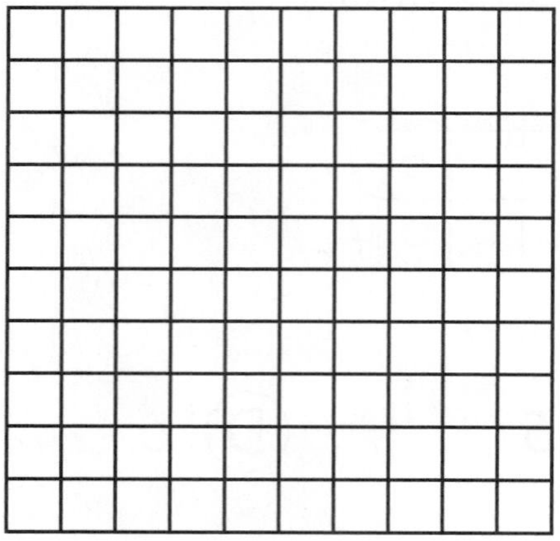

2. Luis is collecting boat stickers. How many boat stickers does Luis have? ______

How many more does Luis need to have 70 boat stickers? ______

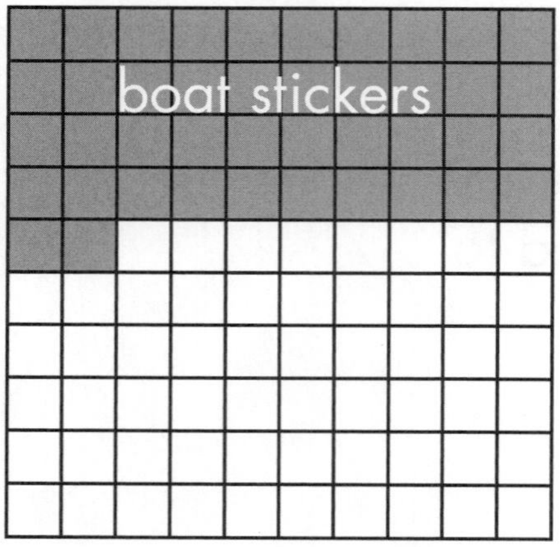

Copyright © by Pearson Education, Inc., or its affiliates. All rights reserved. 2

Use anytime after Session 2.5.

Name Date

More Than 100 Stickers

Solve the problems. Show your work. You can use the grids to help you.

1. Holly has 142 flower stickers. How many more does Holly need to have 180 flower stickers? ______

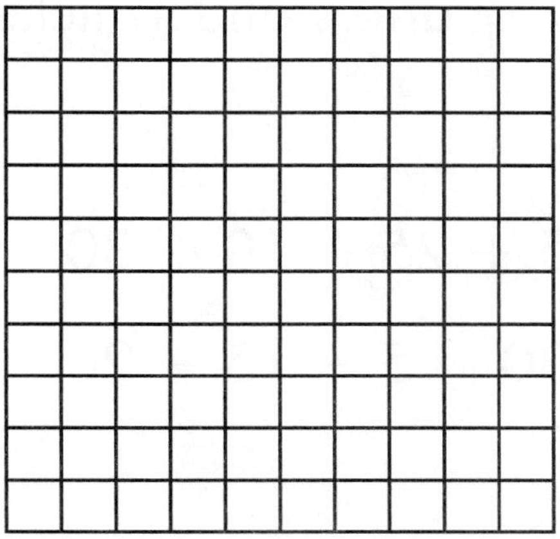

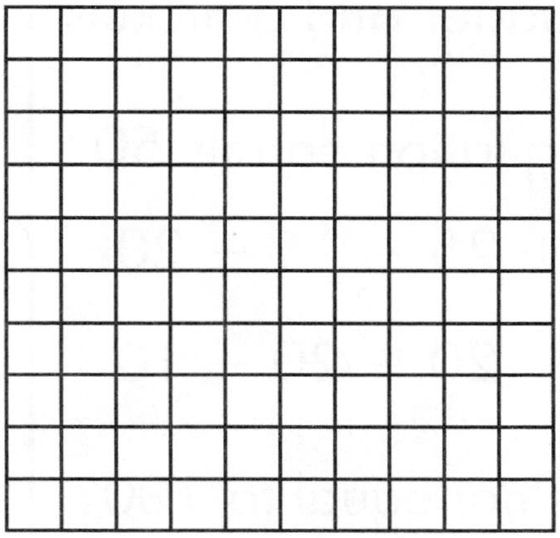

2. Nate has 157 car stickers. How many more does Nate need to have 200 car stickers? ______

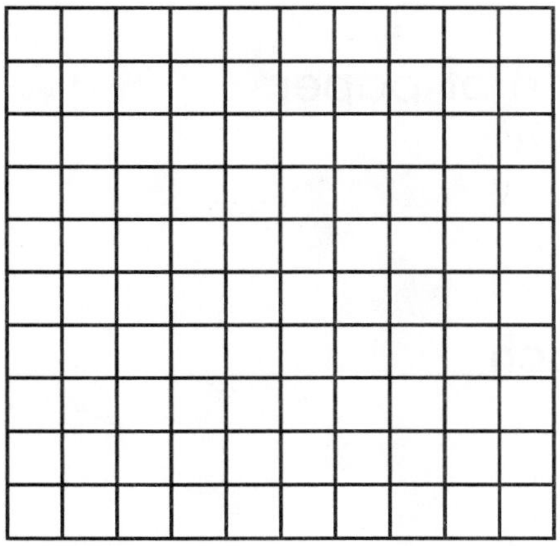

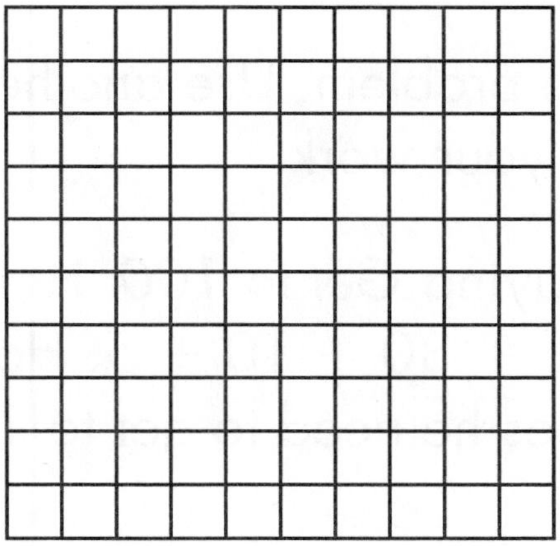

Copyright © by Pearson Education, Inc., or its affiliates. All rights reserved. 2

Quiz

Choose the correct answer.

1. Tia has 5 dimes and 5 pennies. Which of the following coins are equal to this?

Ⓐ 1 quarter and 2 dimes
Ⓑ 1 quarter and 5 nickels
Ⓒ 2 quarters and 1 dime
Ⓓ 2 quarters and 1 nickel

2. Which equation equals 50?

Ⓐ $20 + 25 - 15 - 20$
Ⓑ $10 + 20 + 20 - 10$
Ⓒ $5 + 25 - 10 + 30$
Ⓓ $30 - 5 + 15 - 20$

3. Which is not equal to 100?

Ⓐ 10 dimes
Ⓑ 10 nickels
Ⓒ 10 strips of 10 stickers
Ⓓ 10 towers of 10 cubes

4. Solve the problem. Use another piece of paper to show your work.

Leo is playing *Get to 100*. He rolls $20 + 15 + 30 + 10 + 5$. How much more does he need to get to 100?

Copyright © by Pearson Education, Inc., or its affiliates. All rights reserved. 2

Name Date

Addition and Subtraction Equations

Solve the problems. Show your work.

1. 62 + 10 + 10 + 8 = __	**2.** 45 + 20 − 10 + 5 = __
3. 76 − 10 − 10 − 6 = __	**4.** 98 − 20 + 12 = __
5. 39 + 30 + 11 − 10 = __	**6.** 54 − 20 + 10 − 8 = __

Copyright © by Pearson Education, Inc., or its affiliates. All rights reserved. 2

Name Date

Get to 0

Anita and Darren are playing *Get to 0*. Below are the numbers they rolled. Write an equation for each problem. Show your work.

1. Anita's game piece is on 50. She rolls 20 and 15. On what number should she put her game piece now? ____________

What numbers does Anita need to roll to get exactly to 0? ____________ and ____________

2. Darren's game piece is on 65. He rolls 20 and 25. On what number should he put his game piece now? ____________

What numbers does Darren need to roll to get exactly to 0? ____________ and ____________

Copyright © by Pearson Education, Inc., or its affiliates. All rights reserved. 2

Use anytime after Session 3.5.

Quiz

Choose the correct answer.

1. Nadia is making a counting strip. She wrote 60, 65, 70, 75, 80. What number should she write next?

Ⓐ 81 Ⓑ 82 Ⓒ 85 Ⓓ 90

2. Juan is making a counting strip. He wrote 34, 36, 38, 40. Which tells about the numbers he wrote?

Ⓐ count by 1s
Ⓑ count by 2s
Ⓒ count by 5s
Ⓓ count by 10s

3. How many nickels are there in 75 cents?

Ⓐ 10 Ⓑ 15 Ⓒ 16 Ⓓ 20

4. Solve the problem. Show your work.

Holly counted by 2s to 70. How many numbers did she say?

Copyright © by Pearson Education, Inc., or its affiliates. All rights reserved. 2

Name Date

Skip Counting from Any Multiple

Write the missing numbers on the skip-counting strips.

1.	2.	3.	4.
20	24	30	65
25	26	40	70
30	28	50	75

Copyright © by Pearson Education, Inc., or its affiliates. All rights reserved. 2

Use anytime after Session 4.2.

Name Date

How Many 5s in Larger Numbers

1. If you filled in every fifth square on a 300 chart up to 275, how many numbers would you write?

____

How did you figure this out?

2. If you filled in every tenth square on a 300 chart up to 275, how many numbers would you write?

____

How did you figure this out?

3. Fill in the count-by-5s numbers up to 275 on a blank 300 chart.

Copyright © by Pearson Education, Inc., or its affiliates. All rights reserved. 2

Name Date

Quiz

Choose the correct answer.

1. Which line does **not** show halves?

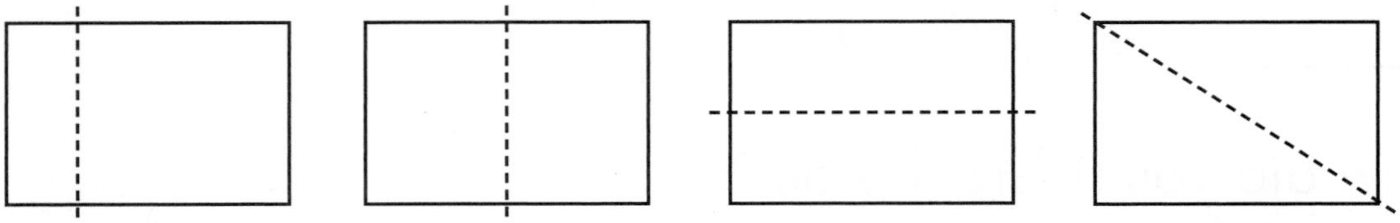

(A) (B) (C) (D)

2. Which square shows one half shaded?

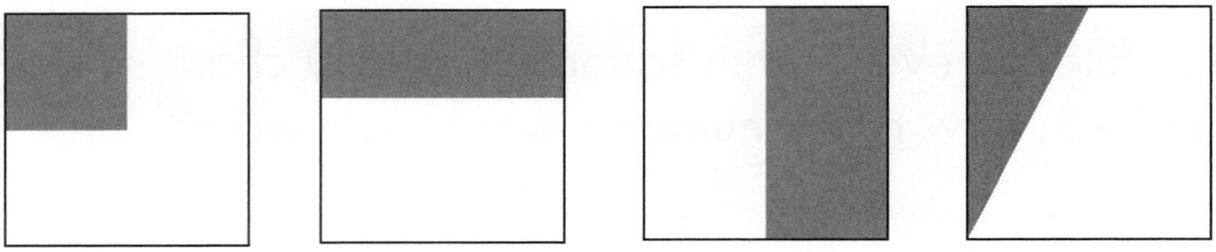

(A) (B) (C) (D)

3. Two girls share 3 apples evenly. How many apples does each girl get?

(A) $2\frac{1}{2}$ (B) $1\frac{1}{2}$ (C) $\frac{2}{3}$ (D) $\frac{1}{2}$

4. What is $\frac{1}{2}$ of 8 tiles? ________ tiles

Draw a way to show the answer.

Copyright © by Pearson Education, Inc., or its affiliates. All rights reserved. 2

Name Date

Halves or Not?

Circle the shape if the line shows halves.

1.

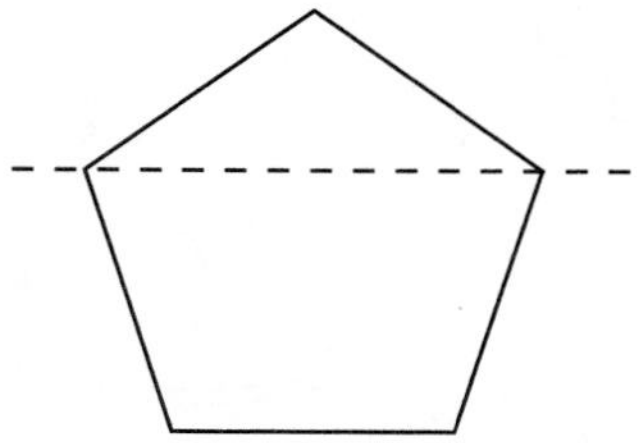

2.

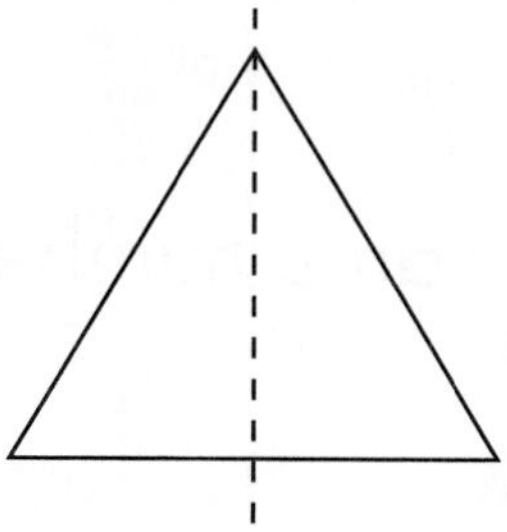

3.

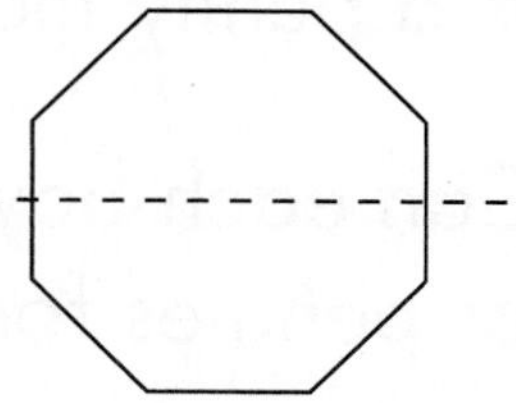

4.

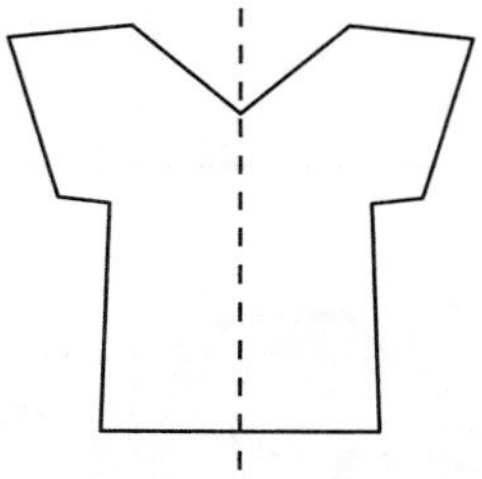

5.

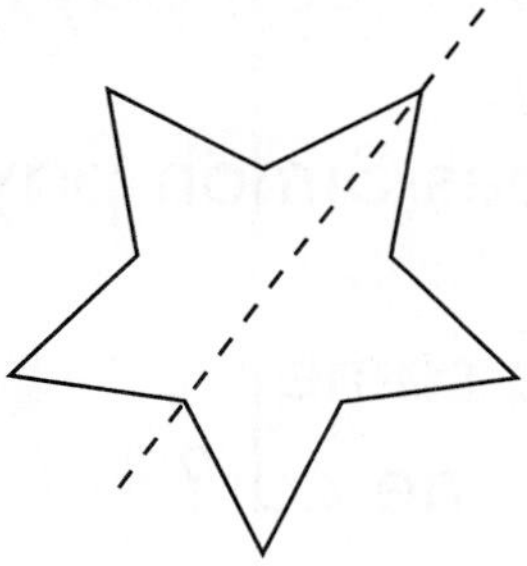

6.

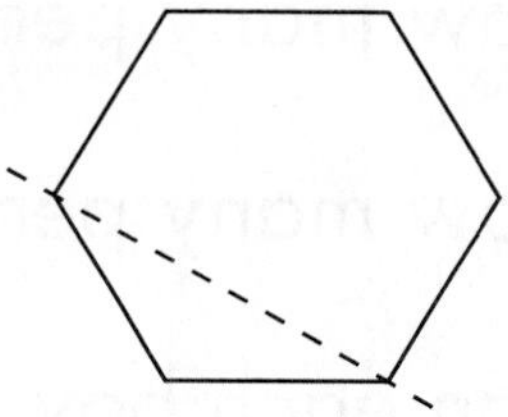

7.

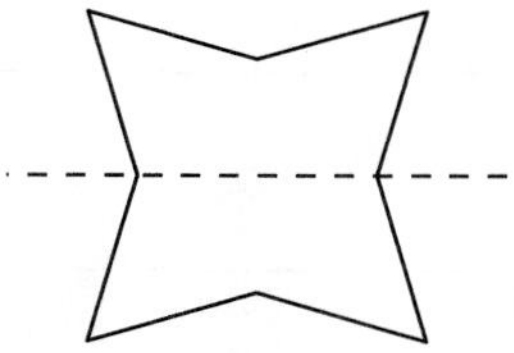

8.

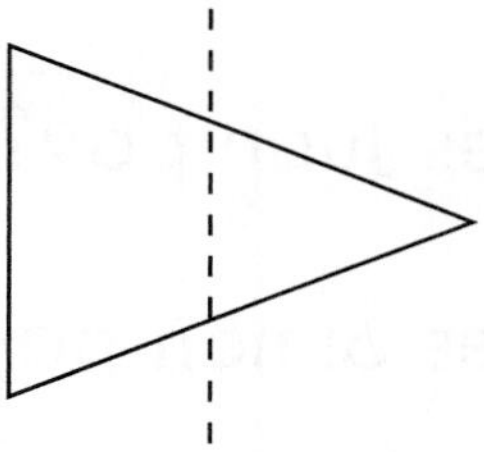

9.

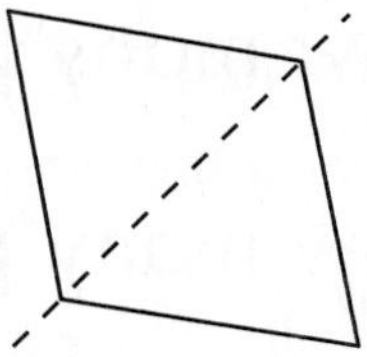

Draw a line to divide the rectangle into halves.

10.

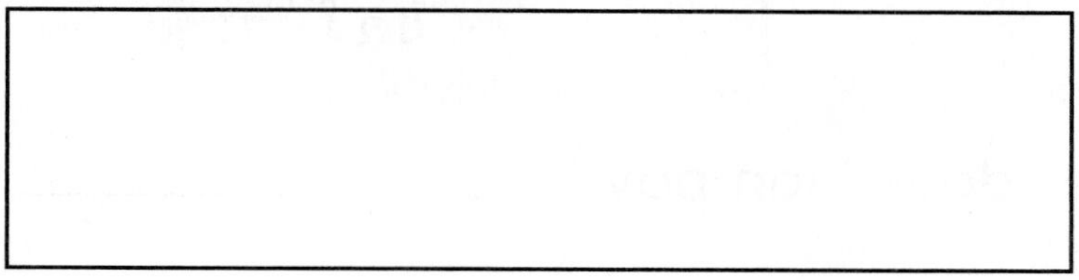

Copyright © by Pearson Education, Inc., or its affiliates. All rights reserved. 2

Name Date

Parts of a Whole, Parts of a Group

Sharing the Cost of Toys

Juan and Simon each have a lot of pennies. They are buying toys to share. Each boy pays half, or one boy pays a penny more.

1. Can each boy pay the same number of pennies for the top?

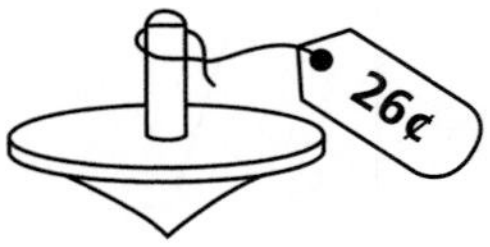

______

How many pennies does Juan pay? ______

How many pennies does Simon pay? ______

2. Can each boy pay the same number of pennies for the car?

______

How many pennies does Juan pay? ______

How many pennies does Simon pay? ______

3. Can each boy pay the same number of pennies for the puzzle?

______

How many pennies does Juan pay? ______

How many pennies does Simon pay? ______

Copyright © by Pearson Education, Inc., or its affiliates. All rights reserved. 2

Use anytime after Session 1.2.

Name Date

Parts of a Whole, Parts of a Group

Quiz

Choose the correct answer.

1. Which rectangle is $\frac{1}{4}$ shaded?

Ⓐ 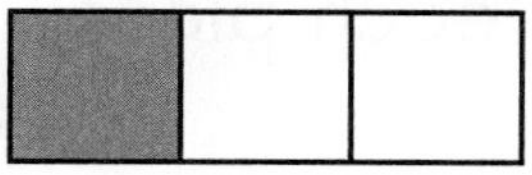

Ⓒ 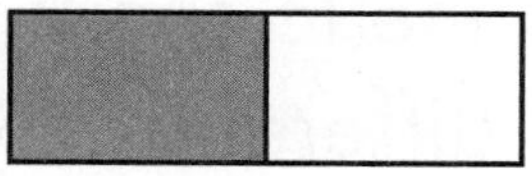

Ⓑ 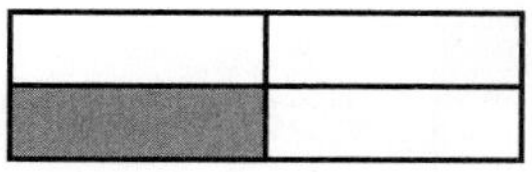

Ⓓ 

2. What fraction of the group of squares is circled?

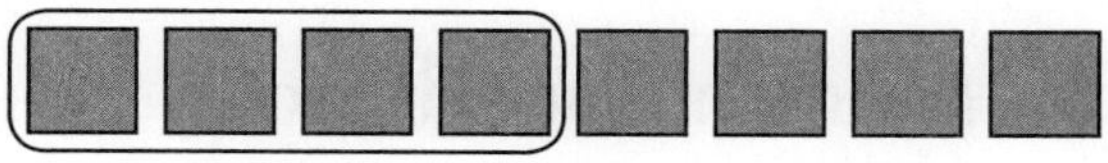

Ⓐ $\frac{1}{4}$ Ⓑ $\frac{1}{3}$ Ⓒ $\frac{1}{2}$ Ⓓ $\frac{2}{3}$

3. What fraction of the rectangle is shaded?

Ⓐ $\frac{3}{4}$ Ⓑ $\frac{2}{3}$ Ⓒ $\frac{1}{2}$ Ⓓ $\frac{1}{3}$

4. Leo's mother has 12 stickers. She gave Leo one third of the stickers. How many stickers did Leo get? _______ stickers

Show how you figured it out.

Copyright © by Pearson Education, Inc., or its affiliates. All rights reserved. 2

Name Date

Making Fractions

Monisha is making a quilt out of some checked cloth.

1. Monisha needs each of these pieces cut in half.
Draw a line to show how she could cut each piece.
Show 2 different ways.

2. Monisha needs each of these pieces cut in thirds.
Draw a line to show how she could cut each piece.
Show 2 different ways.

3. Monisha needs each of these pieces cut in fourths.
Draw a line to show how she could cut each piece.
Show 2 different ways.

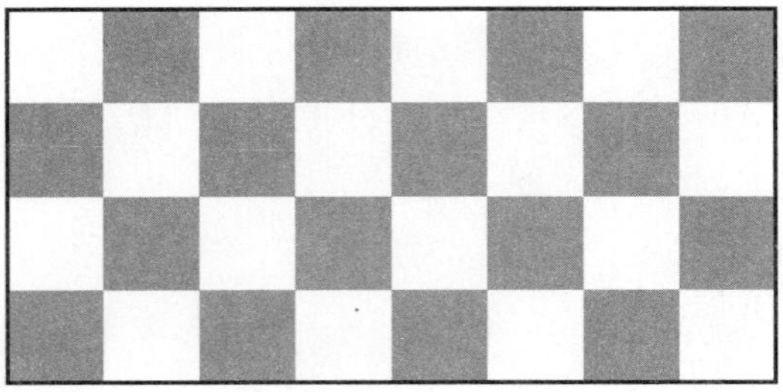
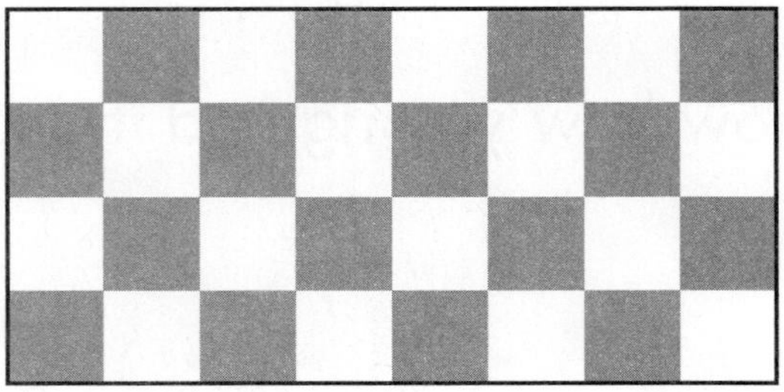

Copyright © by Pearson Education, Inc., or its affiliates. All rights reserved. 2

Name Date

Parts of a Whole, Parts of a Group

Sharing Snacks

Solve each problem. Show your work.

1. Two sisters are sharing 3 pieces of toast evenly. How many pieces does each sister get? ________

How did you figure it out?

2. Leigh, Rochelle, and Luis are sharing a bag of 15 grapes. Each person eats $\frac{1}{3}$ of the grapes. How many grapes will each person eat? ________

How did you figure it out?

3. Four children are sharing 5 sandwiches. Each child eats $\frac{1}{4}$ of the sandwiches. How many sandwiches does each child eat? ________

How did you figure it out?

Copyright © by Pearson Education, Inc., or its affiliates. All rights reserved. 2

Name Date

Quiz

Choose the correct answer.

1. Which number of students can make 2 equal teams?

Ⓐ 7 Ⓑ 10 Ⓒ 15 Ⓓ 21

2. Which combination has an odd sum?

Ⓐ 14 + 13 Ⓒ 16 + 12

Ⓑ 15 + 11 Ⓓ 17 + 9

3. Which combination has an even sum?

Ⓐ 19 + 6 Ⓒ 8 + 17

Ⓑ 10 + 23 Ⓓ 21 + 11

4. Can you make 24 with an even number and an odd number?

________ + ________ = 24

If you think you cannot, explain why:

____

____

Copyright © by Pearson Education, Inc., or its affiliates. All rights reserved. 2

Name Date

Partners, Teams, and Paper Clips

Even and Odd Sums

Solve each problem. Answer each question.

1. 2 + 4 = ________ Is the answer even or odd? ________

2. 10 + 6 = ________ Is the answer even or odd? ________

3. 18 + 22 = ________ Is the answer even or odd? ________

4. What happens when you add 2 even numbers? Why?

____

____

5. 3 + 5 = ________ Is the answer even or odd? ________

6. 11 + 7 = ________ Is the answer even or odd? ________

7. 19 + 23 = ________ Is the answer even or odd? ________

8. What happens when you add 2 odd numbers? Why?

____

____

Copyright © by Pearson Education, Inc., or its affiliates. All rights reserved. 2

Name Date

Subtracting Even and Odd Numbers

Solve each problem. Answer each question.

1. 9 − 3 = ______ Is the answer even or odd? ______

2. 17 − 5 = ______ Is the answer even or odd? ______

3. 35 − 13 = ______ Is the answer even or odd? ______

4. What happens when you subtract an odd number from an odd number? Why?

____

____

5. 9 − 4 = ______ Is the answer even or odd? ______

6. 17 − 6 = ______ Is the answer even or odd? ______

7. 35 − 14 = ______ Is the answer even or odd? ______

8. What happens when you subtract an even number from an odd number? Why?

____

____

Copyright © by Pearson Education, Inc., or its affiliates. All rights reserved. 2

Name Date

Quiz

Choose the correct answer.

1. Which has a sum that is 1 less than 5 + 10?

A	B	C	D
6 + 10	6 + 9	5 + 9	4 + 9

2. Nate and Jacy are playing *Plus 9 or 10 Bingo.* Nate wants to cover a square with 16 on it. Which card does he need?

A	B	C	D
9	8	7	5

3. Jacy wants to cover a square with 17 on it. Which card does she need?

A	B	C	D
6	8	9	10

4. Henry says he can't remember the sum for 5 + 7. Write a clue that will help him.

Copyright © by Pearson Education, Inc., or its affiliates. All rights reserved. 2

Name Date

Sorting and Solving Addition Combinations

Choose 3 pairs of problems that might be hard for you to remember.

4 + 7 7 + 4	4 + 8 8 + 4	5 + 7 7 + 5
5 + 8 8 + 5	7 + 9 9 + 7	6 + 8 8 + 6

1. ______________ is hard for me to remember.
Here is a clue that can help me:

2. ______________ is hard for me to remember.
Here is a clue that can help me:

3. ______________ is hard for me to remember.
Here is a clue that can help me:

Copyright © by Pearson Education, Inc., or its affiliates. All rights reserved. 2

Use anytime after Session 2.2.

Name Date

More *Plus 9 or 10 Bingo*

Tia and Leo are playing *Plus 9 or 10 Bingo.*

1. Tia wants to cover the square with 17 on it.
What two cards would work?

$\square + 9 = 17$ $\square + 10 = 17$

2. Leo wants to cover the square with 14 on it.
What two cards would work?

$\square + 9 = 14$ $\square + 10 = 14$

Chen and Holly are playing *Plus 9 or 10 Bingo,* too.

3. Chen wants to cover the square with 15 on it.
What two cards would work?

$\square + 9 = 15$ $\square + 10 = 15$

4. Holly wants to cover the square with 12 on it.
What two cards would work?

$\square + 9 = 12$ $\square + 10 = 12$

Copyright © by Pearson Education, Inc., or its affiliates. All rights reserved. 2

Quiz

Choose the correct answer.

1. Yama put 36 grapes in a bowl. Carla ate 14 of them. How many grapes were left?

Ⓐ 28 Ⓑ 22 Ⓒ 18 Ⓓ 16

2. $100 - 25 =$

Ⓐ 95 Ⓑ 85 Ⓒ 75 Ⓓ 65

3. Jeffrey had 52 pennies. He spent 39 pennies on a sticker. How many pennies did he have left?

Ⓐ 7 Ⓑ 11 Ⓒ 12 Ⓓ 13

4. Write an equation. Solve the problem. Show your work.

Nadia and Simon were playing *Cover Up* with 45 counters. Nadia hid some of the counters. She left 12 showing. How many counters did she hide?

Copyright © by Pearson Education, Inc., or its affiliates. All rights reserved. 2

Subtraction Problems: Starting with 100

Solve each problem. Show your work.

1. How many bottles of juice are in the case? ________

How many are missing? ________

2. How many cans are in the case? ________

How many are missing? ________

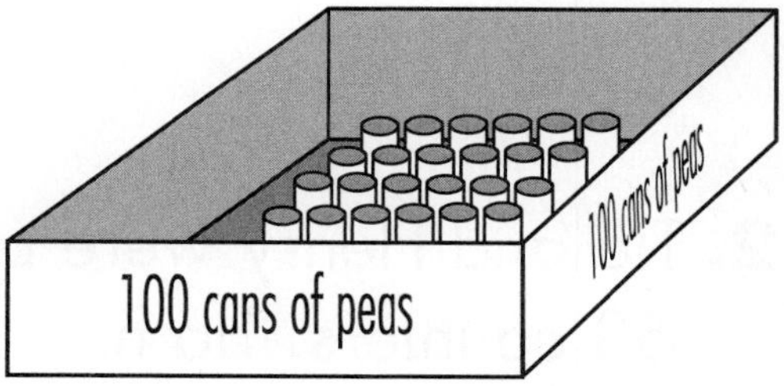

3. How many boxes of raisins are in the case? ________

How many are missing? ________

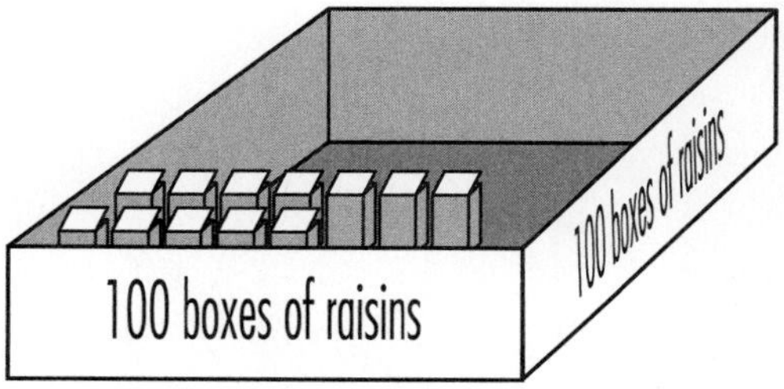

Copyright © by Pearson Education, Inc., or its affiliates. All rights reserved. 2

Name Date

Visualizing Problems, Writing Equations

Write an equation. Solve the problem.
Show your work.

1. Travis had 42 pennies. His brother gave him 10 more pennies. Then he spent 31 pennies on baseball cards. How many pennies did he have left?

2. Tia and Henry were playing *Cover Up* with 68 counters. Tia hid some of the counters. If 29 were showing, how many counters did Tia hide?

Copyright © by Pearson Education, Inc., or its affiliates. All rights reserved. 2

Use anytime after Session 3.2.

Name Date

Quiz

Choose the correct answer.

1. Luis solved 36 + 23 by adding tens and ones. How many tens are in the sum?

Ⓐ 1 Ⓑ 4 Ⓒ 5 Ⓓ 6

2. Which matches the picture?

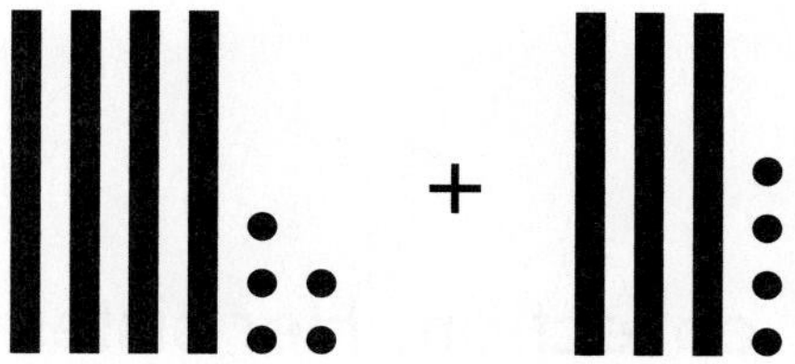

Ⓐ 45 + 34 Ⓒ 54 + 43

Ⓑ 46 + 35 Ⓓ 55 + 44

3. Yama had 57 pennies. Her mother gave her 33 more. How many pennies did Yama have then?

Ⓐ 80 Ⓑ 90 Ⓒ 91 Ⓓ 100

4. Write an equation. Solve the problem. Show your work on another piece of paper.

Juan saw 35 ducks in the pond. He saw 29 ducks on the shore. How many ducks did Juan see?

Copyright © by Pearson Education, Inc., or its affiliates. All rights reserved. 2

Name Date

Adding on Tens and Ones

Write an equation. Try to solve the problem by keeping one number whole. Show your work.

1. Nate saw 21 large birds in the park. He saw 52 small birds. How many birds did Nate see in all?

2. Tia had 45 seashells in her collection. Her sister gave her 36 more. How many seashells did Tia have then?

3. There are 39 guppies in the fish tank. There are 14 goldfish in the tank. How many fish are in the tank?

Copyright © by Pearson Education, Inc., or its affiliates. All rights reserved. 2

Use anytime after Session 4.2.

Name Date

Partners, Teams, and Paper Clips

Two-Digit Addition Challenges

Write an equation. Solve the problem. Show your work.

1. Holly picked up 24 pinecones from the yard. Malcolm picked up 51 pinecones, and Carla picked up 29 pinecones. How many pinecones did Holly, Malcolm, and Carla pick up in all?

2. Leo has 32 baseball cards, 57 football cards, and 19 basketball cards. How many sports cards does Leo have in all?

3. Amaya, Simon, and Anita picked wildflowers in a field. Amaya picked 44 wildflowers. Simon picked 23 wildflowers, and Anita picked 36 wildflowers. How many wildflowers did they pick in all?

Copyright © by Pearson Education, Inc., or its affiliates. All rights reserved. 2

Quiz

Choose the correct answer.

1. Use connecting cubes. How long is the straw?

Ⓐ 4 cubes Ⓑ 5 cubes Ⓒ 6 cubes Ⓓ 9 cubes

2. Use the measurements for the bookcase. What is the missing measurement?

Object	Measurement in Red Strips	Measurement in Green Strips
Bookcase	12 red strips	6 green strips
Easel	? red strips	1 green strip

Ⓐ 5 red strips

Ⓑ 4 red strips

Ⓒ 3 red strips

Ⓓ 2 red strips

3. Tia's jump measures 59 cubes. Nadia's jump measures 71 cubes. How many cubes longer is Nadia's jump?

Ⓐ 9 cubes Ⓑ 11 cubes Ⓒ 12 cubes Ⓓ 15 cubes

4. Luis and Chen measured the length of a window. Luis said it was 9 units. Chen said it was 16 units. Give 2 reasons why they got different amounts.

Copyright © by Pearson Education, Inc., or its affiliates. All rights reserved. 2

Name Date

Find the Object

Find an object to match each length.

Blue Strips	Yellow Strips
Find something 9 blue strips long. Object: ________	How many yellow strips is the object? Estimate: ________ Measure: ________
Find something 1 blue strip long. Object: ________	How many yellow strips is the object? Estimate: ________ Measure: ________
Find something 8 blue strips long. Object: ________	How many yellow strips is the object? Estimate: ________ Measure: ________

What did you notice about the number of blue strips compared to the number of yellow strips?

____

____

Copyright © by Pearson Education, Inc., or its affiliates. All rights reserved. 2

Name Date

More Blue and Yellow Strips

A class measured objects with pink and brown paper strips. All the pink strips were the same length. All the brown strips were the same length. Use the measurements for the height of a table lamp to figure out the missing measurements.

Object	Measurement in Pink Strips	Measurement in Brown Strips
1. Table Lamp	4 pink strips	8 brown strips
2. Cabinet	5 pink strips	______ brown strips
3. Door	13 pink strips	______ brown strips
4. Floor Lamp	______ pink strips	30 brown strips
5. Bucket	2 pink strips	______ brown strips
6. Pencil Cup	1 pink strip	______ brown strips
7. Bench	______ pink strips	6 brown strips

8. What did you notice about the number of pink strips compared to the number of brown strips?

____

____

Copyright © by Pearson Education, Inc., or its affiliates. All rights reserved. 2

Use anytime after Session 1.2.

Name Date

Quiz

Choose the correct answer.

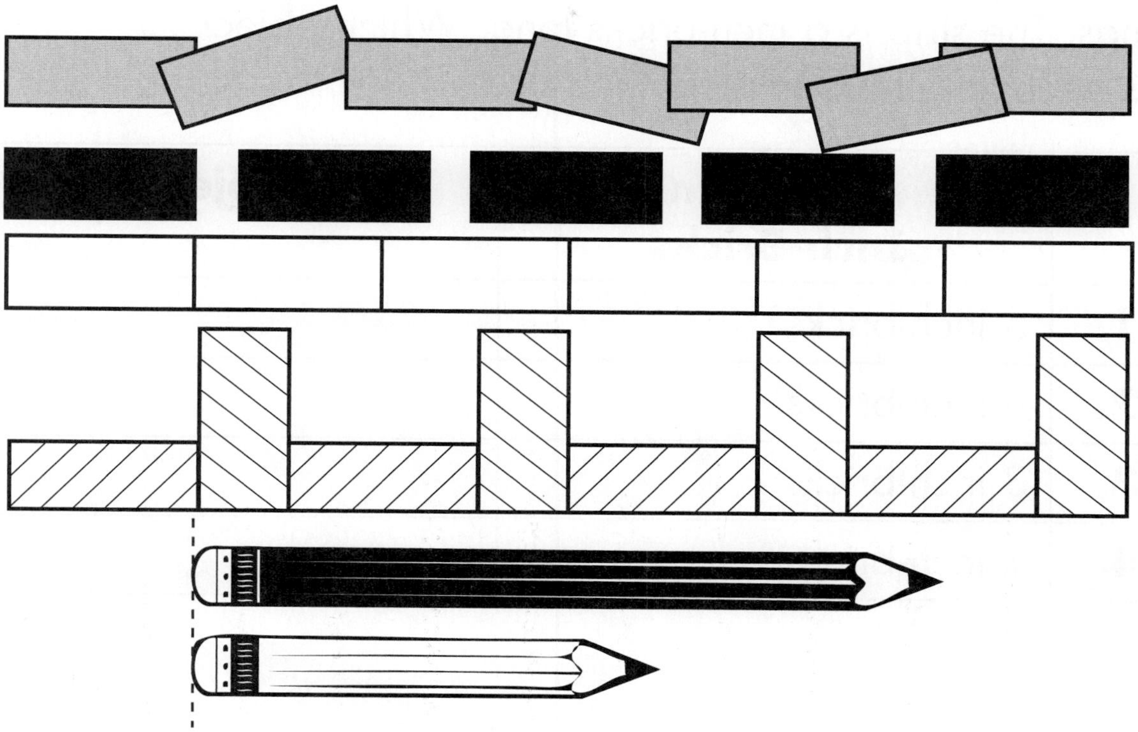

1. One row of inch-bricks above is best for measuring. What color are the bricks?

Ⓐ  Ⓑ  Ⓒ 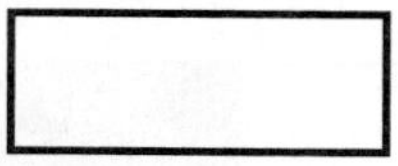 Ⓓ 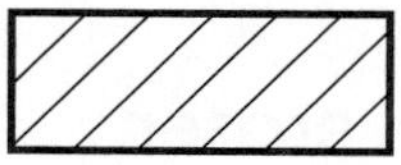

2. How many inch-bricks long is the dark pencil?

Ⓐ 3 Ⓑ 4 Ⓒ 5 Ⓓ 6

3. How many inch-bricks long is the white pencil?

Ⓐ 4 Ⓑ $3\frac{1}{2}$ Ⓒ 3 Ⓓ $2\frac{1}{2}$

4. How can you use an inch-brick tool to measure an object that is longer than 12 inch-bricks?

Copyright © by Pearson Education, Inc, or its affiliates. All rights reserved. 2

Measuring with Inch-Bricks

Use the strip at the bottom of this page to measure things. The strip is 6 inch-bricks long. Which object has each length? Complete the table.

	Length in Inch-Bricks	**Object**
1.	5 inch-bricks	
2.	4 inch-bricks	
3.	3 inch-bricks	
4.	1 inch-brick	

carrot
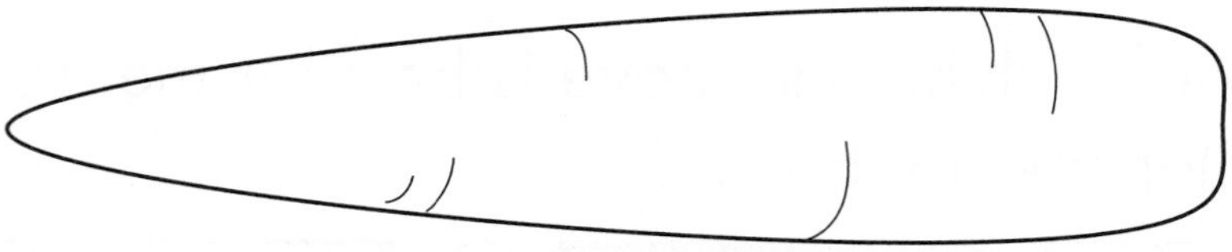

eraser

ribbon

paper clip
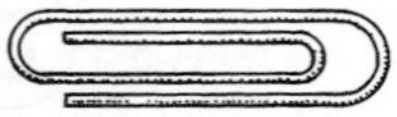

rope

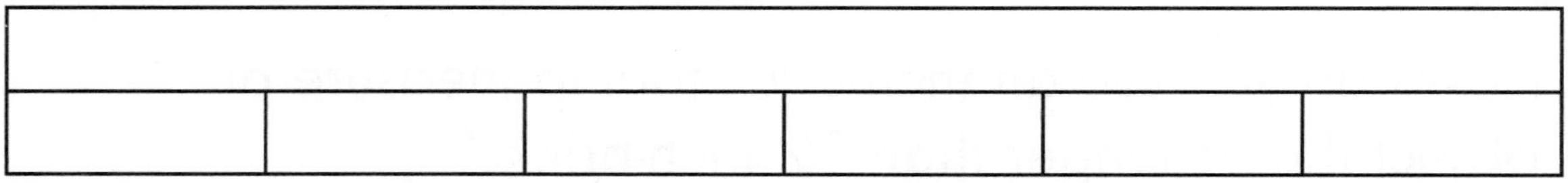

Copyright © by Pearson Education, Inc., or its affiliates. All rights reserved. 2

Name Date

Fractions of Inch-Bricks

Measure using the inch-brick tool.

1.

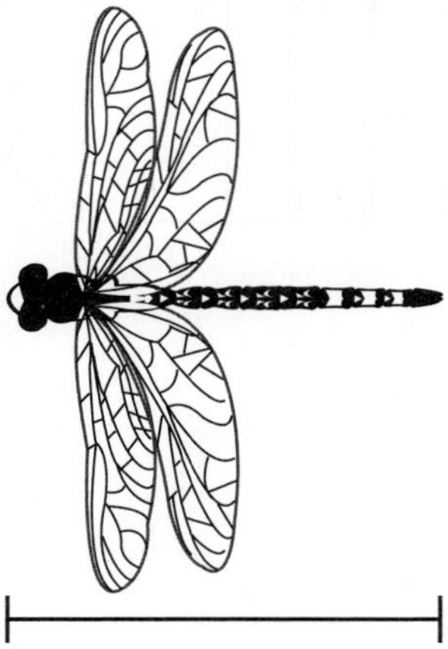

____

2.

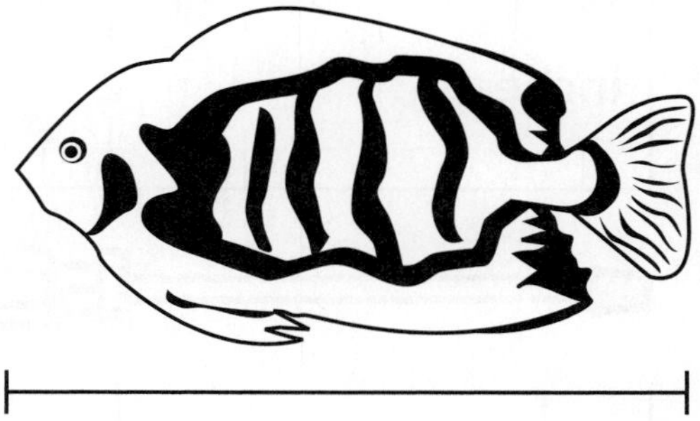

____

3.

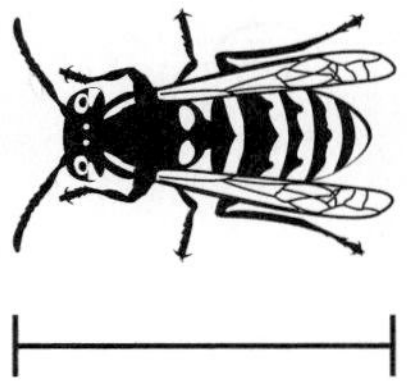

____

4.

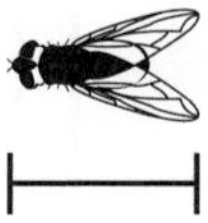

____

5.

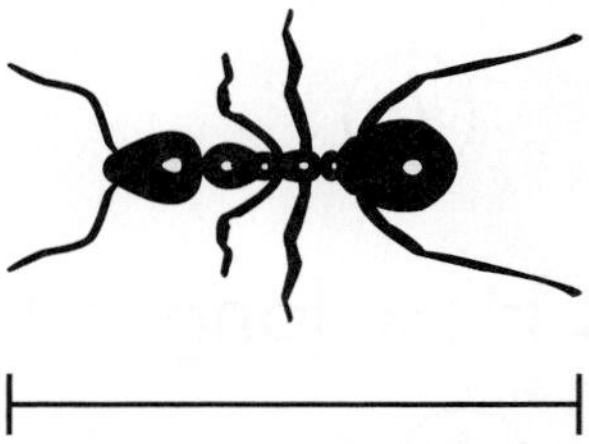

____

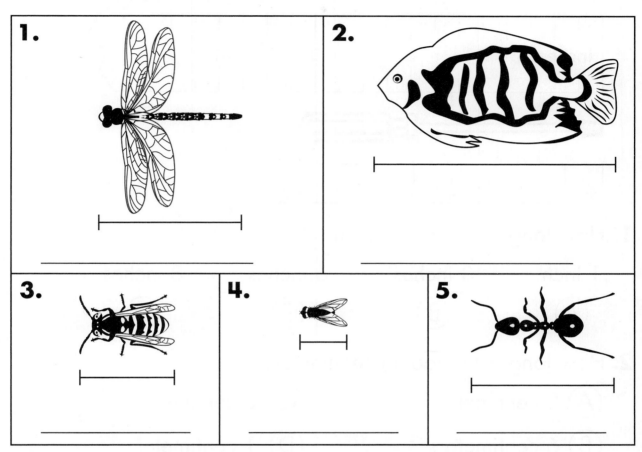

6. Draw or trace around an object that is $3\frac{1}{2}$ inch-bricks long.

Object: ______________________

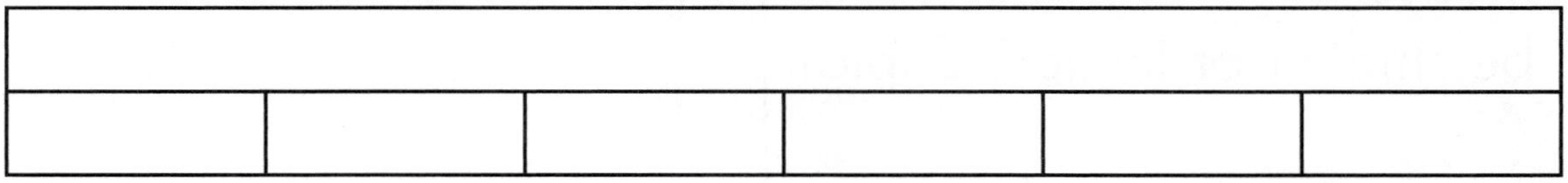

Copyright © by Pearson Education, Inc., or its affiliates. All rights reserved. 2

Quiz

Use the rulers shown. Choose the correct answer.

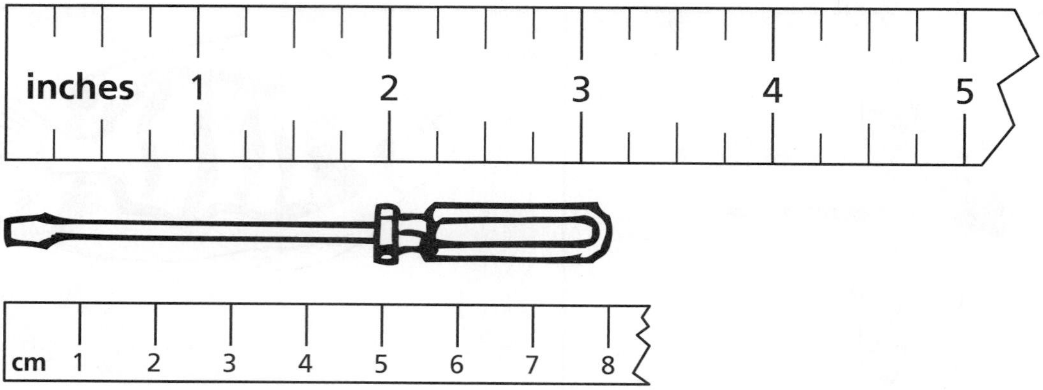

1. How long is the tool in inches?

1 inch	3 inches	6 inches	8 inches
(A)	(B)	(C)	(D)

2. How long is the tool in centimeters?

(A) 8 centimeters

(B) 6 centimeters

(C) 3 centimeters

(D) 1 centimeters

3. How many centimeters are in 1 meter?

1	10	12	100
(A)	(B)	(C)	(D)

4. Measure something that is about 1 foot long. If you measure the object in centimeters, will the answer be smaller or larger? Explain.

Copyright © by Pearson Education, Inc., or its affiliates. All rights reserved. 2

Name Date

Cat Comparisons

A cat is playing on a climbing tower with shelves.
The tower is 1 meter tall.
Shelf A is 30 centimeters from the floor.

1. Shelf B is twice as high as Shelf A from the floor. How high is Shelf B from the floor?

_______ centimeters

2. Shelf C is 32 centimeters above Shelf B. How high is Shelf C from the floor?

_______ centimeters

3. The cat jumps down from Shelf C to Shelf A. How far is that jump?

_______ centimeters

4. How tall is the tower in centimeters?

_______ centimeters

5. How far is it from Shelf A to the top of the tower?

_______ centimeters

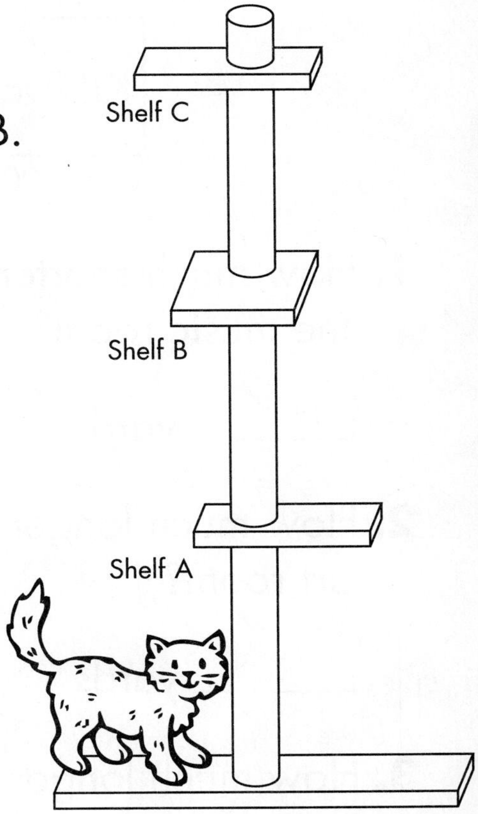

Copyright © by Pearson Education, Inc., or its affiliates. All rights reserved. 2

Name Date

Room Comparisons

The lengths of some rooms in a school are marked.

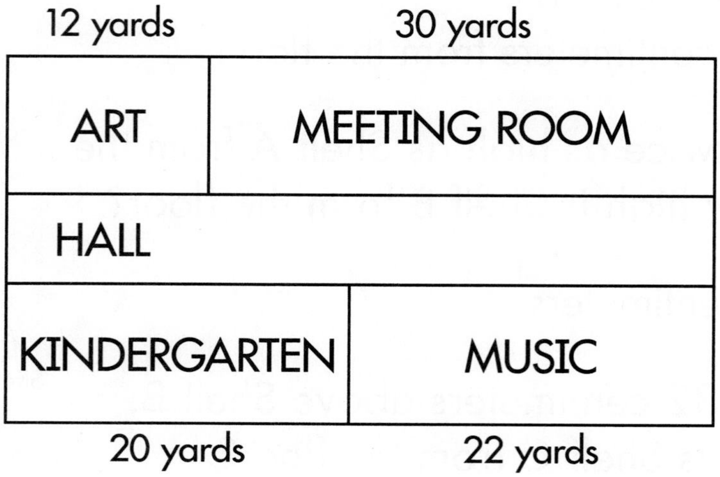

1. How much shorter is the Kindergarten room than the music room?

________ yards

2. How much longer is the meeting room than the art room?

________ yards

3. How much longer is the meeting room than the music room?

________ yards

4. How long is the hall? ________ yards

Copyright © by Pearson Education, Inc., or its affiliates. All rights reserved. 2

Use anytime after Session 3.3.

Name Date

Quiz

Choose the correct answer.

1. A tour began at 5:00 P.M. and ended at 8:00 P.M. How long was the tour?

4 hours	3 hours	2 hours	1 hour
(A)	(B)	(C)	(D)

2. Science class started at 10:30 A.M. and lasted 1 hour. What time did it end?

(A) 1:30 P.M.

(B) 12:30 P.M.

(C) 11:30 A.M.

(D) 10:30 A.M.

3. A game lasted $1\frac{1}{2}$ hours. The game ended at 8:30 P.M. What time did the game begin?

(A) 6:00 P.M.

(B) 7:00 P.M.

(C) 7:30 P.M.

(D) 8:00 P.M.

4. On the timeline below, mark and label the half-hour times. Then mark an activity that lasts for $1\frac{1}{2}$ hours.

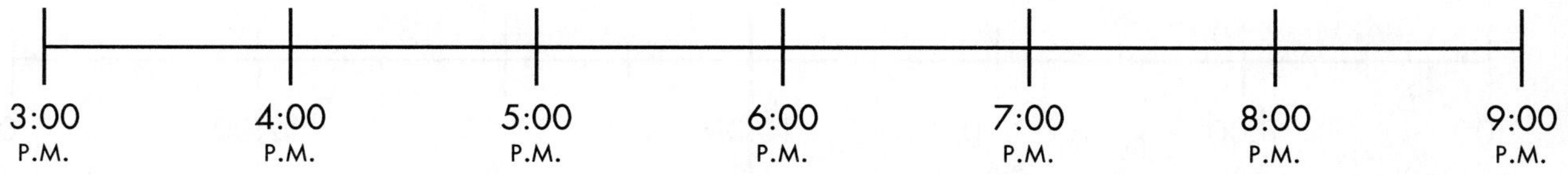

Copyright © by Pearson Education, Inc., or its affiliates. All rights reserved. 2

Name Date

Trip to the Zoo

Mark each activity on the timeline at the bottom of this page.

1. Leave school at 7:30 A.M.

2. Eat lunch at 11:30 A.M.

3. Arrive at zoo at 8:00 A.M.

4. Monkey feeding at 8:30 A.M.

5. Leave zoo at 1:00 P.M.

Show these special events on the timeline. Mark how long they last.

6. Bird show at 12:00 P.M., or noon, for a half hour

7. Guided tour at 9:00 for $1\frac{1}{2}$ hours

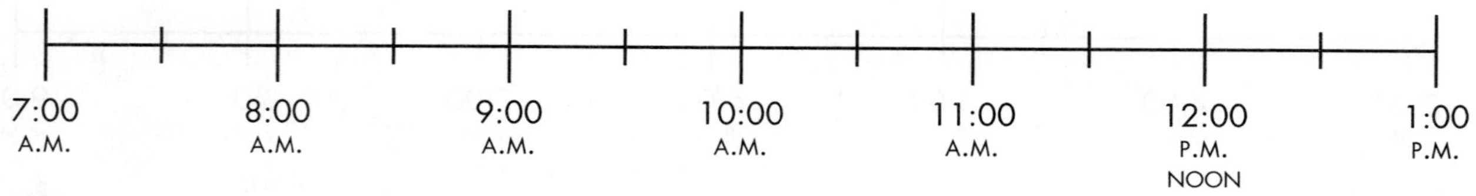

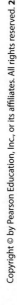

Copyright © by Pearson Education, Inc., or its affiliates. All rights reserved. 2

Name Date

Measuring Length and Time

Garden Timeline

Holly and Henry planted a vegetable garden. At 8:00 A.M., they began work. They planted beans for **1 hour**. Then they planted potatoes for **$1\frac{1}{2}$ hours**.

At 10:30 A.M., Holly said, "Let's take a break." So, they took a **half hour** break. After that, they planted peppers **until noon**.

Holly and Henry stopped to eat lunch for an **hour**. Finally, they planted corn for **2 hours**. When they finished their garden, it was 3:00 P.M. They went home to clean up. At 3:30, they started to play a game. They played for **$1\frac{1}{2}$ hours**.

Fill in the blanks for the missing times.

1. 8:00 A.M.–__________	Planted beans
2. __________– 10:30 A.M.	Planted potatoes
3. 10:30 A.M.–__________	Took a break
4. __________–12:00 P.M. or noon	Planted peppers
5. 12:00 P.M. or noon–__________	Ate lunch
6. __________–3:00 P.M.	Planted corn
7. __________–3:30 P.M.	Went home to clean up
8. 3:30 P.M.–__________	Played a game

Copyright © by Pearson Education, Inc., or its affiliates. All rights reserved. 2

Name Date

Blank Ten-Frames

Copyright © by Pearson Education, Inc., or its affiliates. All rights reserved. 2

Name Date

Addition and Subtraction Equation Cards

1	2	3	4	5
6	7	8	9	10
10	10	10	20	20
30	+	+	+	+
=	−	−	−	−

Copyright © by Pearson Education, Inc., or its affiliates. All rights reserved. 2